GRAFTERS

MANCS ABROAD

MORE INSIDE STORIES FROM EUROPE'S MOST PROLIFIC SNEAK THIEVES

BY MARK BLANEY

EMPIRE
PUBLICATIONS

First published in 2018

EMPIRE PUBLICATIONS
1 Newton Street, Manchester M1 1HW
© Marcus Blaney 2018

ISBN: 978-1-909360-40-2

Printed in Great Britain.

ACKNOWLEDGEMENTS

Firstly I would like to acknowledge the friends that are no longer with us; P Foot, T Corrigan, M Royle (Diller), P Dolan, P Ronan, C Donnelly (Divy), Martin Young, D Richardson (Cat), P Murphy, M Dixon (Dicko), J McKee, G McCulloch (Ronnie), S Snowdon (Reggie), Coco, Bambi, Joe Pesci, Essy, K Eastforth, Sully, Toby, Clint, Rabbi and Martin Gallagher from the Young Munichs.

Thanks to Rick Milnes for his work on the photos and Stuart Campbell, Fraz, Jocky and Pey for their contributions.

Also to my brother Colin; without his support and encouragement you wouldn't be reading this story. To Empire Publications, in particularly Ashley for being patient and putting up with me and not giving up and my group of friends in the local who all urged me on, even on the sober days!

Finally to David Adamson for his proof reading, editing and interviewing and J Langstaff without whose help as my PA/secretary this book would be just slang and jibber language.

And last but not least to my mother who thankfully hasn't read this, well not yet!

CONTENTS

FOREWORD

In the mid 80's, if you were from the North West, you would have definitely known a grafter or two; it was like a fashion or trend to get away from the UK at the time when the country was ruled by mad Maggie Thatcher.

They came from all over the north of England: Manchester, Liverpool and Sheffield - these areas all had their own set of thieves that were regularly 'at it' to earn a few bob.

Later, when we toured Europe, all the travelling grafters were onboard too and these guys did exactly what the label said - carrying wads of cash or chunks of hash and bags of jewellery too.

They caused mayhem all over when we were on tour: one night we played in Paris and it was all going fine until McEvoy from Salford emptied the place by spraying everyone with an over the top canister of CS gas. On another night, all the takings went missing from the box office and we never found out who took it but we knew one thing for sure, it had to be a grafting Manc!

I suppose we got our own back on them as they were always shouting "Call the Cops" as some form of anthem so we jibbed the saying and added it to our tune "Step On".

As I write this forward I have recently heard that Stuart "the live wire guy" sadly passed away, he was such a loss as he was a really good lad and will be greatly missed by all who knew him.

RIP Stuart.

Shaun Ryder

THE GRAFT

Stuart C.: Sometimes crime is easy; everything within the team runs like clockwork and you come away with a nice fat wedge of cash with very little effort. But the bread can't always land butter-side up and every now and then, all you're left with is hairy toast.

"They've got our kid!" yelled Colin, a fellow grafter, as he legged it back to the car.

We'd done hundreds of thefts on jewellers all over Europe and beyond over the past two decades but perhaps we'd become a bit too relaxed on this one, maybe we hadn't spent enough time sussing it all out. So what had gone wrong? We hadn't done anything different; I guess the big man upstairs had decided this particular job wasn't going to run smoothly today.

Col threw the briefcase full of goodies into the back of the car and said "I'm going back in for him!" He had sweat pouring into his eyes and a look of steely determination plastered across his face. "Chuck me the flick cosh and a canister of CS gas and listen Stupot, if I'm not back at this car in three minutes, reverse the backend through the main entrance, trust me it's been done before."

"Okay, B" I shrugged. It was Col's brother Mark who was in Shit Strasse, so I had no right to say no. At the end of the day, anybody with an ounce of self-respect would have done the same for a brother whilst working away.

Colin got off – back in the direction of the jewellers...

Fuck me, those three minutes ticked by on my watch at a snail's pace, a million different thoughts were racing round my head.

What if I end up killing someone? I don't want to end up getting lifed off in my fucking prime for god's sake!

Two prolonged minutes passed...

I don't really want to be responsible for the death of some innocent straight-goer who's just doing their job either.

Two and a half...

Wait a second, what if I hit Colin or Mark or both of them at once? There's just as much chance of that happening.

The three minutes were up…

Oh well, fuck it. Here goes nothing, wish me luck boys.

As my foot hovered over the accelerator, ready to plough the getaway car through the front of the jewellers in what could have been the most ill-conceived rescue mission of all time, I wondered how my life had come to the point where I considered this normal. It was a crazy situation but I had been in others that were just as surreal and dangerous. If I had come from a criminal background then it would be understandable but both of my parents are dibble! How had a copper's loving son ended up as a jewellery thief with a spot on Interpol's list of undesirables?

I hit the accelerator and headed toward the shop…

Marcus B.: While Batman and Robin pondered my escape, I was lying flat on the floor beneath two blokes who were holding my neck down with their knees. There was no way out of this. What had just gone wrong?

It had all been business as usual: I had entered the shop and engaged one of the staff in a cock and bull story about wanting a present for the wife. Col and Stu had given me a few minutes then entered the shop after they had seen that I had taken the shopkeeper over to the desired spot. Their target was a cabinet full of watches out of view from where I stood, chatting away happily. All went well until the cabinet door slammed shut with a mighty bang.

Clumsy twats!

With that the dynamic duo made a bolt for the door and were off out of sight. Immediately the other shopkeeper grabbed me sussing (correctly) that I had something to do with it. Now I was in lumber, pressed down by the weight of two burly blokes.

Luckily for me after a few minutes they decided to drag me up while one of them went to phone the police. The other guy had me in what he thought was a tight grip.

I then decided to use the 'dying fly' routine, basically dropping down to the floor making him lose his grip on me. I'd done it before and it was always a great way to get out of someone's grasp. Having evaded the guy I ran out the door. He was gobsmacked, with his mouth wide open and my jacket still in his hands as I hit the street.

Within a few yards I almost knocked our Colin off his feet. He was holding a cosh. "Lively Colin, he's a big twat!" I shouted and we then spotted a car driven by Stuart belting towards us. We both dived in. I was relieved, gasping for air and missing a jacket. However Colin soon cheered me up by showing me the watches we'd just acquired. A whole bag full of silver linings.

In truth, this was a rare example of a graft gone wrong. During our two decades grafting across Europe we robbed thousands of jewellers, department stores, back offices, petrol stations, builders' merchants and other likely targets and rarely got into trouble. We made our living thieving across the continent and usually we'd be in and out without the owners even realising it. Until Interpol got their act together in the mid 1980s there was a significant gang of us for whom the grafting lifestyle made us very comfortable and almost invisible to the police. They were chasing murderers and drug gangs, we were fuck all in comparison. The most they'd do was deport us back to Blighty. The British coppers were sound with us because we weren't shitting on our doorstep. Margaret Thatcher probably approved, it all helped with the Balance of Payments, we were net importers after all…

Life was carefree, a million miles away from the humdrum nine to five we were supposed to knuckle down to. Amsterdam was our base; The Netherlands our protector with its liberal laws and lax approach to petty crime; Switzerland, Germany and Austria were our targets, the 'land of the wedge' as our Colin termed it – lands stuffed full of money but with very little security to protect it. And our markets were continent wide from the gold dealers of The Dam to grateful Spanish bar owners who couldn't afford Video Recorders and cameras at shop prices.

Watches, diamond rings, necklaces, all types of gold chains and coins, cash boxes and safes; anything that wasn't screwed down would be carried away. We'd send a bit back to Manchester and sell the rest, then do it all again the next day and the next. For years we lived like this but how did a humble lad from Manchester fall into this life of crime?

We were from a lost generation. When Thatcher took over, anyone who didn't fit snugly into place in British society was outcast. Rather than sit on the dole and rot away in grimy Manchester we got off to the continent where the beer and the birds flowed.

OUTCASTS

"ONCE known as the notorious Racecourse Estate, Sale west has often been unfairly stigmatised in its 40 years history as little more than a crime ridden suburban ghetto"

MANCHESTER EVENING NEWS

We had it tough from the start.

I was originally brought up in a run down area in north Manchester called Collyhurst. Unfortunately the flats we lived in were condemned and we were moved to the other side of Manchester, the posh south. For some unknown reason, the council decided to build what was called an overspill estate (or as I'd call it an 'overspew') between three estates of expensive private houses. In their wisdom they plonked our crappy estate beside one of the plushest parts of Sale and called it the Racecourse Estate. It would probably have been better if they'd put a big wire fence around it and posted machine gun nests on each corner as a finishing touch.

Unsurprisingly, we were outsiders and instantly disliked. A lot of the new Racecourse residents had been transplanted from slum dwellings in Manchester's inner-city. From the neighbourly world of freezing flats to plush Sale was quite a contrast. Talk about two worlds colliding! We had gone from our rundown areas to this brand new, open and very colourful world – now there were flowing rivers instead of dank canals and green fields instead of a tyre-strewn red rec. All in all it was like stepping straight out of a Lowry landscape to a Van Gogh in the blink of an eye. All the other lads on the estate must have felt as alienated as I did in our new surroundings.

I had to go to primary school for the last few weeks; this was when it really hit me that there was another kind of human being on this planet – the posh kid. They wore smart uniforms, blazers that held ten or more pens in the top pocket and wore clean shirts. No holes in their shoes here or jumpers with snot all over their sleeves and I bet nitty Nora (the bug explorer) wasn't a regular… at least not yet.

On my first day in class I thought all the kids were really ill or sick as they all had their hands up as if pleading to go to the toilet. As it turned out they were all desperate to answer a teacher's question. "Sir, sir… me, me please" they pleaded, cupping their elbows to make their arm stretch to the limit. Others stood up on tip-toe "Me! Me!". I stared – is this normal? I was accustomed to keeping my head down in class, I don't recall any questions at Saint Malachy's back in Collyhurst, unless it was about a collection for the new church or for poor African children who had even less than us. They were always collecting for the new church, as at the time the church was in the basement of the school, which made it feel to a kid as if we were in church all day as it was run by nuns. The only thing on our timetable was the bible. The other two things I remember was watching the moon landing on the school telly and staring at Strangeways from the playground where we all told each other they still hung people under the steeple. The prison really stood out on the grey landscape. What I definitely don't remember is being asked real questions unless it was calling your name out at registry and then you just said "here, Sister Veronica" - that was it!

Growing up in the 70's was so different to today. We played out and went anywhere we wanted. The only thing you'd be told was not to talk to strangers and make sure you have clean undies on in case you got run over so as not to embarrass your mother. Those were innocent times and kids didn't have much but we knew how to enjoy ourselves.

The same year that we moved home, our Colin left school at the age of 14, which was the educational standard back then. Plus we had a new addition to the family. Our Jay was born, this took the attention off me, leaving me free to do as I pleased more or less. I would often find myself aged ten on long bus journeys going back to Collyhurst for the youth club every other Friday. Our Colin, who still more or less stayed in Collyhurst, just came home on Sunday or midweek but he always made sure that I got back on the bus home with a nice crisp pound note for my spends. I will never forget Colin was up at 4.30am each day to go down to work on a fish stall in Manchester's famous Smithfield market. He'd be so boozed up at weekends that he'd often tell me he'd get woken up by bus drivers at Altrincham interchange, the final stop on the Sale bus route. Being a couple of miles away he'd end up having to get another bus back and would sometimes fall asleep again and wake up in town, just in time for work on the Monday morning! It's fair to say neither of us had adapted to this new environment, Sale was just so far from the city centre.

The Collyhurst flats were still there but hardly anyone was living in them now, it was really strange to see the streets I'd grown up in so desolate. I half expected to see tumbleweeds blowing by. This area was in my blood and I missed it. Simple things such as looking forward to bonfire night, which was always so much bigger and better than Christmas. We would go raiding other areas for their wood. You'd see lads carrying front doors and planks for weeks before, we'd be marching around like an army of ants. To protect the bonfires the older lads would leave us younger ones to watch over it so that no one raided our precious wood while they went off and raided other stockpiles from surrounding areas. We would make sure we had plenty of ammunition for 'chucking duckers'. This was basically throwing stones, rocks, bricks or anything that we had gathered for such an attack. The bigger lads had real dens built inside the Bommie but the younger kids weren't allowed inside because the older boys said we were too young. When bonfire night finally arrived you wouldn't see many fireworks as you do today, just rip wraps and bangers – I can't really recall seeing any big displays of rockets in the air with the fancy razzmatazz seen at organised events today.

Then there were the fights with the local gypsies. If I'm being honest I didn't really want to partake in these as they were pretty scary – we were still only kids after all. So to annoy them we would go chucking duckers into their camp and run off like the clappers. The gypsies had a reputation of being hard and nobody messed with them but throwing stones into the camp got a good chase out of them and gave us a little bravado knowing they would never chase us into Collyhurst proper, they would be just happy chasing us away from their site, though shamefully I must admit we often taunted them with vile comments. In our defence, as kids we didn't realise how bad some of the remarks were, we were just being kids trying pass time and get a rise out of them – to have a chase and a laugh – nothing serious ever happened, it was just banter really.

As kids we wore Collyhurst clogs and actually used to have kicking competitions while wearing them. You were only allowed one kick each, usually to the shins, until someone gave in. Initiation to a gang meant running through the kicking machine where two rows of lads would form a line and you had to go through it trying not to get kicked too much.

Going into the town centre on Saturday was a test of nerve. We'd dare each other to nick daft things just to prove you had bottle. Collyhurst was such a deprived area that during the six week school holidays everybody had to go for their dinner in the local community canteen, which ensured that at least the kids ate something nourishing that day. Whit Week was as big an occasion as Christmas back in those days and every kid went on the walks. They were very religious and we were separated between Catholic and Protestant – everybody knew everybody. Parents would look on, proud as punch at their kids who would be very pleased with themselves in their new clobber, if not a little bit embarrassed at the attention they received from their mums.

One woman, I can't recall her name now, was there every year stood on Rochdale Road shouting "cock yer lily up". I only found out years later it meant "stand straight and be proud". Every adult we knew in this community was called aunty or uncle and I really thought I belonged to the biggest family in the world. When the council destroyed communities like this they ripped the heart and soul out of people. They promised pastures new and housing with all mod cons and we were told everything was going to be good. What we got was a soulless, disappointing modern seventies housing estate that had nothing going for it at all.

After my first summer on the estate I was off to secondary school. The first morning was like a scene out of the film *Kes*. Morning assembly with everybody coughing and spluttering, pinching each other and pure chuckles while pretending to sing boring hymns like *Morning Has Broken*. Most teachers outwardly hated everyone from the estate and the headmaster was a nasty piece of work with his bald head and a slight limp. He was nicknamed Mr Whippem by the lads - he'd always rant on and on "since that estate has been built..." It was clear that the new estate was going to change the face of posh Sale forever. The headmaster just couldn't wait to use the strap on us heathens, he tended to favour the cane; six on your palms and it burnt like fuck too. We were just the new arrivals but we were just the start of his nightmare! He'd seen nothing yet as this estate was still only half built, he'd soon have a queue of scallies outside his door on a daily basis.

After a few years they built a couple of pubs and shops and we even had a bus service going around the estate making it easier for us to get into town. I'd made a good few friends by now and we all had the similar backgrounds. Most people from the estate were looked upon as refugees. You really can't picture this and where it was built, it still amazes me to this day. I suppose they were being built all over the UK by the hundreds at the time - little estates full of future criminals, footballers, boxers, thugs or shady characters. Looking on the bright side, the newsagents on the way to school was a dead cert for five-fingered discounts. This shop had never seen the likes of us before - we could help ourselves to anything but the cigs, you had to get the older lads to buy the 5 Park Drive and a book of matches for you.

Unbeknown to us at the time, this estate would become infamous within the Manchester criminal world a few decades later.

I'd started going to the football by this point. I can recall my first derby game at Maine Road. Although I was a United fan, I was also a big fan of Frannie Lee, the best diver in the game, he made my day when I saw him actually do a dive in this match to earn a penalty. He even did a tackle on a United player and mimed to the ref afterwards that the United player (George Best, I think it was) had dived. This was all on the half-way line and funny as fuck to watch. The game was brilliant, ending 3-3. Sammy McIlroy, who would take over from George Best as a United hero, scored on his debut – what a cracking player! I knew every name on the pitch that day, even Bobby Charlton was playing with his famous strand of hair combed over his noggin.

United at the time were going from heroes to zeroes. Although they had been a great team, they were a spent force. We eventually got relegated by none other than Denis Law a few years later but football on the whole was brilliant in that era with "Bite Yer Legs" Norman Hunter, Chopper Harris, Billy Bremner - all nutters by today's standards. They would never last a full match without being sent off nowadays. In fact they were just as bad as the real hooligans that followed their teams to all the matches.

We had grown up knowing most of the football hooligans, as this was the time of the boot-boys who were really skinheads that grew their hair into the fashionable Rod cut. I think the book 'Skinhead' by Richard Allen was influential at this time and violence was just an everyday event really. Even as youngsters you had to be blind not to notice it. It was just the world we lived in. I'd grown up watching the older lads going or coming back from games filling my imagination with stories of it "going off" everywhere they went. All my mates had older brothers and our Colin would regale us with tales of Red Army away days and I'd just listen silently loving it all.

United weren't that good on the pitch but off it they were top of the hooligan league. Theirs was the largest hooligan firm in the 1970's and became synonymous with some of the biggest kick offs in football history. Obviously I'd seen the United fans going to away games but was still too young to travel myself and often wondered what would be happening.

Apart from football, music was a second influence on my life; *Top of the Pops* was the only program worth watching, the Top Twenty being a big deal back then. The top three bands at the time were, T-Rex who looked camp and *"rode a white swan"*. A band called The Sweet who all looked gay as 'parie' but their lyrics were totally different to how they looked eg. *"and the man at the back said everyone attack and it turned into a ballroom blitz"*. Even Elton fuckin' John sang *"Saturday night's alright for fighting"* for fucks sake!

The next couple of years flew by as I made new mates while still adapting to our new area. A new kid arrived at our school called Craig Donnelly. He was from Wythenshawe, at that time the biggest social housing estate in Europe. It was known as an area full of rough 'uns. For a bit of banter one day I called him 'Divy' Donnelly as it seemed to rhyme plus I thought it would get a laugh in class. Craig didn't like me calling him Divy and went to punch me but missed so the name stuck straight away. He would then try and dig anyone else who called it him but after a while he had to reluctantly accept his new nickname. Divy and I would be top mates for many years to come but he'd often slag me for that name as the word Divy was a new word coming out of Liverpool at the time and meant daft or not clued up but there you go. The Divy was a loose cannon being skinny as fuck yet he would twat anyone knowing that he couldn't fight his way out of a wet paper bag but he had another mate called Woz who lived in one of the posh houses who really looked out for him.

Me, Woz and Divy would go down to Piccadilly every Saturday to do the photo booths. We learnt that to make some money all we had to do was block the money slot up with card so the coins didn't go into the machine and the change wouldn't come out of the return end. As both ends were blocked up when the customer tried to get their money back, they couldn't because all the coins would be jammed up in the middle. We would go around doing five or six machines and leave them for a few hours. We were just kids but it was a great way to make money and no risk at all really. With the proceeds from the photo booths we would go on a Monday dinnertime to Old Trafford and buy tickets to sell for a little bit of profit. We would usually get rid of them at school but preferred to sell them mostly at the game itself as obviously you could make more money.

One day the police turned up at school. A cigarette shop on Washway Road in Sale, close to where Wozzer lived, had been burgled and relieved of loads of packets of Embassy Regal. Woz and me were the main suspects and were taken to the police station for a chat. However we both kept quiet and couldn't be charged. Due to our ages we were considered juveniles so my mother and Wozzer's dad had to come down to get us released. It didn't come as any big surprise when Wozzer's dad instantly barred me from ever entering his posh house again - this always happened, the parents would always blame the estate kids, never suspecting their own little darlings could be responsible. Back at school we got suspended for two weeks even though the old bill had not charged us, yet the school deemed us guilty and suspension was seen as an appropriate punishment. Looking back, this decision wasn't surprising since half the school were smoking Embassy Regal and the cig butts were there for all to see on the school grounds and around the bike sheds proving our circumstantial guilt.

With Woz being my best mate, hardly anyone would start on me except for one lad who fancied his chances. So after school at 4pm we arranged to meet on a field opposite the school and I remember thinking "shit I've got no chance here". So, as this lad is walking ahead of me I took my chance grabbing his jacket to restrict his arms so he couldn't punch or grab me. This earned me the reputation of not fighting to the rules, which is a square on fight. Being only 5 foot 2 at this age I had to use every dirty trick in the book. If the same happened to me on the estate, I would never fight fairly but I didn't take advantage of anyone if I got the upper hand and more than likely they would become mates after a fight, that was how it was back in the day.

As we got older it became apparent that we weren't from North Manchester anymore. All my mates and I were more like ex-pats who had not lived in our old areas for about four or five years. Sale was unheard of in North Manchester in those days, although most of us all still knew someone from there. We were now self-proclaimed outcasts from the 'townies' as we now started to call them. Not far from Sale was the Wythenshawe estate where Divy was from and it had a reputation. This was the only place anyone in north Manchester people had heard about, mainly because a lot of their relatives had been decamped there. My dad lived close to a shopping centre called The Civic; I'd go to see him sometimes and I would often get into a few scrapes just because I wasn't local. I used to hate going and soon stopped altogether. I was chased around the place almost every time I went. Even just standing at the bus stop got you targeted, it was as if they could smell you weren't one of them. I know it's still the same today, it had the nickname 'Little Leeds' back then.

Divy and me both went to Collyhurst one night to the youth club, by this time hardly anyone I knew lived there, most had moved out to Langley and Hattersley but we all still met up at the youth club to moan about the areas we'd been shipped out to. I was playing table tennis and saw Divy getting ganged up on but being the lad he was Divy got stuck straight in. His head was down throwing punches windmill style then scuffling all the way down the stairs then outside where the fight got split up – but we still had to make it to the bus stop. "He's a fucking nutter," one of them told me, "what you brought him here for Blaney?"

They continued to follow us to Rochdale Road. While being okay with me, they continued to take turns half-heartedly chasing the Div around. At the bus stop Div got a farewell dig from one of the lads and comforting his sore chin and soon to be black eye he looked a bit the worse for wear mumbling, "I'm not going there again," he said, then protested "they started it yer know."

"Did they fuck! You threw the first punch so you started it' I laughed, 'yer Div!" continuing, "anyway, it's the same for me in Wythenshawe mate." Divy never went back to Collyhurst with me again after that.

★

My ever first jib to an away game I was with a mate, Tony Madden. United were playing at Burnley's Turf Moor, so we jibbed on a Ribble bus from town, where we both just hid under the seats without any hassle, funny thing is I hardly remember the day, only that 'their end' was like the Kippax on the side of the ground as opposed to behind the goal. I don't recall any fighting; I just remember United fans everywhere, it felt more like a festival to us than anything else.

After the game we headed for where the coaches were and thought we were well lucky coming across a kid's dad we all knew. Plus he drove all the coaches from The Vine pub in Sale to all the away games; it was Roger Palmer's dad (Roger would become a professional footballer later playing for City and Oldham). Tony asked him if we could get a lift back home.

"No problem" he would get us back to Sale he told us, what he didn't tell us was he had to make various drops all over north Manchester, at one point we thought he was going into fuckin' Yorkshire somewhere, though I now know it was only Glossop. We eventually got home around ten o'clock, we could have done a "jib on the rib" bus back again if we had known, "walking back would have been quicker" we chuckled as we walked home.

'THE OLD GUARD'

The Barmy Army, Doc's Red Army, The Tartan Army, Doc's Thieving Army, when we were out and about with them, this was when I would get involved doing little earners for our kid as and when. He'd do a till or turnstile and he'd hand me his cash as I'd be unlikely to get stopped and searched as I was so young. I would just watch the Red Army rampaging everywhere they went, it was pure mayhem. "Taking ends" it was called. I remember a game in the Second Division at Bolton. It wasn't as much taking their end as I saw it but more like one hundred plus hooligans staying in the end for ninety minutes. I watched the fights and scuffles before and during the game, these guys were in their element causing pure mayhem wherever they went.

What stays in my mind most is that all of them were grinning and laughing even when getting kicked, punched or nicked! After half time I was handed another wedge of notes that had been liberated from the bar. Now I started to flap a little, I was out of my comfort zone here, with two separate wads of money down me keks and surrounded by a load of beer monsters in full swing. *"Beer, beer we want more beer, all the lads are cheering get the fucking beers in"* they were singing… but then I knew I was safe as houses with this lot, as they all knew I was Colin's brother. They looked after me, mostly by twisting my ears and pinching my nose plus over the top back slaps that fucking hurt.

For home games, these lads took up residence in the Scoreboard Paddock and they were reputed to be the hardest firm in the ground. Most were from North Manchester and it seemed every last one was a beer monster, with their Rod Stewart haircuts, flared trousers with side pockets and mad five buttoned waistbands, star jumpers and shirts called penny rounds topped off with very fashionable platform shoes. I really don't know how they managed to fight in their chosen footwear but they did – they came to be known as the Collyhurst Cowboys. Today I'd call them 'The Old Guard' and they would *"fight any bastard that got in their way"* as the song says. They were the *"cock of the north"*.

It would be fair to say the casuals hadn't yet arrived!

One memorable match was Leeds away, up until this game the Yorkies had terrorised United whenever they played at Elland Road. According to the lads who went, Leeds regularly chased United the four or so gruelling miles back to the station from their ground. On the last trip, the Yorkies had pelted our fans with bricks and concrete from a new bridge that was being built over the M62 and would prey on stragglers who were unable to keep up with the red hordes. I was told by our Colin that if I ever felt opposing fans getting too close for comfort, I'd be wise to trip up a scarfer. Of course our Colin and his crew didn't wear scarves as it was too easy to spot a fan wearing colours. It was snide to trip a fellow red over to be left to the thugs but there you go.

The day of the match saw everyone gathering at Victoria station – this was a ragtag bunch of thugs and thieves led by George Lyons, Mickey Farrell, Willis and Gaftney (OG), it was early and the beer was already beginning to flow for the older lads. Apart from them, coming up through the ranks were a new contingent of United fans; all manner of sneak thieves and pickpockets gathering on the station platform awaiting the arrival of the next train, poised to relieve the passengers of their valuables the second they spilled on to the platform.

As the passengers stepped from the carriage, hordes of kids would swarm past them, dipping people as they passed. The minute the coast was clear they would reappear ready to repeat the scenario on the next train to arrive. This went on for a good hour and the lads I knew, one called Ritchie the Cat, were all around my age. We all dressed differently from the OG with semi-flared jeans, desert boots, crew tops, sweat-shirts or rollneck jumpers finished by a cagoule jacket. Grafting went hand in hand with football but Ritchie the Cat and his cronies were the new kids on the block – they were ruthless. They would snatch takings from shops, pubs, turnstiles – you name it. Okay, all these things were being done by the older lads but the new generation weren't drinkers, we were too young for boozing just yet.

Finally, at 12.30, everybody piled onto the Leeds train. Most Leeds fans wouldn't be expecting United before 1.30 when the Football Specials arrived. So about 100 United fans filtered out of Leeds station free to go and do bit of shopping before the match. I lost our Colin but later found him in the ground where he handed me his takings from the day, "right, you better stick with me now as it's going to go bonkers after the game." Sure enough, after leaving the ground a little early, more or less the same firm that had left together earlier in the day had all regrouped. We made a beeline for the area where the coaches were parked then after waiting what seemed like ages Mickey Farrell started the "everyone stick together" speech and we were off. I didn't really know what was going on as I was too young to be a hoolie, so I just kept Colin in my sights as best I could.

After hiding for a few minutes and giving the police enough time to escort the United fans back towards the train station, we headed back towards the ground and emerged behind the Leeds fans who were following the police who were herding the United fans. Fuckin hell what a sight! I couldn't catch my breath. About 300 Leeds fans had their backs to us in a big broad line and beyond them were the police on horses chasing the reds back like cattle to the station. Then on cue the chant went up "UN-I-TED" as a hundred or so reds steamed into the unprepared Yorkie twats. The Old Bill were gobsmacked to see United giving Leeds a good hiding and then continuing to run on through the police lines we joined our own fans where we ran through a park. I remember a mixed race Leeds lad called Charlie, a well known thug of the time. He was wearing a green boiler suit. He came right up through the police escort, he wasn't after a fight – he'd been in borstal with our Colin and he wanted to hug our kid. Then just as quick as he arrived, he jumped back but just before he reached the police, he twatted a scarfer just for show. The Old Bill even made a gap for him to return to his firm! It was surreal; either way that year United didn't recieve the traditional run back to train station.

On the train back everyone was having a real knees up and stories of the day were exchanged along with the odd show of the wedges earned. The whole point about the day seemed to be to get home with more than you left the house with. Pay for nothing and take what you could get away with; either from sneak thieving or dipping. This was the beginning of what later got called the Perry Boys era, who all dressed differently from the Old Guard.

WORK? WHO ME?

Back at school shortly before Christmas I was called to the headmaster's office one day with two other lads and told we could leave school as we were now 16. I remember asking…

"When?"

"Today, Blaney."

They were the best two words I'd heard in five years of school. We were told we could go on an apprenticeship instead of going on the dole, the wages being a whopping £19.95.

I was lucky as my step dad, who was pure Northern Irish and had a thick accent, was working at Clean Walls with Colin. Colin's mate Gagzy and Frannie Clerkin from Collyhurst did sandblasting. Jimmy had been there for years and I was told the boss, Russ, would take me on. So off I went for an interview along with my mate Carl one Thursday afternoon. As we walked into his office there was what looked like a million pounds just sat staring at us on the table. Oh dear. It was wages day. After a successful interview, as we got back on the bus to go home Carl just pulled out a wad of £1 notes that he had skimmed off the top from the massive wedge that I'd been trying hard not to stare at while Russ was chatting away to me about the job. "Yer fuckin daft twat! I'm bound to get nicked for that!"

After a little argument Carl said "So, you're saying you don't want any then?" Suffice to say, after nearly talking my way out of a share of it, we split the money up - £60 each. I was flapping to fuck really and waiting for the inevitable visit from the police or even Russ himself but unsurprisingly I never heard any more about it. Carl had been correct saying they wouldn't know the money had even gone, what a start to my first ever job!

I was to do two weeks at each job, sand blasting and pointing walls but really all I did was sweep the floors. After four weeks of sweeping I finally got to work with Jimmy and our Colin cleaning hospital walls. Jimmy set me doing the toilets on my first day. After a while he came back and said "what yer feckin doin?" to which I said "I'm cleaning the walls" with him looking at me puzzled. "No, no! We don't clean the feckin walls" then with a worried look on his face he shouted "Colin, he's cleaning the feckin walls in here!" Our kid is laughing his head off and explains to me what I should have done in the first place which is only cleaning the hospital wards he told me "the rest we skim as Jimmy's got to get to the pub."

Then he showed me skimming. He got a wet soapy rag, ensuring he left plenty of soap suds on the floor as proof of a job well done. Even in my first ever job I was being shown the short cut to making easy money. Nothing would stop Jimmy getting to the pub for dinnertime and he was sure to show me the tricks of the trade. The trick being you chose a high corner of the room and made a big 'X' mark on the dirty wall. It was always easy to find a dirty corner because the walls in the hospital were filthy anyway. A square outlining the X could be seen clearly showing the dirt yet outside the square you would clean about half a metre down then lightly rub the wall with less and less pressure the further you went way from the 'X' making a hard job very easy and quick. Presently, Jimmy would shuffle a member of staff in to see what a great job we had done and be off to the pub in time for dinner!

Jimmy and his mate would have a good few beers giving Colin and me the chance for the old five-finger discounts at nearby shops. Van Gils suits were our main choice of the day – ready made, straight off the peg but with quality a cut above the average. Everyone wanted a Van Gils for the weekend. You wouldn't need to go home – it was straight on the piss with a new whistle on looking dash. Colin would go into the shop ahead of me and by the time I followed he'd have about three or four suits nicely folded waiting for me. I'd hardly have to break stride – just open my bag and he'd throw in the goods and then walk a few yards behind me just in case I got stopped.

Another favourite to make quick money were tenor saxophones and Gibson guitars. I'd walk in having given Colin his usual couple of minutes to secure the bounty. He could always be found lurking in some corner of the shop with the sax or Gibson already removed from the window or wall display ready for me to throw a black bin liner over. Then, timing it right, we'd walk out. Sometimes we'd exit without covering the item as we weren't always prepared for any opportunity that came our way. Gibsons were and always have been the most expensive and therefore the most popular guitar in the world. Colin had a long list of bands in the North who were very happy to take goods off our hands, no matter how paranoid they were. A sax or guitar at a knock down price usually eased the paranoia for them. Listen to any bands of the day and you probably heard our grafted items being played, just ask "*Guitar George, he knew all the cords*".

Our rewards were plentiful as we were soon working all over the UK. By now there was more grafting being done than actual work. Mini bronze ornaments were popular with the poachers – they loved the greyhound or hunting scenes depicted on them. Capo de Monte figurines for the Miss Buckets we knew. For the housewives; bed sheets, curtains or any type of household goods were easy sellers on the estate. We would pinch anything from A to Z and it would sell. High fidelity stereo systems had been in demand and everyone thought they were the dog's bollocks. That was until they were superseded by stereo rack systems – these fuckers blew our minds; where you put your own separate system together with a turntable and, later, a cassette player. We mostly robbed them for ourselves – you were the DJ in your own home blasting out Pink Floyd, Lou Reed and Dillingers CB 200.

Everything was going well until Colin got arrested for a burglary on a shop in Yorkshire. It gave Russ no option but to sack him and thanks to Colin I was then moved back to shitty sandblasting at some office block in Old Trafford. One day at work my mate Lou came down to see if I was up for going to see Bob Marley in Stafford. Much to my own surprise, and lifelong regret, I said "no I've got work". What the fuck was happening to me? Putting work before fun! I've never forgiven myself for not going and as the song says "I never got to see Bob Marley". The job didn't last long after Colin got the sack. So I decided to sack myself and never went back after payday, I'd had enough.

To keep the peace at home I carried on getting up and pretending I was still going but I just went straight round to my mate Kev's house every morning to drink tea and smoke spliffs. I had wagged church at Saint Malachy's, wagged school at secondary, now I was wagging fuckin work! Not long after this and for some mad reason which I can't remember now, a few of us made our way to Jersey. It didn't last long though as I couldn't get in any of the pubs and after getting a job in a hotel I got sacked for throwing garlic in the bin. What the fuck did I know what garlic was? On top of it all, being ordered around was getting right on my tits. After my experience of Jersey I was on my way back home. I'd only had two jobs but I knew deep down I just didn't have the so-called 'work ethic' in me. I was never going to be doing a nine to five, it just wasn't for me.

JUNK & PUNK

After my brief working career I started hanging about with some older lads just to get me out of the house and to see what they were up to. I imagined them all smoking spliffs and listening to reggae and having a good old laugh with a few beers but I couldn't have been more wrong. Instead they were all just dossing around each other's gaffs listening to Pink Floyd, Lou Reed or Santana getting mashed up, being sick and 'goofing out' on junk. One of the lads, Pete, had a car, a mini with blacked out windows that made them all look like the Ant Hill Mob on a bad day!

During the week they would suss out which chemists they could burgle for their next bit of graft. They would look for old buildings that would be easier to get into. Once inside they'd go straight for the cabinet that held the heavy drugs they craved. There seemed to be plenty of chemists to rob, as I remember they'd be doing at least one every other weekend. However, the atmosphere between them all after a burglary was very tense. They'd become very paranoid and the place had a horrible vibe as if it was going to be raided or the door was going to be kicked in at any minute. In reality these lads were as safe as could be, as it was a tight, secretive circle and drugs weren't really out in the open like today. The drugs fed their paranoia and nobody would go out for the next few days as they would do what they liked doing best 'goofing out' on what was to them the best drug in the world Dykonal - pink tablets that were crushed up put on a spoon then filtered into a syringe - they would almost fight over the *pink critters* as they became known. After the pinks had finished, they'd turn to whatever other pills they had left; palph, df118s, fortral and last but not least valium, which monged them all out like they were really drunk.

A couple of weeks later the process would be repeated all over again and they'd go to the 3bs (Bury, Bolton, Burnley) as these areas were easier targets and carried less jail as opposed to South Manchester where doing a chemist in Knutsford, Wilmslow or Hale would see you looking at real jail time if caught. If you were in the know, it was obvious a chemist had been done because afterwards the usual suspects weren't seen out and about on the estate for about a week. The lure of the demon drugs created such bad characters that by now they would track down friends who had family members who were seriously ill just so they could get their hands on their medication hoping that these pills would be morphine-based. The lads would mither the hell out of whoever lived there to get them.

Most parents had the attitude that if you weren't on drugs then you were the one selling them; they had no idea about the local chemists being ransacked every other week. I did try junk (opiates) even though the thought of taking it never appealed to me and, as expected, I hated it. After every cigarette I smoked for the next three days I spewed up. Every drink sent me straight to the toilet. Taking drugs to be ill and say it was good seemed strange and baffled me - it still does today. Sadly the first but certainly not the last casualty I knew was a great lad whose nickname was 'Foot'. Paul was a big user and died from an overdose. You would think it would make people stop but it didn't and still doesn't.

Luckily the drug scene wasn't for all of us, punk was better than junk but even at that young age we knew punk was false as fuck, with bands selling out as soon as they could to get on *Top of the Pops* and sort themselves a record deal. We had been into punk since it started, though we didn't dress punk, I'd wear drain pipes and a borstal shirt - we played our style down. We listened to the music though and went to the concerts as we could at least get in the places being young. Most were held at student halls, town halls and of all places The Electric Circus in good old Collyhurst.

On Jubilee Day 1977, I was looking forward to returning to the place I'd grown up. There was a concert being held that night and I knew our Colin and the Collyhurst Cowboys were having a day's drinking; so Woz and me went down for the day. Nobody lived in the flats anymore but everyone would congregate at the local boozer called The Manhattan right in the heart of Collyhurst and it was one rough pub. Anyone dressed as a punk would be getting pure abuse from everyone stood outside. Most had to walk past dressed in punk garb, their heads down. The odd brave one would give us the V's and get chased and beaten up. They all got taxed on the way to the famous Electric Circus and even going home afterwards they were picked on, although I doubt any had any money on their way home, it was just intimidation and for a laugh really and a kind of sport to give chase to some middle class punks. I got drunk for my very first time that day, getting drinks given us left, right and centre. With the mixture of different beers I was soon spewing up as I wasn't a drinker. Luckily for me Woz liked a drink, and helped me to the dreaded bus station in town on the way home.

Waiting at the wrong stand at the bus station could cost you - after a concert most punks went to Piccadilly where getting home without incident wasn't easy as it was always shady with small gangs of lads roaming the stops looking to see who they could beat up just for being from a certain area. You would get targeted from around ten o'clock onwards and had to be very wary about standing too long at stops as this just gave away to everyone where you'd be heading. I've seen so many people getting battered for just standing at the right stop, only to find out that it was the wrong stop. There would be a quick opening line of "Where you from mate" followed by a sucker-punch and a kick to the ground for amusement. Salford would usually be the main culprits as they went out of town a different way from Piccadilly, although we never had any mither as bullies only target vulnerable, helpless people.

The Clash played at the Apollo in Manchester that year and a few of us got in for free round the back, along with about twenty other lads. Soon as they played *White Riot* the place got wrecked, all the seats got ripped out and thrown around the place – what a great night. The Clash were our favourite band at the time. Although the negative side were punk fans who, like most of the bands, were false to us. The music was great but it ended there. *Never Mind the Bollocks* turned into just that - a load of bollocks! In the end most sold out, the twats.

JIBBERS

Virgin Records had a popular shop in Manchester at the time. Lou and me were on the mooch in town and were attracted by this new record shop just near Piccadilly blasting music out where all the punks met. We saw an inviting envelope on the other side of the counter looking lumpy – we assumed it was cash but it was just out of reach. The staff looked busy and had their backs to us, so I did my best pogo over the counter, grabbed the envelope and was back over on my side in one spring. A split second later we were trotting down the road, nobody shouted or chased us so it was sweet to look at what we'd got. There were 200 tickets to Knebworth that coming summer in that envelope – we thought they were a great result... until we tried selling them.

Sully, our kid's mate, got pulled a few days later with fifty tickets when he got stopped and searched in town. My name got mentioned so the Old Bill came to question me but I just said "he must just be throwing names in, didn't Sully mean my brother Colin? I don't know him, it couldn't be me, look I'm only 16." So we quickly sold 100 the next day to a well-known tout called Vase who dressed and stank like a tramp but had pure money. The other 50 Lou took to Knebworth where he sold them; I didn't go with him as I'd already had my name tied to them but regardless we were buzzing from the money we got.

By this time our Colin had come home from an extended holiday and all the talk was of going abroad. He'd been to a game in Saint Etienne and we were told it was so easy over there to rob anything you wanted. At this time, almost every other night in the *Manchester Evening News* they would be reporting a wage snatch or stolen takings from staff outside banks. We'd know almost all the jibbers by the descriptions in the paper. Such a lad who was always described as a "tall, skinny man with long dark hair and prominent nose..." this would have been Skinny. "Man with mouth wide open looking lost holding a rolled up paper" would be Sully and so on.

Cash tills were everywhere back then and an average 'Jack and Jill' would usually see you through the next few days as they actually had money in them, unlike today. Shopkeepers would turn away in fright when they saw a bunch of thieving football hooligans unloading their tills. The hooligans on away days didn't really have to conceal what they did. So long as they made it out onto the street, they were safe. A quick change of the ever faithful cagoule which helpfully came in various colours and were often reversible, and there was little chance you'd be caught.

Around this time everyone was dressing up a bit more and started to look smarter. Fewer reds were wearing the colours; semi-flares, desert boots or hush puppies, Fred Perry T-shirts, Slazenger jumpers, Lois jeans – these were all hitting the scene. The flick was well and truly part of the fashion and we became labelled the Perry Boys. On away days, small groups of Mancs would be walking around towns like it was open season – they'd be in and out of every other shop looking for their beloved cash tills and even the back office for the day's takings or some clobber. Manchester's thieves were now really taking the piss left, right and centre – it was a great scene to witness. I used to really buzz watching them go at it in the turnstile areas then inside the ground. At half-time they'd raid the tea stall. I used to love watching it all, it was a top buzz. It was soon given the name 'mobbing and robbing'.

"Everywhere you go-oh people wanna know – oh, we're the boys in red and white who love to sing, love to fight"

Football and grafting were just made for each other in those days. This was a time before CCTV, mobile phones, TAG and ASBOs. In the mid to late seventies few people had credit cards, it was all cash. The tills were so full it was unreal by today's standards and the temptation was huge. Every shop was a target from big stores right down to the little corner shop.

★

Home matches at Old Trafford were a case of running the gauntlet for away fans. Even scousers, who could take the piss all over the country, found this out on many occasions visiting Manchester. Here's a description of a typical United/Liverpool game of the period...

The famous Oasis shopping centre was where all the main United lads hung around in the centre of Manchester. All the thieving thugs would join up with Salford around 12pm, about 20 lads left the Oasis to meet up with them in a pub opposite Strangeways prison, less than a mile walk from town. Now with their ranks doubled in numbers, filling the pub to capacity after a few swift pints and observing the scousers from this great vantage point, they knew that the scouse had decided to come out the back way of the station, which was a big mistake as only around 70 of their lads had got through the police cordon. Now this meant they were all heading into Salford/Cheetham Hill territory, which was a bad decision on their behalf. Though the scousers had a good contingent out that day it was a pity for them that only around 70 got out as about 600 were left behind in the station. Of all the exits they could chosen that day they chose the wrong one, although the scousers had the advantage of being on higher ground, this didn't put off a United mob who steamed into their ranks again and again until the Old Bill got between them, shuffling the Scousers back to their mates now locked in Victoria Station.

This left United all hyped up with nothing else on the menu as it was still too early to go to the ground. So they decided that as they were near Deansgate, which is the plush part of town, they'd go mobbing and robbing. Clearly the phrase "don't shit on your own door step" wasn't going to apply that day. First on their list was the obvious one, Paris de Sept in Manchester's Deansgate, where Kicker boots and Lacoste shirts were sold, it got completely ragged that day. The building had 3 Floors: Coco, Colin, Sully, Spud, Miller, Dessie and Rabbi plus every other top thief in town stormed the place. They did both tills within seconds and took as much gear as they could carry out. The staff were in a panic, apart from one bloke, who stood his ground to protect the stock which was being snatched before his eyes. Colin was at the centre and the bloke was now wrestling him shouting "call the cops I've got one" it took a good few blows before he let go of him but credit where it's due, he was brave to face that crew alone. Now all the lads were running amok; snatching handbags and wallets from people just stood at bus-stops while muttering in broad scouse accents – they just took the piss really. But not everyone got away - a few lads were nicked and charged as they swanned into Piccadilly where the plod were waiting to round them up.

It seemed that everyone wanted the clobber they had in France without actually going there or paying for it. A pair of Kickers at this time would cost half a week's wage. It still baffles me today that Kickers are cheap in today's market, the company mustn't have got onto how popular they were in the UK as their sales must have looked shite. Lacoste T-shirts too, I mean, whoever paid for them? None of us lot that's for sure. You'd be publicly humiliated and would have to endure constant ribbing with the likes of "how much did you pay for that again?" and "he's paid for that you know!"

TO PAY WAS TO FAIL

Three of us jibbed the train and made our way to Kings Road, Chelsea. Jibbing a train was easy, all you needed was wit and nerve. Before the train left you would just see where the ticket inspector was positioned, if he was stood at the front we would walk past him and get on at the back of the train and vice-versa. When the train departed one of us would go and see if the *Uncle Hector* was collecting tickets yet or sat on his lazy arse in the cabin. If he was collecting, it was every man for himself. Me being five foot nothing, I could easily hide under a seat. Another way, if he was heading toward you, was to pass him telling him your girlfriend had your tickets at the back of the carriage. If you had drinks in your hands he would always let you pass without asking for your tickets as he could see your hands were full - the trick was timing it just right to get past him without being seen.

On arriving in London's Kings Road we couldn't believe that you could get any colour of Kickers you wanted. I asked to try a blue pair on and just waltzed out wearing them, the shop was so busy I bet she never even noticed. Meanwhile Divy and Kev took theirs from the window display where they were on show in pairs just ready to go. We met up again at Euston where they told me politely to "fuck off". I wasn't getting a penny for the shoes they got but I wasn't arsed, I had my Kickers and was more than made up. I remember that everyone would rough their Kickers up straight away to look like they had really been wearing them for ages. Our Colin and his mates went abroad regularly now, mainly on missions to Swizzy, The Land of the Wedge. He'd always come back home looking as happy as Larry and proper wedged up telling us of his adventures and exploits. It was a bit different to what we were doing at the time, grafting dismal Yorkshire...

★

Sid, a mate of ours, had a rust bucket Morris Minor that shook and rattled when it got to 40 miles per hour, but it was a car, just, and this was our first trip out of Manchester to graft. Naively and unbeknown to us, Yorkshire had well and truly been battered and we were arrested shortly after our arrival. After we split into pairs I noticed this massive bloke looking at the two of us, me being me I stupidly went up to him and asked "can you tell me where the cigarette shops are please?" Bang! The bastard twatted me hard on the side of my napper and threw me against a wall "Yuv come here ter do tills you lot" he growled in a real Yorkie accent, turns out he was a copper who had followed us since we'd left the car, oh well. Back at the station, when I was asked what we were doing in Barnsley I just said I had fallen asleep in the car in Manchester as I'd been out all night and was knackered and "I never even knew I was in Yorkshire and not had chance to wake up before getting twatted, by you! I only wanted a packet of cigs" that was my cover story anyway. I kept with this same story for the next 30 years.

One of the other two lads had got nicked and had hidden a cine-camera he'd pinched in the police car. How he'd managed to hide it God knows, it sounds far-fetched but it's true. Either way it wasn't found and as we hadn't done anything we were released but only after being subjected to a few hours of intimidation from the Yorkshire Old Bill. One copper tried to say my boots must be stolen as one sole was red and the other green "why's that's then lad?" On our way home the lad who had hid the camera said he thought one of the Old Bill must have found it and kept it for themselves, yet a few weeks later they drove down to Manchester and arrested him as his prints were found on it. We definitely would have got a good slap if they'd found it when we were in the cells, there's no doubt about it. It was normal back then to get a dig or two from the dibble, this was the seventies and the Yorkshire dibble hated Mancs or anyone who wasn't local.

★

By now Colin and his crew were on a roll and they were very much at the forefront in town and on the football scene. I was still helping to carry things for him, as he and his mates would be getting pulled and searched all the time. Once, just before I was due to meet him, he had got pulled with something and was charged with *"committing or possessing a stolen item from an unknown theft at an unknown place trying to sell to an unknown person!"* He ended up at CDC holding cells in town. I went to visit him there to take him some clothes and stuff. Just outside I recognised the copper who was always on our Colin's case. I only asked him "was our Colin in the cells" and he walked briskly up to me and just clouted me snarling, "fuck off, you little bastard". He stunk to fuck of booze. Ignoring him I walked into the police station to drop our kid's stuff off, only to be told "he's been charged and let out". I was relieved when I went back out to see that the drunken copper had gone, probably to the nearest pub, as it was teatime. A copper would never get away with slapping Joe Public while drunk nowadays and right outside a cop shop too! Even getting a slap or just clipped on the head by the police was normal then – after all this was the seventies...

I knew roughly where our Colin would be at this time as the shops were closing. So I marched down to Oxford Road where there was the then famous Grosvenor snooker hall where everyone inside was just an out an out crook. Everyone was puffing away on big fat spliffs, as I entered there were massive clouds of Afghan hash or Jamaican weed drifting by. The smoke was illuminated by the lights above the tables. The place was managed by Mary, an Irish woman who was always so happy and friendly that everybody treated her like they would their own mother. She had real respect from everybody and the place ran itself with her in charge. I had been in a few times, mostly with Divy or Lou. We would all put together and buy hashish from a Scottish guy called Donnie. I remember he used to cringe slightly as I didn't really buy enough! I would only be getting a quarter at most but I knew he'd serve me up, as I was Colin's brother. Pubs weren't open all day back then, plus lads like me who didn't do pubs yet could go to the Grosvenor. It was always full of characters and every race and creed would be mingling together – there was never any friction in this mish mash of streetwise *fun loving criminals*.

They all had nicknames: Beaner, Swift Neck, Dicko, Fat Neck, Skull, Cat, Snowy, Long leather Joe, No neck, Dirty neck, Paki Pete, Paraffin Pete, Daffy, Two bob Tony, Norman the Nose and T-Bone Terry. To the older lads I would end up with a really original and well thought out name 'Beaner's brother' or just simply 'B'. I didn't mind one bit being known by this name as it got us in places we wouldn't get to see otherwise. Plus the places and people we got to know through Colin were jaw dropping at times, though by now, me and my mates were on our own little crooked road. We loved hanging round with the older lads, especially for the club scene. With the end of the punk era, funk started to hit the scene, although the likes of Blondie, Ian Dury and The Clash along with a few other bands made it past punk, we all started listening to reggae or funk now with a band called Parliament whose lead singer George Clinton was as mad as he looked. The style had really gone back to Mod with the Perry look and everyone seemed to have a flick haircut.

Mainstream music was all daft discos and it was really irritating listening to it all in the clubs, watching the girls dancing round their handbags while we waited for the smooch at the end of the night to move in on some girl you'd been eyeing up. If we wanted our own music or club scene Manchester had Kloisters, The Cyprus Tavern, the student union bars, The Russell club and Reno's, which was rough and shady as fuck but played great music. I remember going to see Santana at the Palace Theatre being supported by Earth, Wind and Fire. The latter were kings of disco at the time and I was mesmerised by their live performance – we had actually only gone to see Santana but EWF were amazing. Half way through their act the whole drum set including the drummer levitated into the air and began turning as the drummer continued to play throughout – it was unbelievable or maybe I was stoned. It was after this night my mate Greg would attempt to become a singer and over the next few years he would do our heads in singing and playing Earth, Wind and Fire. I remember he had a flat on Springfield Road, Sale which had a large student/hippy population. For a laugh just outside his flat I sprayed on the church wall, where everyone could clearly see from the main road, *Greg's Disco -10p!* With an arrow pointing towards his gaff.

It was fair to say he wasn't amused and punished us all by playing EWF every chance he got. From then on he was known as Earth, Wind and Greg.

SALE SET SAIL ON THE SEALINK

Inevitably when we reached the age of 17 we got itchy feet. It was high time we got passports and ventured abroad. Six of us were up for going: me, Div, Donnie, Paddy, Kev and Sid. Donnie and Paddy had been to Amsterdam before. You couldn't really sneak passage onto a boat so we bought cheap Transalpino tickets at the Students' Union on Oxford Road and went to buy a smoke from the Grosvenor snooker hall nearby. With a Transalpino ticket, plenty of weed and a one year passport we were off, with hardly a penny to our names. This was the first journey of many that would be repeated so often over the next few years.

Getting off the train at Dover we split up and tried to look like we weren't with each other. Fat chance. For a start we were all in the same clobber, plus the Gestapo had seen it all before - small groups of lads dressed the same but trying to look they didn't know one another. A big brute of a man who had clearly seen us trying to duck and dive past his customs colleagues, yelled out, "Right – you, you and you, come over here! Where yer from and where you lads off to then?"

"Grape picking" and "we're from Cheshire" blurts out the Div.

"Are you taking the piss you little cunt! Grape picking!" said the official.

He took us to one side and searched our empty travel bags, "I'll ask you again where are you going?"

Still avoiding his question the Div asked "How come you're stopping us anyway? We can go abroad if we want can't we?"

"Not till I've checked you three out you're not!" He took our passports and disappeared into the office.

We knew we weren't wanted for anything so we weren't that bothered apart from the size of the bloke. He looked like he wanted to beat us up there and then the twat! He had hands like shovels and well over the top sideburns. This felt like we were back at fucking school being bullied and intimidated by Mr Whippem. Anyway, he came back actually laughing "Cheshire, that's a new one, you mean Manchester don't you?"

"No. Cheshire." Divy said, the customs officer just had to chuckle, Divy had that effect, like him or not he was a rum fucker.

"You would be wise finding a better attitude in the future" he informed us before telling us he would be keeping his eye out for us coming back, "especially you!" he ended, pointing at Divy. This little sketch would be repeated over the years...

It felt like the great escape or something. If this was what leaving your own country was like, then what was it like getting back in? So we were let on our way to board the ferry and as soon as we got on Kev and me gave Divy a nice friendly but hard dead arm each for being a div! Packs of cigarettes were our first stop in Duty Free. After a while Divy the dipper (as he thought he was) went *jibbing* which was really in and out of all the cabins looking for tired drivers who were fast asleep. Either way he got nothing as it goes but we were all buzzing from just getting out of the UK for now.

We reached Antwerp train station at 7am and I'll never forget the sight of people in the buffet bar drinking beer for breakfast on their way to work. We all sat down to ham and eggs with real coffee. After a quick look out of the station we decided to jump on a train to Amsterdam as Antwerp looked a real drab moody place – we even nicknamed it Gotham City as it looked so gloomy.

Arriving in Amsterdam about 12ish we checked into a dormitory at Bob's youth hostel, which is still there today. Everyone got showered and changed ready for grafting. We were all brassic now, so we decided to split up and go on the mooch. Paddy and myself got on a train to Harlem about 15 minutes ride away. After nipping in a few shops we soon found ourselves in a wool shop. Now why would two young lads be in a wool shop for fucks sake? Just underneath the till was a draw with 500 guilders in so it was enough to call it a day plus we were well knackered from travelling the previous night; we made a 'U turn' and went back to the train station.

We both felt relieved because at least we had enough money to see us through the next couple of days. We felt even better when we got to Amsterdam as I hadn't even seen it yet, as Paddy had been there before and said he knew a coffee shop where we could go. So we had a quick walk through the red light area - I'd never seen anything like it before, all these women were half-naked gesturing towards us. Wahey!

We managed to walk past without giving into temptation as we were more interested in getting weed. I remember it seemed ages before we eventually found the place to buy hash. It wasn't like today where coffee shops are on every corner, we ended up in a hippy tea house shop just past the Waterloopleine. Inside was a blackboard with all the names of what they sold and after reading the list we bought something I had never seen or heard of before called *Red Lebanese*. I had been stoned before but fucking hell this hit me like a ton of bricks - the walls were zooming in on me. Everything felt like my first ever spliff but ten times stronger. Then we had to get back to pay for the dorm, we were lucky in the first place to check in without money up front but we had said we needed a bank change and would pay him within the hour or so and left him a passport. Me and Paddy had only been away a few hours and we were well relieved and chuffed as fuck with ourselves that we could now relax and enjoyed a nice big spliff with the hippies. We had a joint from this newly discovered hash we had bought while we waited for the other lads. Still buzzing that we were finally abroad, Amsterdam was another planet, worlds away from Manchester's culture, it was brilliant and I'd only been here five fuckin' hours plus I'd already got a bit of expenses - bonus!

Divy and Kev came back not long after. They had gone on a tram around Amsterdam's outskirts and had got a few hundred, we felt better now and started up another big joint. Then Donnie and Sid came in not long after. Donnie looked like he had seen a ghost or something - he flew past us ushering us to follow him back to the dorm. We were made up to announce we had all earned but soon felt deflated when Donnie threw a big load of cash on the table; 15,000 fucking guilders, the equivalent of £3,000. In amongst the notes were thousand guilders notes worth £300 each – what a result! None or us had ever seen this kind of money before but the day actually ended up as an anticlimax for four of us, as it was only agreed to split expenses and not wedges. Okay, it wasn't written in stone but the four of us were secretly gutted. It was clear that as far as graft went, this wasn't "all for one and one for all".

Anyway, onwards and upwards. We were all made up that we were finally abroad. Although we did slag Donnie and Sid off behind their backs for a bit. If the shoe was on the other foot would we have shared that amount of money? I doubt it. That night we ended up in a club on the Liedsepleine called The Milky Way. You went over a little Amsterdam drawbridge to get to it. Inside there was a cinema, a theatre and a big hall that was for bands at the back which is where you bought hash and weed. It all looked like Willy Wonka's hashish bash to me and strangely it wasn't full of criminals like I'd expected to be but dead average hippy dudes sat about smoking pipes, bongs and chillums. After chatting with a few locals they told us that the entire weed and hash that was sold in this place came from the police station across the road. That meant the police were actually selling weed and hash! No way did we believe any of it, although later I discovered this to be true. I'd heard Holland was a top country. Fucking right on! We all went straight in for that super-tasty, lovely-smelling Red Lebanese hash; we were like kids in a candy store. You could also buy a variety of weed - Columbian gold or Red, Thai sticks, or Afghan Black, Nepal Temple Balls, Manila or Kashmir. The list was baffling to read as we had only ever smoked Afghan and Jamaican weed before, back in sunny Mancland.

Amsterdam was mad and you were lucky if you didn't get run over either by a tram, bus, car or cyclist, the last being the worst. It seemed bikes would come silently from any fucking direction, I swear. The same could be said for the street dealers who hassled people non-stop as soon as you stepped out from your hotel or bar. Within a few metres you'd hear it! "Pssst hey you! Hash, coke, smack?" We soon learned not to acknowledge them as even if you said "no" or made eye contact they were on you and then they followed you for ages.

There were far too many Surinamese dealers to say fuck off to or fight, especially around the station, Damrak or red light area, so it was best to ignore them if you could, even though you'd be getting shadowed, then within 100 metres or so they would spot someone else to mither instead. All in all it was a funny experience as long as they didn't get too near, after all they were only grafting! Apart from the Surinamese, the other street dealers were Moroccans who got right in your face. They were too close for comfort. We instantly disliked them as every last one thought they were hard. So too, it seemed, did the Surinamese.

There were eight of us now (Lou and Terry had arrived) and we had only been in Amsterdam about a week and taken to it like ducks to water. Eventually we went toe-to-toe with the Morrocans, much to the delight of the Surries. We stayed around the area where there are a few English bars such as The Flying Dutchman. This place could have been below deck on Black Beard's pirate ship, it was full of rum cunts. Eventually, we liked and got on well with the Surinamese. Yet it was the opposite with the Moroccans, we didn't like them one bit. We were soon well onto all the goings on we witnessed in this criminal paradise.

★

Within weeks three of us got off to Copenhagen with a bag load of acid tabs. Donnie had been before and said we would easily sell them at a place called Christiania which was a hippie commune and is now a 'freetown'. It was another sight to behold as we had taken half a tab of acid each early on before leaving the hotel. The snow was knee deep, everyone had big fur hats on and all the taxis were big American style cars driving down the widest roads I'd ever seen before. Tivoli Gardens right in the city centre made everything look like New York and it felt like Starsky and Hutch would drive by any minute. We were tripping out, gobsmacked by it all.

We managed to get in a taxi, somehow, and told the driver to go Christiania, a few miles out of town. It was more relaxed here as we took the sights in for a short while then Donnie said "wait til you see this place, it's fuckin mad here". The taxi stopped in what seemed to be the middle of nowhere. It was a dimly lit area and I saw what looked like a big gloomy prison from the outside. This had been an old military base for a German army garrison back in the war. It felt to us like being taken back to that period and the state I was in it could have been the Berlin Wall for all I knew.

Going into the place you had to walk through a big open gateless entrance. The old army base had now been taken over by thousands of really well-organised anti-government, squatting, anarchist, drug dealing Vikings. The snow was 4 foot deep and small paths led on to the barracks where the ground floors were turned into cafés, pubs and canteens. We were tripping and slightly spaced out – it felt great. The only downside was I felt like a dwarf as I remember everyone was so fuckin tall. I'd gone from New York to World War II in the last hour, now I was in Wild West territory, only populated by giants... Outside the main bar it looked to me like the 'OK Corral' and instead of horses tied up outside, there were packs of massive dogs that looked like wild wolves. Some breeds I'd never seen before. This wasn't the acid either. Inside confirmed we were in the OK Corral. The only thing being I couldn't, luckily for me, see any guns. Instead everyone was carrying fuck off bowie knives and openly playing with them stabbing at the tables they sat behind while waiting to sell their hash. Each dealer had a table and each one had a massive guard dog at their side. It all looked very surreal. We made our way to the bar to catch our breath a little.

Observing everything we saw the dealers with big chunks of hash showing customers what they had, then cutting off whatever grams you wanted with the over the top bowie knives before tossing smaller chunks onto the fishing scales. The place was a hive of activity – dogs and people milling around, beer being consumed, food roasting on skewers – and to us sat watching offside they definitely were Vikings, growlers every last one. This wasn't friendly Amsterdam that's for sure, this was the roughest place that I'd ever been to. Anyway, after buying some smoke the whole place felt a lot more sociable, even though they didn't have my favourite Red Lebanese. We started chatting with the dealer, a top guy. He told us about the history of the camp and the people that lived in cottages originally built for German officers, while others lived in the barracks built for the Wehrmacht. The police never came inside the base as they would "get fucked up bad" he assured us and they had regular riots every other week when the police would turn up in full riot gear and try in vain to close things down. We stayed in the bar and soaked up the atmosphere, just watching these Hells Angels/Vikings! The only things missing from this bar were guns and Viking helmets. It was fair to say George Lyons and the Old Guard would have loved it.

The next day we got back to reality and went to see the bloke Donnie had met previously, who lived right by the railway station. When he saw Don he was well made up but when we said we had acid to sell he wasn't impressed. "Eh man you can't be selling that shit here, nobody likes tabs" turns out that apart from hash everybody was pretty much drug free in Denmark. We spent a full day at this guy's house, he was about 40 years old and he loved what we did. His advice was sound, "always dress in neutral colours" i.e. dark blue as you get less noticed and "don't ever look a copper in the eyes from a distance, they'll get right on to you". I for one took his advice and started dressing down and I rarely looked at a copper in the eye from a short distance especially the Gestapo (customs). After a day or two he gave us an address of some hippy he'd tracked down for us who might want the acid. He happened to live back on that Christiania commune, Don's mate was right - nobody else wanted to know.

We might as well have been selling heroin from the reaction we got. "You're mad even trying to sell them" this other guy told us plus we shouldn't let too many people know what we had as only hash was allowed there, everyone on the compound were very anti-drugs. It was more than we needed or wanted to know really! We decided to leave the tabs with his Danish mate who was asked could he post them on to an address when Donnie wrote to him after he got back. The Danish guy, who I don't think even wanted anything more to do with them, reluctantly agreed and we decided to graft some ex's to go home with. It was mid-winter and fucking freezing, the streets and shops all seemed empty compared to Holland where, by now, I wish I'd stayed!

THE FLYING DUTCHMAN

By the time of our next trip to the Dam, nine of us were up for the off and we ended up in that same dorm at Bob's. The same six as before were on the trip plus Terry, who was a nephew of Joe Corrigan, the Man City and England goalkeeper (yet he looked the spit of Norman Whiteside a United player), Earth, Wind and Greg joined us plus Diller – we were all from Sale. Whatever things had in store for us, we were all young and with no master 'grafting' plan we were in no rush to get home, so we just soaked up the everyday scene going on around us in Amsterdam. Although I'd been the winter before, it was now summer and full of tourists walking round stoned. Inside the pubs people took their time and relaxed, yet once out on the street it turned into mayhem – it seemed every bit of transport wanted to run you over and every hustler wanted to have you over. It was like getting rained on from every angle, just like at a big football match.

As we had before we took up The Flying Dutchman as our new local. All the Brits that lived in the dam seemed to be Scottish, the majority being rum fuckers. We met three rum guys, Chappie being the most popular. The Scots even had a bar just off the Zeedijk, one of the roughest streets in Europe, which says it all really. It was positioned just before you came into the red light area. We got to know more people over the next few weeks and as usual everyone likes a bargain. We could sell them jeans or whatever they ordered within reason. Right next to the Dutchman is a massive pedestrianised street with shops on both sides that went on for a good distance.

Soon the local English in the pubs started asking can we get this or that for them. Okay, it was all petty stuff by later standards with its junkie image but back then it was money and money's money, innit. We were all happy getting at least a week's wages in a day and Amsterdam suited us all just fine. It was the most crooked place we had ever seen before, not that I'd seen that many places yet but there you go. We were all on a high that's for sure. I remember Col's mate Dicko came over. He was much older than us. Dicko had just got out of Strangeways and was over on a busman's holiday. He said "if you're here for a while, don't you get a gaff?"

I don't think that thought had ever entered our heads, so we decided that was the way to go, we didn't want to go back to England, there was nothing for us there. Dicko summed it up when he said, "England's shit, Amsterdam is the place for us". He then told us about the squats in Holland where Anarchists took over whole streets that were usually set to be demolished. They were known as kraak houses, and the squatters were kraakers. They all looked fucking crackers to me, I remember that much! Most were punks and looked like Sid Vicious with a big 'A' printed on their backs but I thought at least they were against the establishment and government and stood up for their rights, unlike the UK punks who seemed like middle class sell outs. When he'd said they taken over entire streets, he wasn't kidding. In a town in the east of Amsterdam, Miuderpoort, a full street looked ready for war. It was some sight! Just off the main road was Tudlerweg. Nearly every flat on the block was squatted with banners hanging out of most windows declaring such. The street looked as if it was just missing a barricade but I suppose you can't have everything.

Surprisingly the flat wasn't as bad as we had thought, we thought it was going to be minging. Okay it wasn't the Ritz but we moved in the next day and the electric worked too, what a result! We arrived with a single mattress and after robbing our bedding, pot, pans and things, we were in. Dicko had already been coming to the dam for a few years and knew more people that would buy our ill-gotten gains. We carried on getting our wares and Dicko was selling them daily just like it was all in a normal day's work.

Arriving back one day I smelt something that went right through me and I nearly vomited. There was a new kid in town, "Mr Brown". Bits of heroin were getting sprinkled into what they called a *chillum* pipe brought round by a group of Dicko's mates. They went regularly to India and had got a taste for it. Kev and

Div had dabbled before and Dicko too but Paddy and I hadn't. One night I got offered a toot. I responded by mimicking a junkie pretending to goof while rubbing my nose and starting to mumble and gargle like they do. Dicko wasn't impressed with my taking the piss and it put our new friendship on hold for a good week or so. Soon Div and Kev would be going out for toot money so me and Paddy would go out working together while Dicko, being more a ticket tout, would go to Rotterdam or Köln buying and selling.

If we were the artful dodgers then Dicko was Fagin. It was like a modern day Dickens novel with Amsterdam's historic buildings as a backdrop set against an electric atmosphere in the back streets and ginnels. Sometimes we even got money without trying with help from whoever worked at a place. Once, in the red light area, Paddy and I popped into a hippy hash café one morning to buy a gram of smoke. We went upstairs where the door creaked open. Inside it was just like someone's front room done out in a hippy style. A guy shouted out that he was in the shower and he'd be out in a minute but we could wait and make ourselves a tea or coffee, which was a nice gesture from the guy. "Oh, ok thanks" we said as we quickly emptied 800 guilders from his wallet and took all his hash. "Tell you what mate, we'll call back later" he'd not even seen us and 800 guilders was a right result for our breakfast, plus a chunk of top Afghan, it was a good little wedge back then.

Video recorders could get you a thousand guilders or £300. The first video we got in Amsterdam there were four of us. There was a big hi-fi store on the Damrak, the shop was massive and the videos weren't even chained up. Paddy set it up, taking the leads as well as they were important - then the Div got the guy out of the way and Dicko was in with a perfectly sized box to put it in. Not needing to do anything myself I just kept an eye out for any staff coming our way. Timing being the key to such things it went smoothly. I remember turning to watch the guy after he'd realised he'd been blagged go out of the shop with a confused look on his kipper. He was staring up and down the Damrak in the forlorn hope he might get his video back somehow, or that Dicko and Paddy would leave it outside. The guy was scratching his head as his prize exhibit had just vanished.

With the money from the video me, Paddy and Dicko soon jumped on a train and went to Rokslide, a massive festival in Denmark where we started buying and selling tickets, then went inside the festival, I can't even remember who was on. But after a top weekend we knew the memorabilia stalls would soon be packing up to leave, so we went mooching around. One stall had been selling souvenirs and a guy was counting up his weekend takings and shoving it all into a big travel bag. After a quick nod to Dicko, I went round the back while he got the attention of the assistant to get him away from the tent wall so I could ease myself under it. I dragged the bag from under the canvas wall and was away with it. The fucker was heavy – I thought it must have a massive cash box inside as it rattled about like one. We met and found the wedge was a good one so that made the festival even better. The noises I heard from the bag turned out to be a small press machine for making badges and all the stuff that went with it plus thousands of badges that had Mick Jagger's lips or cannabis leaves printed on them. We kept the bag and took it back to The Dam, I thought I'd sit back and just sell badges in Vondle Park, flogging them to the hippies floating round while I sat around getting stoned doing nothing but thinking I was going to make easy money. But after a few hours I realised I would sell nothing and decided not to bother again, instead swapping it for slabs of hash from a punk we had met down our street. He was really made up, he probably made a load of badges with that simple 'A' for anarchy printed up on them for the 'never to come' revolution. Though Sid Vicious had died earlier that year, it looked like the fucker lived on in Amsterdam where almost all punks had adopted the Sid look. Although punk rock had fizzled out back in the UK, it was still massive with the Dutch, especially the squatters.

Colin came and stayed for a short while one time and did the till at our local laundry. As we used the laundry most days and Colin kept saying he was going to do it, even though we asked him not to, it was a pain in the arse. The woman who worked there was okay with us but he just told us he couldn't leave it there 'crying out to be emptied'. He told us no one saw him but that was a blag as the vibe in the shop after was a bit strained towards us. She knew what had happened, I'm in no doubt, but it's not like you can just give it back, though being Amsterdam we could have tried… Instead we chose to go to a different laundrette - Divy was willing to "half admit to it" in order to give the money back to her but that doesn't come easy, so we had to dodge her from then on in.

Fucking Colin!

There was a cockney guy who drank in the Flying Dutchman we called 'Bob on yeah' cos that's all he ever said. 'Bob' was really sound with us and I remember he gave us a car up front that we could pay him for after we had earned. So we went out of our way and managed to get him a video, "good on yer lads" he said grabbing the video with both hands from the boot, he was a massive no nonsense bloke making light work of the weight of the fucker. I could just about lift a video, they were as heavy as a slab of concrete and as big too.

Another character was Irish Tony who sported a great big long red beard and looked every bit the typical funny upbeat Irishman. Being the official dealer he sold his hash from his tobacco tin and did top RedLeb, plus he even started giving us tick before long. The Flying Dutchman was buzzing back then, it was always full of characters who seemed to have been abroad and done most things already, just like the lads at the Grosvenor Snooker Hall back in Manchester. The only people who looked out of place in the pub, funnily enough, were a couple who were always in there - the owners. They were the only people I never spoke to either, yet to be fair they let us sell our wares and never once said a thing to us. With them seeming odd and aloof, I don't think any of us actually tried to sell anything to them.

That winter, along with Lou and Greg, I made off to the Alps, only not to Switzerland but Austria. We ended up at Innsbruck station at close to midnight - the snow was knee deep and the three of us weren't dressed for the occasion that's for sure. We got a cheapo hotel and counted up enough for some chips as that was all we had on us.

Having arrived at night I didn't notice the scenery until the next day and at first I thought the clouds were very low and looked strange, only to be told they were the fucking Alps! The way we were dressed we stood out like sore thumbs looking like the Three Stooges surrounded by arctic explorers. Everyone was pointing at us when we crossed the road which made us well paranoid. We quickly got into a big store and got ourselves completely rigged out. We looked like right wallies but felt better and the pointing we sussed was all about us crossing on a red light rather than our clothes. We were still tip-toeing round this snowed in city in snide shoes and managed to get a waiter's zap we had seen left about. It contained little as the restaurant had only just opened so it was just a float but it was was enough to get off with as we didn't like the look or feel of Innsbruck. We jumped straight on a train to Bregenz near the Swiss border.

Lou figured we had enough money for a room, so we hid our bags and went hunting down much needed boots to go with our new jackets. Ski shops were plentiful so getting canvas snow boots on our feet was a relief. Up until then I'd naively arrived in midwinter Austria not thinking it out at all, wearing a black Harrington jacket, jeans and Kickers. We went out that night and met a group of hippies who liked the fact we had hash on us from Amsterdam. We shared a joint outside a bar and they gave us their address. The next day we met them again while out mooching in the town. They asked if we had more hash on us, which we did, and they invited us to their 'hippy pit'. We had maybe ten grams on us, they were in heaven when Lou gave them a good little piece to build up with. Graft done for the day, we managed to get a place to stay after telling them we were struggling money wise and were waiting on money from the UK.

Having a place to doss felt ten times better than a hotel and they treated us fine with plenty of food. We went out for two days telling them we were waiting on money. They lived within walking distance of the small town so me and Lou ventured out on the third day at getting on for closing time. We ended up in a big store.

The Flying Dutchman

It was that late it was almost the only thing open on the street. I saw an assistant empty a till putting the contents in a cash bag then she went and opened another till 20 yards way and another then another… then she put the money bag right underneath the till in a drawer. I frantically found Lou and told him what I'd seen and with no time to lose he flew over and led her away from the money. She wasn't a bit wary as she hadn't even seen me. I crouched down and ran for the drawer. Bingo! It felt wadded to fuck. I kept my head down and made my way towards Lou just letting him see I'd got it and made my way out. Lou caught me up down the street and we proceeded towards our hippy gaff. As soon as we got there the idea was to declare that our money had arrived from England. Handing the bag to Greg when we got back, we hadn't had time to check its contents as we'd had to get back to the flat quickly. We knew the scream would be up back at the store - it was only a small town and the sirens were already out. The hippies might have felt our unease as they got jumpy too - it emerged the old bill always went to theirs as they were the only smokers in town and we also started getting the jitters when Greg said it was a massive wedge, £3,000.

After an hour or two a girl who lived in the flat came back looking at us but telling everyone else in the room there'd been a robbery in town. They were hippies but that didn't make them stupid. We had been separately nipping in and out of town for three days. After a long silence and only knowing them a couple of days, I spoke up. My light-hearted version of events ran that it wasn't a robbery, I just tripped over some money on my way back. I said I found it but never stole it, that was my story and I was sticking to it. In the end they were sound as fuck and loved it, chuckling at my story after a little translation! So after giving the main honcho £300 they phoned a friend who lived locally and when he arrived, he drove us to another town nearby. That night they all stayed with us as and we had a top night out in a Bierkeller right up in the mountains, about ten miles up it felt like. Greg, Lou and me were buzzing now; drinking beer and schnapps for the first time, we were dressed not in our tourist gear but odd looking hippy clothes.

It was like a spy movie. We were stoned to fuck and this being my first grand and it not being long after my 19th birthday, I was made up with our new friends. They had been sound with us, they were a great set of hippy anarchists and never stopped smiling at us that night with that "we know what you did" look.

Wisely, the next day, we got the fuck out of the area and went back to Holland for Christmas. Apart from the hippies and that lucky wedge, we didn't like Austria. I never went back. The one thing registering to me at this time was how different the people were in Europe as compared to England, they seemed to have a good standard of living but were ignorant as they never spoke or wanted to chat like people would back home.

Not that we knew it but they didn't celebrate Christmas in Holland. Their Christmas was on December 5th (Saint Nicolas Day). New Year was brilliant though with massive firework displays plus all the bars and clubs open 24/7. We had spent nearly all our money in a week. We would soon get used to spending what we earned, that part came quite easy, that's for sure! Spending it felt just as good as getting it I suppose, I loved it. Pulling a nice wad out at the bar made you feel great, I can tell yer. There seemed to be two types of grafters; the ones who spent and the ones who banked it all. I couldn't relate to the latter one bit. I was out for a good time, so too were all my mates from Sale. With nothing to return for other than a crappy estate, we seldom went back to Maggie's Farm.

By the start of 1980, the squatters were in full swing and brilliant at organizing riots. Forget the football fights I'd seen up to now back in England, they seemed lightweight after seeing these punks who really got stuck into the Old Bill, not like back home where we normally ran from the dibble – these fuckers ran into them instead. They would take the police on at full throttle. Posters started appearing all over Amsterdam saying that they would be defending a street due to be demolished. The thing was this street was where we lived!

So the night before everyone occupied the buildings that had been targeted. Barricades to all the entrances were put up and squatters started major parties with all kinds of music blasting out from the flats with the ever-present banners hanging out of all the windows, then the next morning the police arrived bang on cue at 9 am.

One trick the police would use to gain entry to the buildings would be to arrive with a massive 'cherry picker' with around ten riot police inside it which would then be raised to the top floor where the dibble would have a good old go at gaining entrance; smashing the windows and throwing tear gas in to get the squatters away from the windows. There would be major scuffles all the way down on each floor until they emptied the building. This went on all day until they had cleared the occupants out of one building after another onto the street. Then there would be around 200 squatters all stood around bricking the Old Bill who were stuck inside the flats. So now you had the riot police stuck in the flats with all the rioters on the streets until reinforcements arrived. This went on for hours until nightfall. We would be getting pelted with tear gas in return; all the squatters wore helmets and gas masks. With most squatters having no place to call home anymore, it made sense to carry it on, the scenes at night were brilliant - just when things were dying down a bit you'd see four or five missiles fly over to where the riot police were stood in groups, and it would erupt again, the police trying in vain to clear the street. Although the police always won in the end, these streets were never given up lightly, I can tell you that for sure. After a full day and night rioting me, Kev and Divy were filthy and well knackered.

With no place to live now, we moved in with this cockney we'd got to know called Alan who said he'd put a few of us up for a while. It was really good of him but before long we had taken over his luxury squat. Even Karen, the girl from Crawley, came with us. Six of us ending up staying there. About two months later his personal money went missing - Greg and Skinny took it from under his pillow one night as the poor cunt slept. And he was no longer sleeping with his darling little girlfriend from Portugal at the time, as she was now going out with me on the sly. The next day he moved out, vowing never to speak to another Manc ever again. So the poor cunt lost his money, flat and his missus. It wasn't planned or meant with malice, it just happened.

The anarchists never gave up and were at it again at the beginning of the summer of 1980. The main controversy was that their queen was going to marry a German. Now, the Dutch hated the Germans more than any other European country and this riot went on for ages with no respite whatsoever. The Dutch punks showed up our punks ten times over. Taking over the town from the central station right back to Dam Square, the police actually got run into the red light area and were in full retreat and eventually caught up on a small canal wedged into an alley. Missiles were launched at them and all this took place just outside a Hell's Angels pub. I couldn't believe what I witnessed next. Around a dozen or so Hell's Angels came out wielding chains and blades at us in order to help the riot police! They steamed right into the rioters and backed them off to the nearest bridge. This gave the Old Bill a boost and they joined forces with the snide bastard Angels. Albeit for a short period they saved the day for the dibble. I used to sell gear in that pub too, though after that I didn't, the collaborating fuckers. Who would ever think that the Old Bill would be saved by a dozen or so Hell's Angels?

The riot lasted well into the night and was all over the news as I found out later when I got back to the pub as big cheers went up for me. Apparently I'd been spotted on the news trying to get into a hi-fi shop, then being stopped by the squatters who told me in no uncertain terms that we weren't there for thieving, just rioting. It baffled me that they never went mobbing and robbing like back home but then again I wasn't back home, although I still went on riots whenever there was one and got to know some great anarchists along the way. I would have loved them all to be in England to show our punks a thing or two about rioting. Our punks back in England were an embarrassment; from this time on I hated the middle class twats, although it only confirmed what I already suspected.

If I hadn't been so wrapped up in our thieving lifestyle, I could have got into this Dutch punk revolution, I loved it. The anti-establishment stance appealed to me 100%. One time I twatted a plain clothes dibble right in the face with a cobble stone. He pulled out his side arm waving it about till everyone scattered. A few minutes later, we got onto the canals and the police had followed our little group riding motor bikes with coppers in side-cars beating their batons on the panels to intimidate us and almost surrounded us. I was fearful I might get nicked for the brick incident, so I got a pedal bike and just threw it underneath the fucker. It skidded up and two dibble nearly ended up in the canal.

My punk mates said enough was enough after this telling me to "get the fuck away, you're going to get arrested". So I melted away and went to the Dutchman that was just in sight. I would still turn up now and again but after a few riots they more or less banned me saying that I was just a thief and a "mad English hooligan". Though I still had friends who went out to riot, I now only met them socially as even I knew I wasn't in with their political plan. So I got back to reality, I had just got caught up in it for the moment really but had a great time all the same.

THE GOLDEN TRIANGLE

HOLLAND-SWITZERLAND-SPAIN

Our Colin came over and said his mate Roufy had DJ work in Spain for that summer and did I fancy it? So off we went. We got a massive boogie box fitted with a little television screen, which back then were the must have item on the shelves, plus two nice cameras and we were on our way. Colin had been before and said we would get close to half whack returns on the items as electric goods and gadgets weren't on general sale in Spain yet. Former dictator Franco had only died a few years before and Spain was almost like a third world country. True to form we sold the boogie box, that was nearly half my height, to a complete stranger on the beach at around 7 am. The two cameras we got half price for later on from Roufy. This was more than enough money for a week's good living at the time as Spain was so cheap. It was hard to spend two thousand pesetas a night and that was a tenner. All the peseta notes were massive, making any wedge we had look exaggeratedly loaded.

Roufy's mates in Lloret were mostly cockneys and a few Scots. They loved the highlife. Tim was a DJ at St Trop nightclub. Frank was the main wheeler dealer and Geoff was just a typical cockney socialite and a barman in a Dutch bar called The Mont Blanc that we used as our local.

I'd been away on and off now for a couple years and everywhere I'd been was full of dodgy characters in one way or another. I thought nothing of it at the time, the fact everyone seemed to be a crook seemed normal somehow. It didn't make me stop and think about what I was up to myself, I had no time – I was too busy having a great time soaking it all up. I loved Europe, I knew that much. England was too cold and grey for me, especially now that on my first ever holiday to Spain we had got 90,000 pesetas, about £500, which was an absolute bundle at the time. It looked and felt like a right old wedge for two fuckin cameras and a boogie box to me.

Spain was yet another eye opener; Sid, Paddy and Terry arrived a few days later. Our Colin had already left on one of his grafting missions to Scandie. So after soaking up the sun and great atmosphere in Spain, the four of us headed off to Switzerland on a shopping expedition. It would be my first time in Swizzy and I remember being a little apprehensive. I'd heard that it had been ragged by now as the tales from grafters who had already been there were legend. Once you're there however, you can't let yourself think like that.

In Geneva I couldn't believe it walking round with all the tom shops closed but lit up looking like a ram raider's delight. It looked like Christmas. These were big tourist shops, I couldn't catch my breath. The first day of graft me and Paddy went and got the biggest boogie box we could steal and went to the station to put it in a locker then went back out on a rattler to somewhere while Terry and Sid went the opposite way on the map to us. We were in our first town and sneaked a cash box out of a shoe shop. It was still summer and Paddy managed to slip into a back room where he found the cash box but, unable to open it, he dangled his coat off his shoulder to hide it. Standing on the platform it felt like hours as we stood apart from one another getting all paranoid until a train finally arrived.

Sat by the famous fountain on Lake Geneva we examined the cashbox. It was a fucker to open. I went off to find a screwdriver and finally popped it open. Bingo! We didn't need to count this fucker, it was loaded. With the box emptied I threw the first of many cash boxes into a Swiss lake. We went off smiling after a decent day's work under our belts. We met up with Terry and Sid later; they'd also had a good day so we had enough of a wedge to call it job done. We knew we had to get to the bus depot out of Swizzy quickly and back to Spain after just one night there, I was buzzing to fuck.

At the bus station we went into a souvenir shop for batteries for the boogie box we had shoplifted earlier in the day, when Terry decided to go up some spiral stairs smack bang in the middle of the shop, nobody batted an eyelid. Fortunately the place was packed with tourists. Terry reappeared and practically flew down the stairs, quickly darting out of the shop and onto our coach which was about to leave. We caught up with him at the back of the bus where he was holding out the biggest wedge of dollar bills you could get your palms around. We didn't even count our money until we arrived back in Lloret, we knew we were wedged and that did us, it felt like the ten hour drive back to Spain took ten minutes, we were buzzing that much.

Back in Lloret we bought a massive piece of Moroccan from Tom and the next day flew to Las Palmas which wasn't built up like it is today – there wasn't much there. So we flew to Ibiza which in hindsight we should have done in the first place, as we'd been told it was buzzing but you don't know till you go yourself do you? Austria, Ibiza, Barcelona, Amsterdam, Geneva, Copenhagen I'd not really been anywhere yet, but what I'd seen, done and witnessed so far was a thief's delight.

After a great month or so in Spain, and with a little money left, we headed back to Amsterdam to meet up with whoever would still be there. Lou and Greg had got a flat by now. Dicko was still in Alan's posh squat so I crashed there while Terry went home as usual. Terry was a bit of a homing pigeon, he loved getting off home. Divy had been deported with Kev for dipping, although I don't know how they could ever charge Divy with dipping as he couldn't take candy from a baby in a pram, although it never stopped him trying. Obviously he got some results but they were few and far between as I recall. Donnie, Kev and Divy had taken to street life in Amsterdam very quickly and were soon 'in' with all the Surinamese street dealers, so much so that one time when I went with Divy for a scran just off the Zeedijk, everyone was letting on to him.

We called the canteen we went to 'the gold fish bowl' as from outside it appeared like fish feeding time when you looked through the windows. Being white lads we were often surrounded and hustled and it felt like we had to swim into the café but we'd just chuckle and squeeze past them - they never stopped hassling the tourists. We were young but not daft. We'd grown up with this shit. We had the attitude 'chin up, chest out' that is in-built in most Brits I think. We looked them in the eye without aggression just getting them to smile. I quickly worked out that the best way to deal with these guys was to ask "if it's free, I'll have it" or simply stop dead telling them "yeah okay I'll take a kilo, hurry up I'll wait here." That always got them laughing. We'd never been in a place like this before, they were nothing like the Jamaicans or Africans we had grown up with and most played salsa music rather than reggae in their bars. There was one Surinamese pub right in between The Three Musketeers and The Flying Dutchman. These were the funniest hustlers I'd ever meet. After the scuffle we had with a group of Moroccans the year before just outside their pub they loved us, so we gladly went from waving them away to greeting them now instead.

However we still had the shady Moroccans gawping on - we couldn't take a liking to them. They were as shady as their reputation suggested. Luckily we were never alone and safety in numbers definitely applied around the back streets of Amsterdam as they were well known for stabbing you. Due to mixing with the Surinamese so much, the local dibble were getting to know Donnie, Kev and Div's faces. That's why the 'three' were constantly getting pulled and deported for one thing or another.

On my 20th birthday I walked into The Flying Dutchman and all the talk was of John Lennon who had been shot dead on the steps of his apartment in New York. Everyone was in shock, it was a real strange day in and around the red light area, all you heard in every bar were John Lennon tunes - *War is over…*

So too was our wedge from the Alps and we needed more cash to live on. So I started grafting with our Colin and Spud, as they were in Amsterdam at the time and had a car. Up to this point I'd only really grafted on trains, trams and buses, so having our own wheels was a big step up for me. That was good enough for me, so I climbed in. Colin hadn't really grafted Holland yet. Half way through the week he called me over to look at his map of Holland. For some reason he couldn't find a town or some big gaff he'd seen signs for everywhere. I had to laugh at our kid while he was scrutinising a map of Holland.

"What's up Col?"

"Oh I'm looking for this place, I've seen it on all the road signs *Doorgang verkeer*, it must be some big tourist town or something but no way can I find it."

"That's because it's not a town Colin, it just means *through traffic!*"

"Oh right no fuckin wonder I can't find it then, eh"

From then on he never bothered with the map again!

Graft with our Colin was a bit turbo to say the least after working with my mates. We used to more or less sneak around all day waiting for our opportunities without being seen or even talking. Colin just took whatever was going and it was very different from grafting with my mates, who wouldn't mind waiting it out until we could sneak the takings. Colin just made things happen, "Get the assistant over there!" he'd bark, "now move them, I wanna get in there!" My nerves were shot after a week's graft with him, I swear. He'd been at it for years, so finally after a week's work and much to my relief, we were going back to England. We'd bought a monster piece of hash in Rotterdam and drove to Ostend in Belgium.

My visitor's passport was looking more like a dog-eared piece of cloth by now, as they wore out very quickly or would separate at the seams with the pages having to be held together with tape. Just for the hell of it roaches would be made out of them for joints too. As long as a photo was still visible they were valid in our eyes. So me, Colin and Spud were on the ferry home. In reality it was supposed to be a booze cruise as our jibbing was over for now, we'd already earned so it was happy days and we weren't really looking for more graft.

Spud went off for duty free, then Colin bowls over to me at

the bar, "Go and change some money at the bureau; the purser's got the office door behind him wide open and the safe's open on the floor. I'll skim a wedge when he's busy with you." Sure enough it was open. So, as I'm rambling on with the guy I can clearly see our Colin in a crouched position making the short distance to the safe just half a yard from the guy's back. No sooner than crawling in there he was back out, with a cracking wedge of Deutschmarks. A nice earner on our return home, a right result. Spud carried the Deutschmarks with him so as to not tie me or Colin up to the theft if the money had been noticed missing. Suffice to say we had doubled our money for the trip home, happy days.

STREET LIFE

Manchester was still worth coming home to; the whole town was buzzing, or at least it was for criminals. The Gallery was another top little club where you walked down steps to get in, it seems everywhere we went clubbing in Manchester had steps going down for some reason. In here I met more rogues, in particular Spud from Salford. I'd just been grafting with a lad from Rusholme called Little Brian (better known as Dangermouse) and Rabi from Salford, who was even smaller than me. Brian had already done prison in Karachi for trying to smuggle hash out. They were all older than me, around 25, but if you knew Roufy you went to the Gallery – it was a top little scene in there, there was no friction at all and everybody got on well together.

Roufy was the DJ when it opened, it was run by a Morroccan guy called Omar and Pete, a Manc who liked all the lads who had adopted his club. It wasn't a club as such at the beginning, more like a little bar with a pool table and good tunes. You could spliff up in there too; in fact back then you could have a spiff almost anywhere you went, unlike today where you can't do anything anymore. This bar would soon become the 'grafters' local; it was on Peter Street just off Deansgate. I would meet many more of our kid's mates there. K'Ob was another I'd met previously, he looked like the actor James Coburn and all the women fancied him like mad, he loved the playboy life along with thieving, fighting and football. He had a tattoo on his hand of 'The Saint' a popular TV program of the day. This tattoo was ironic, seeing as he was the total opposite to one; the kind of guy who would be buying girls a drink at the bar with their own money having just dipped their purse while chatting them up, insisting he buy the next round and "no expense spared for you darling – waiter, double whatever the lady wants!" There were countless amounts of all kinds of criminals, all the older lads seemed to have MCFC or MUFC tattoos, most self-made, along with the ever familiar borstal dots on their knuckles.

Another club, Kloisters, was one big mad house and, although most people knew one another, it would still 'go off' every Saturday night. It was a place you went to try to cop for a bird and if you didn't then a fight would normally do. Whatever, this was the only club I remember from back then that had uniformed police posted outside it, it was that rough. It was a funny place decorated with suits of armour all over for some strange reason - if you stood still too long your feet would stick to the fucking floor. All the birds had 'flick' haircuts and they'd be flirting as their ex-boyfriends were getting wound up as the other lads chatted them up – you knew a fight wouldn't be far off. The club was 100 miles an hour - everyone knew someone, a real growler's club. It was funny at times but could get very tricky and you had to keep your wits about you. If you got neither a bird nor a fight it would be a visit over the road to the 'Star of India' for a scran, where we would claim a seat in the window to watch the ensuing carnage every Saturday night!

Another place we frequented was The Reno, a West Indian bar in Moss Side. This was one hell of an eye opener to us. It was £1 entrance *if* you paid. Even at this token price we would try and jib in, albeit just for a laugh. Though to be fair you could just as easily be let in free anyway if you went early. Walking down the steps you could feel the heat, smell the spliffs, and most of all shook with the bass! On reaching the bottom you'd be asked if you wanted weed – £1 wraps in brown paper, if you bought a fiver's worth you could get six wraps depending on who was serving you up. Then on the right there was an area for eating rice an' peas or chicken and dumplings. To the left was a bar that sold warm Newcastle Brown Ale or tins of Red Stripe. Most people it seemed would be drinking brandy and coke because at least you got ice in the drink! Then in the far corner would be the DJ pumping out tunes that you could feel vibrate on your face. In the back room you could have a game of pool or gamble on the cards run by friendly Jamaican guys, this place was another world to me and my mates and we fucking loved it!

It was just like the snooker hall - full of characters. Irishmen still in their working clothes, pants tucked into their boots, even the Old Bill came down and got a free drink as the clubbers puffed away, exhaling over the top clouds of smoke from their spliffs. We were still young and well aware of it, so we would just be happy to get in the place and settle in some corner or most times cling to the pool table in the back room drinking coke and enjoying the atmosphere while getting stoned. Some of my mates had relatives in Moss Side which was great as we had finally come across people who, if nothing else, would have at least have heard of Sale! After a while of going down the Moss we would get taxis to take us home. Not only was it a good fare for them, they all seemed to know somebody living in Sale and with us looking so young back then, I think the taxi drivers actually went out of their way to take us shouting "Racecourse Man, over here!" It could be murder to get a taxi in Moss Side and I'll always remember them for sorting us out when most people were waiting in vain for one.

Most nights people started getting in around 1'ish till quarter two. Now and again most likely the only friction you felt would be when plain clothes dibble arrived. They would try and look normal, the hard-faced fuckers. Then they would have a quick drink looking around then go, leaving half the club wondering if they were wanted or not for something. I never saw an arrest in there. I think they waited outside or followed you home later probably. To me and my mates there was never any tension in The Reno. Getting bad vibes for being young or white never happened to us, there were no barriers of race or class back then, plus me and my mates were a mixed bag ourselves really, so to us Moss Side was heaven on earth.

The police seemed unaware that a mass thieving sub-culture even existed. I suppose we were unaware of it ourselves, we were all just mates who happened to be doing the same sort of graft but from day to day this sub-culture of thieves and vagabonds was growing. At best I think the police regarded the older lads like our Colin as clueless football hooligans and thieves who just stumbled into the Moss on weekends for a late bit of clubbing. It wasn't like the police were observing all these new white or mixed race lads as, after all, they seemed more interested in getting free booze, back-handers and brass out of the local population. Most dibble wore plain clothes back then and more than once I would see them getting in unmarked cars with a brass to get a quickie. They were just hypocritical parasites.

The only racists I would see around this time were the police themselves. If you were white they hated you for being in the area, if you were black then they just hated you. On top of all this we had shebeens (The Kitchen, being the most popular) and pubs. These places were rarely raided or very seldom anyway and were real places of disrepute. The police had a 'hands off' approach on these premises due to the fact they had no bottle whatsoever. It's not so much that these were 'no go areas' more like 'let's not go' areas! The only time you really saw the police was at around 4am when they would bravely pull cars over that were on their way home, this way the police outnumbered you.

"Where have you been, where are you going? Is this your car?" they would ask. Then the customary search for a bit of weed and with a bit of luck you would be drink driving as well. "Oh we'll *have* to take you back to the station" more than likely someone in the car would be wanted for one thing or another. So it was wise to jump into taxis instead when leaving Hulme or Moss Side in the early hours - on the whole the Old Bill were getting rings run round them and they knew it.

One trip back was beset by complications from the off. Before leaving the pub someone suggested a bit of coke because we had been in the boozer a while and needed something to wake us up before the long drive. We took what we assumed to be Charlie but it ended up having the opposite effect and almost caused Colin to fall asleep at the wheel halfway to the ferry port. He almost hit a wagon but leapt back into consciousness just in time to swerve out of the way, which had us all breathing a huge sigh of relief. We somehow made it onto the ferry and sat about scratching our heads for a while, trying to work out why we felt so knackered. Everybody agreed that the powder couldn't have been coke because there's no way that you can nod off whilst driving with a beak full of Charlie. We knew it wasn't smack so we concluded that it must have been morphine stolen during a raid on a chemist because a lot of chemists were being burgled at the time.

None of us fancied a repeat of our narrow miss so we had a kip on the boat and stopped for another sleep at a hotel in Ostend before plodding on through Belgium towards the Dutch border. We woke up at around four and decided to take advantage of the late night shopping in Holland. We had a browse round some shops in a little town called Etten-Leur and then went into a bakery to get a bite to eat before we started our graft. We were just approaching the counter when we heard a voice from behind us saying, "Lads, if you could all get into the van, I'd like a word." We turned around to see that a police van had been backed right up against the entrance to the shop so that we had no choice but to walk into it.

The owner of the voice was a little policeman with a Scouse accent who looked the spit of Bobby Ball from the '80s comedy series *The Cannon and Ball Show*. The first thing that went through my head was, what the fuck is a Mickey copper doing in Etten-Leur? Closely followed by, fuck it at least I'll be able to get some shut-eye in the cells. Not everybody was as resigned to their fate as I was though; McKee shouted his head off until we arrived at the dibble shop. He was the only one of us that the morphine hadn't subdued because he was into smoking brown, which meant that he was used to its effects. John hated being locked up. The minute he was faced with time in the cells, he would start bellowing at the Old Bill, claiming that he was innocent. He was right on this occasion, we hadn't stolen a thing.

Once we had arrived at the station, Bobby explained that he had nicked us because we were English. Our nationality marked us out as being suspicious as English thieves were constantly targeting Etten-Leur. "It's the first place most Brit criminals come to when they enter the country," he told us. "I'm not saying that you lot are necessarily on the rob but you can understand my concerns."

"Fair enough, but what's that got to do with the Scouse Old Bill?"

"I'm actually with the Dutch police," he said, "I married a girl from Merseyside, lived over there for long enough to pick up the accent and then moved back over here."

He was quite sound for a copper and had a pleasant chat to us for a while before getting down to the nitty-gritty and asking us what we were doing in Holland. We blagged him that we were on our way to Germany and he advised us to go straight there upon our release from the cop shop in order to avoid getting picked up again by the ibble in Holland again.

"Yeah," we said, "we'll do just that, Bobby."

"Well just to be on the safe side, I'll keep you here for the night while I check out your names see if you are wanted," he chuckled. All that he succeeded in doing was giving us some time in which to sleep the morphine out of our systems and the next day we were released. This would be my third arrest in Holland, getting let out again only reinforced my opinion that their laws were so lenient it was untrue!

When we got to Amsterdam we went to see Dicko who was now living on the fucking Zeedijk! We didn't know what number but all we had to do was shout up to the flat windows and eventually one of the dealers sussed we were looking for our mate and weren't tourists. He even told us the number of Dicko's flat and the four of us blindly followed this guy who assured us it wasn't a trick! The Div's head pops out from a window saying "now then lads" and as soon as this happened all the Surinamese started giving us big smiles expressing to us how much they loved the Div! We spent most of the day watching the street from the flat above, it was better than any movie; people were getting mugged and dipped all day with deals openly getting done in full view. This street was lawless, like something out of the wild west! If you were to stumble on the Zeedijk you would be very lucky to get out unscathed, I can tell you that.

This was the same street that Tottenham fans had stumbled onto a few years before. A major battle had ensued with the street dealers and Spurs fans. It was still widely talked about and must have been some battle, as I knew Tottenham had a decent firm of followers then. They had been playing Feyenoord at the time. I don't think things went well at the game or the next day either with a good few Tottenham fans getting stabbed up in Rotterdam.

Back in the dam, video recorders were still a good earner and we got to know the owner of a small bar. The Dutch guy ordered one so we set the price and told him the next one was his. Playing videos attracted more customers as they were a new entertainment, though he didn't want to pay the standard price of a thousand guilders. Spud opened the boot of the car. Then the guy got cocky saying "here you take 700 guilders English, okay". "No, not okay" came the reply. Then Spud took hold of the video and half crouched/walked towards the guy struggling to carry the fucker as it was half his size. Then to our amazement he just threw the fucker in the canal! The Dutchman's jaw dropped at the sight "Fuck you, you twat, I'll throw you in next" the Spud shouted as the guy retreated to his pub! We all found it hilarious and what has always stayed with me is the sight of him throwing away a good video! Suffice to say we didn't go in the guy's bar again and there were discussions about mugging the fucker or beating him up as a lesson but time moves on and so did we.

We found a new local a stone's throw from The Dutchman called The Tomaso owned by a Surinamese guy and his missus. They were a great couple and as they had no customers yet we soon filled it up for them. You couldn't buy beer over the counter in a coffee shop so she used to serve Heinekens in big milkshake cartons. It had a small section upstairs where Tosca, the wife, would even let the lads that tooted use it to smoke their shite! Tosca had been in blue movies before she got the café and openly told us about it.

Coffee shops were taking off in Amsterdam now and we all used to chill. A few of us would get stoned rather than booze really. We'd chill out to Level 42 or blast out UB40. There was loads of reggae music, the Dutch love it. We all started going to the Paradiso and reggae clubs too, though they couldn't work us out at first – a dozen white lads in a corner and the place just full of Surinamese. It all changed when the Div was about, by now he thought he was

Dutch. Literally everybody would know him in a reggae gaff plus a few of our lot obviously got on as they would buy from them. They were happy anyway until Dicko starts up the big weed/ Charlie spliffs. The DJ would shout "who smokin de Charlie man, put it out!" Dicko knew he would cause a commotion. Either way the simple case was the Surinamese were our kinda guys!

We were in Amsterdam when we heard the riots breaking out in the UK. Big cheers went up. First for Tottenham, then nearly every other town in England followed suit. I remember we were waiting to hear Manchester had gone off and we were gutted that Liverpool was first. It was like following the football results on a Saturday afternoon just waiting to hear Manchester had started one! When it came we heard the great news that the police station in Moss Side had been besieged locking the fuckers up in their own pigsty!

★

Report

On 8th July 1981, a crowd of more than 1,000 youths besieged the police station at Moss Side, Manchester. All windows in the building were broken, and twelve police vehicles were set on fire. Police reinforcements equipped with riot shields and protective crash helmets were deployed around the station. A second attempt was made by crowds to attack the police station and during this a policeman was shot with a crossbow bolt through his leg.

Spud

The night before the riot a few shops had been set alight just for fun as the lads had come out of The Reno. The next day was really sunny and all the lads from the estate had gathered together looking at the damage from the night before. Everyone was really chilled and there was quite a gathering with plenty of spliff and Red Stripes being passed around. By about six o'clock there were 1500 people milling around and after about an hour or so we were getting a bit bored so decided to have a little march to Moss Side Police station. When we arrived we proceeded to smash all the windows in. The police station was in chaos with cop cars and vans parked outside, leaving the police locked in their own station. Someone had a petrol bomb and threw it straight at the station, the cops must have been shitting themselves.

About half an hour later we could hear the sirens of the reinforcements coming to help their colleagues. So off we went up Princess Road looting all the shops as we made our way to Claremont Road leading towards Withington Road where every shop was looted, especially the jewellers. It was total mayhem for twenty minutes until two police vans turned up. As they drove up the cops jumped out with batons and shields and began to charge us. Apart from about 300 of us who stood our ground, mainly consisting of United and City hooligans plus a few mad heads, the rest of the dickheads ran off. The 300 Spartans made our move and charged back at them. One van managed to drive off leaving the other van unattended full of riot gear, helmets and shields - we proceeded to smash the van up and made our way back to Moss Side. We made our way to the Alex estate and sat down on the grass knackered and lads were skinning up. Ten minutes later around 200 cops arrived banging batons on their shields to intimidate us but we just sat there laughing at them drinking and smoking and generally taking the piss. Anyway two cockneys, not sure where they came from or who they were with, had a crate of petrol bombs which we were more than happy to throw at the police line which chased them off and then we just went rampaging around the estate for about 4 hours.

By now, the police had blocked us all onto the estate and there were no exits out so we had to disperse in tiny groups and try and make our way home. It took me until about 2am before I got home. One funny event I remember clearly - we were locked into the estate and as we walked round a corner we came across a lone policeman. What he was doing on his own I could never understand but he spotted us and made a run for it, the chase was on. We chased him up an alley and we nearly caught him. Looking back now I'm glad we didn't because god knows what would have happened. The cop had a great escape plan and ran up some path and dived head first through someone's window into their living room. We surrounded the house but luckily for the copper the guy who lived there came to the door and most of the lads knew the owner of the house who said he wanted *no trouble at his gaff. Because we all knew this guy, we fucked off leaving the copper shitting himself in the house. He must have been thankful he went through that house that day, any other house and he may not have been so lucky.*

Over the next few days the coppers took the streets back bit by bit by driving around in clusters of vans with the back doors open and verbally abusing any passersby and conducting the stop and search routine. This went on for three days but started to filter out once the streets started to calm down.

★

After the riots more and more northwest criminals left England to stay over in The Dam for longer periods. They all said the same thing, it was fucked up back home. Maggie was having a big effect. She was fucking the place up real bad with her Nazi policies; making the working class pay for insubordination and not doing as they're told, while expecting everyone to work for peanuts. The average wage being so low it wasn't worth working, so it seemed to me that half of Manchester and Liverpool's scallies were in Amsterdam now. Teams of thieves just came over on busman's holidays collecting all the best clobber all week while enjoying the sights of Amsterdam, then going back overloaded with Lacoste, Sergio Tacchini and Adidas.

I would go grafting with most of them as I knew my way around Holland. Also I didn't mind the blagging job that I had taken on, as I seemed good at keeping the shop assistants at bay while someone did the sneak. I'd just chat shite until I got the nod to move on.

Most grafters still preferred the Alps to the Flatlands, however. The Dutch speaking perfect English put off some grafters from working in Holland plus they seemed a bit more clued up in the shops than the Swiss and ze Germans. I'd now been arrested in Holland three times; twice for suspicious behaviour in a village, with three other young Mancs roaming the town, although they nicked us both times before we had done anything so had to let us go. The other arrest was for shoplifting. Luckily we were just seen as petty criminals, Europe didn't seem to have thieves like us and we didn't warrant any attention just yet, we were more than happy being treated as such!

Lads from Wythenshawe started coming over, with Snowy and Gordon being the funniest pair that came over regularly. They soon got the nickname Ronnie and Reggie from us lot, as they were the spit of the Kray twins. I even grafted with them a few times and once saw a shop assistant look away when she see saw Snowy blatantly coming out of the office with the takings. One glare from him and you would look away too! He looked like a real nutter with big mad jet-black eyebrows. It was fair to say you knew when they were in town, they were ruthless. Another time I went out with them we had got some money but half the village was onto us and had surrounded the car we were in. We soon got off without running anyone over, ditched the car and got a taxi. After a couple of miles the traffic stopped dead, although it was only a canal bridge going up, as they do in Holland. Snowy, thinking it was a road block, opened the door and 'did one' legging it over a field towards some village with the taxi driver looking puzzled. We just said he'd taken some drugs and we should just leave him to it, saying he will be just fine and giving him the impression that he always did such things. The driver was smiling "crazy English on holiday yes!" "Oh yeah, that's it" we said. The bridge came down and we left him on some field in the middle of nowhere!

John McKee had lived in the Dam years earlier. Now he teamed up with some Surinamese from the Zeedijk and started ripping off drug dealers. The gangsters would offer to sell drugs to foreign (usually German) dealers. Then John would turn up partway through the deal with a fake police ID and pretend that he was doing a bust. He had a huge mop of ginger hair that made him look like a copper and very convincing. After handcuffing the buyers, John would confiscate their money and tell them that there would be no further charges if they fucked off back to their own countries. He did this over and over again, buzzing off what an easy graft it was!

Soon we moved on to tom shops with great results. When in

the shops I'd just ask for necklaces first then after being shown them I'd simply say I didn't like them and now I would like to look at some gold bracelets. The shop keeper would put the necklaces in an unlocked cupboard, usually right by where they sat at the desk. So we now knew where they were stored we would go back a few days later again, this time asking for bracelets although now I would place myself at a different table well away from where the cupboard was while the staff were serving me. Colin would ghost over to the cupboards, usually covered by John, and relieve them of their gold. It was so easy it was untrue by today's standards but it worked well for years and years. In Germany and Swizzy we would do the same scam.

Selling the tom was an experience; we used to go to a place called the Waterlooplein where they had two or three bars. On entering it looked like a hash dealer's café with all the dealers weighing out gold in full view on old-fashioned scales. Gold was openly bought or sold at the day's prices that we would check out first in the paper so we weren't being ripped off. There was never any Old Bill in these pubs and they were a real result for us. We could walk in with what we regarded as a little parcel and come out shocked at the wedges we would be paid. We soon got to know a good few dealers in there and never once were we disappointed with our proceeds. Most Swiss rolls would get us around 20,000 guilders (about £4,000) all in nice green thousand guilder notes. After a short while we soon had a man who would tell everyone else in the bar we were his clients and wave us over to himself. The man we had befriended had himself a nice little cabin on the Waterlooplein where the flea market is today. We sold this guy our gold for the next ten years! Not once did we have to haggle about prices, which in Holland was a result as the Dutch are known for being tight-fisted. Gold was gold and the prices are set each day and this guy was delighted with his steady supply from us. He was quite old and his son took over after a short time and he was just as happy to buy from us too. However any gold watches we got usually went back to England with us, as we had to keep in with the buyers back home.

One of our dealers back in Manchester was as gay as Parie. A Scouser called Graham, he lived and worked in town. He was harder to get money from than the Dutch and took days to haggle with on prices, which is why we preferred to get gold as it was a set price unlike watches or shitty diamonds, they always became a pain in the arse, as what the shop charged and what they were really worth was the real crime. We could have a diamond ring priced at £5,000 thinking we would get a third of that price but we seldom did. We ended up not even wanting diamonds after a while. From a tray of diamond rings worth £30,000, we would end up getting a shitty £5-6,000 rather than the expected ten. In time we got to know the prices paid in a shop. It was scandalous what people paid for the work that went into making them and most were chipped diamonds rather than carats so they always became a hassle really. Getting them sold privately in pubs was the best way to get a third of the price but it took too long that way, although we still took trays of rings that were on offer to us as it was still money plus "take it while you can" was one of our main rules.

Amsterdam was still the place to be for me, it was just one big bubble of criminal activity and the Dutch, it seemed, loved anything that was cheaper than in the shops. We had also a good earner getting cameras. We soon sussed if we got hold of a certain key it would normally fit all the other cabinets in the other shops too! These shops had all the cameras on display but right underneath the displays there was always a big drawer with the same cameras boxed up ready to be liberated – Canon, Nikon and Hassleblads. We got to know two locals that had a shop on the walking street in Amsterdam but they only bought cameras that weren't ousted from Holland. As long as we said, "no they're from Germany, honest" that's all they wanted to hear. The next day we would go past their shop and see all our cameras lined up neatly for sale in the shop window.

By now we had got to know a car dealer called Yankee Bob, he would even lay cars on costing around 500 to a thousand guilders, or he would take the ever-faithful video recorder as payment! Bob was a top guy and treated us well. He loved all the lads, although a few years down the road he probably wish he'd never met us as most of the cars were traced back to him but at the time he was more than happy to serve us up with these two-a-penny throwaway cars! He was probably selling around three to five cars a month to various Mancs, maybe more; every time we went for a new car from him, we always got the same response. "Hey you guys, the police have been here asking about you all" this was usually when we had had to ditch a car somewhere. It would get traced back to him, although we always knew we could trust him to keep his mouth shut as we were never questioned about him or heard his name mentioned by the Police.

With all the numbers coming over, deportation was inevitable for a good few lads, Divy being the first within our group from Sale getting the treatment ten times. The Hook of Holland was where you would be sent back from, then usually the person deported would get back within a few days via Belgium and the rattler back to Holland. The sooner you got back, the more street cred you'd get with big cheers going up when you entered The Dutchman again.

The Queen's Police at the Hook of Holland knew us all in the end. "Eh you fucking English hooligans again!" While being strict, they were still funny with it, they didn't fuck about. If you were a twat with them, they would be a twat back. They were the big boys of the force and you could sense it too.

The holding room you waited in on arriving at the port had a big glass window where you waited like a monkey at the zoo. The only entertainment was reading the graffiti on the walls. The main slogans were MUFC, MCFC, LFC or EFC, which kind of summed it all up! Here you had to wait until the passengers had boarded and you would be hurried through last but not least. Sometimes the dibble would cross over the channel, putting you in a cabin which they would sit outside treating it all like a big thing and going right over board with the procedure. Though I think they were just on training duties really. Once I said "I'm starving I've not eaten all day" and the Old Bill very kindly went and got me a massive tray of cheese and ham butties and a big bottle of coke which was a top result – I even left the crusts as there were so much food.

Other times they would walk you on the boat giving the purser your 'ID' and you would be free to roam the boat and the duty free for much needed cigarettes, then return when it had docked. Then an English bobby would escort you to be checked out. If you weren't wanted, they weren't bothered about what it was you were sent back for, usually asking if you had been treated okay over there. I think "not shitting on your own door step" was okay with the English customs. Anyway, hadn't robbing abroad got England its riches in the first place?

With all the travelling on your own name leaving a trail, everyone soon started getting false passports. You could give some lad, who had no intention of going abroad, £20 for his birth certificate and you were sorted. After a couple of years we were getting visitors' passport printed up. Even Transalpino tickets were getting printed up too, as the people who printed them used to also print up false tickets for big games or concerts as loads of Mancs used to work the concerts with all the flags, magazines, scarves, posters - you name it. False security passes were the best earners. You could walk four or five people in for nothing and plonk them back stage, they would pay great money for that. The fights with security were the highlight of a good night's grafting. Concerts weren't like football, at concerts back then you hardly saw the plod. On tour the security were usually the same guys who had been involved in the previous fight in some other town so either side always had a bone to pick with the other.

This was the life for me and my mates, that's for sure. It was nothing new to us at the time, just pure mayhem everyday, it was just the world we lived in, a batallion of rag tag grafters all hungry for life's adventures, good times and money!

PEY'S PERFECT DAY

Sitting in the Bulldog Coffee Shop in the red light district, smoking the best hash in town from water bongs, Lou Reed singing 'Perfect Day', more colour shining from the cut than back in grey, grimey Manny – it had to be the move.

Right then, first move; get a roof over my head. Second, get a job. Third, enjoy the country and the day.

The first came heaven-sent. After a few nights I found myself in the Qxshoff Nightclub on the Herengraght. A Cockney bird took a fancy to me and invited me back to hers. Well you don't look a gift horse do ya? In the morning the electric man came round to turn off the power as the bills hadn't been paid. So I went to the flat upstairs with an extension lead so we could get a coffee on. Knocking on the door, it just opened – it was empty, vacant, nothing. Squatting being legal I legged it to the Iron Mongers, got two fuses and a new lock and made myself comfortable in my new Amsterdam Pad. Happy Days.

Next move – a job. I trekked round agency after agency, Snide labouring out in the sticks in the wide open freezing fields. After a couple of months I'm thinking "fuck this". So I do a little shoplifting which started to pay the way. A new thing had just come out on a commercial basis - suitcases on wheels that you could just pull along. They were easy to fill up and these little jibs kept me busy and wedged for a while as I got to know my new environment; places, characters and faces. Working early morning before the shop staff had even woken up proved very profitable, it was on these early morning mooches I kept bumping into a lad I'd met a few years earlier when I'd gone to the Dam for a holiday. He was a game kid called Divy. I'd have had two quality jackets away, while it wasn't unusual to see him pushing the whole fucking clothes rail through the streets. "Morning Div", "Morning Pey". You gotta laugh! Mancs abroad eh!

When I first met him a few years earlier he was barely sixteen, the other kid also from Sale called Diller was even younger than him. When I'd asked them how they were gonna get back to Manny being on their arses after blowing all their money on Amsterdam's nightlife, Divy just said "Oh Pey, we'll just go to the Cop Shop, don't worry I've done it a few times, I just tell them we've been robbed again and they'll put us up for the night and get us back home on the following night's ferry."

As more and more lads from the North West and beyond heard the call of mainland Europe, the numbers getting deported back for being naughty and undesirable became a weekly event. The Div was the first to demand a goodie bag, the rum cunt. He would be a thorn in their sides for over 18 months non-stop causing grief to the customs, customers and staff on the boat trip back home. See, every time he was deported back over that ugly sea he would be boarded on last by customs, he'd then make a bee line straight to the duty free and rob it blind, get a quick earner selling backie, whisky and perfumes to the lorry drivers. Now the reason he was so keen was almost every time he was slung back there were others and they were all were skint and just wanted to look after them booking a cheap double room. Only problem was almost every time once the lads got half way over the sea they'd nip back up to duty free on the jib with enough Dutch courage to threaten that they would throw any of the staff that were lippy overboard. See, what you find with most northern lads who are from other parts is we soon bond and look after each other. Sadly on them trips Divy and his motley mates ended up going straight from Sheerness to the dibble shop. This went on for over three years, in the end they asked Divy can they do a deal, by sorting out everyone being deported with a hot meal away from the tourists in the staff canteen. After the scran they'd wait about an hour to see which rooms were free so they were well away from the paying passengers. To make things easier they were given a pack of cards, a six pack of cola each, bags of crisps and a few butties in a nice strong bag. Hence The Divy Bag was born, and believe me that bag became a life saver because most people were fucked, tired and in disarray after days or weeks in police detention all over Holland waiting to get back to the Grey and the Grime as it was still grim up North. Good on ya Div. R.I.P

Another earner the cockney girl (who I was now living with), got me onto was the 'Methadone Man'. She explained you just turn up, talk shite, tell him you're on 4 bags a day, show any kind of dodgy ID and you got a pocket full of pills that had a value worth the effort. So off I went to the outskirts of the Dam to meet the 'Methadone Man'. It was *so easy, it was laughable. Now then, considering I didn't know jack about Class A's or where to move them, an education was to come my way via a French Avant-garde philosopher I met in a bar off the Damrak one afternoon. This guy was a source of untold knowledge, a quick course in Existentialism, Albert Camus, Jean-Paul Sartre and Dutch Surinam street lingo were among many interesting topics we discussed. Pointing out as he did that every tyrant, dictator, Head of Government, industry, King, Queen or Sheik almost always had a Jew as their right hand man and advisor. He laughed when I pointed out that perhaps that was where Hitler may have gone wrong. Talking to me, he educated me about the Amsterdam streets, what to do, what to say etc.*

With my new education I headed for Class A Central - The Zeedijk. A lawless no-go area for the cops. Almost getting pounced on every other step by thieves, rogues, junkies and dippers. I hit them with their lingo. "Mi Sab Be", meaning, as the French guy had explained, "I know your game, I know who you are, so leave it". They all seemed to be amazed and dumbstruck by these words and others I'd learned, to the point their eyes lit up with a smile, as they let me past. On one corner I noticed a half caste kid who looked British (well you can sense these things can't ya?). He was from Dublin and obviously an addict as he was scraping brick dust into paper parcels as his girlfriend set off to sell them as smack wraps to unsuspecting tourists. Striking a deal for my pocket full of pills, we then met up for a long time thereafter on a regular basis, until one day he was gone, never to be seen. As was half the brick on the street. There must have been some disappointed people over time.

Another little earner I got onto, again, via my cockney girl, was when she introduced me to a couple of ex-public school guys who lived on a houseboat - No. 1, the Singel. You couldn't get more central. They'd been bringing in dope from Nepal and India for years and were now doing a brisk business selling acid to the Spanish Basques who were mad for 'em! It became my job to paste the little mothers onto T-shirts and then front the deal somewhere away from the boat. The dope these guys had was among the best you could get.

One night they gave me some 'Manali' pointing out on a map, not only which part of India it was from but the exact fuckin field. What an amazing smoke! A single skinner but a 12 hour trip. That night I floated into a bar, The Flying Mancunian, sorry, Dutchman, for a game of pool and a wee chill out. And it was buzzin. Hearing all the sharp accents I thought I was back in Salford or over the river in Manchester. Everyone was dressed in navy blue Paul and Shark tops, "is right" all on form having a right good old chin wag, blown away on readymade joints of Sensi weed. So having waited a while to get a game I was soon on top form potting away and just as I was lining up the black for the seven ball shuffle, right in my beady eye-line was this guy's mug shot, swear he had the most beatific, top of the world, Cheshire cat grin I've ever seen. He saw through my Manali haze. Turns out this was your author Mark Blaney along with the rest of the Wide Awake firm who'd just got in town, a good night was awaiting later in Mazzo's. Moments like that were ten a penny, looking back we were all living the dream, a tight, keen crew of working class lads that all knew how to party.

SHORT SHARP SHOCKS

In 1981 Adam Ant was huge in the UK and a few off us got programmes copied up for his tour that winter. After the graft I'd been used to, I soon discovered this wasn't for me - it felt like real work. Too many times I'd be sat on my programs just getting stoned waiting for a grafter who'd be buzzing on his way back to the car for more "here, you take these, I'll go back for more I've just got them but here I don't mind" knowing we all tallied up in the pub later on anyway. It took our Colin and McKee about a week to suss I'd not sold a program and it got a good chuckle from John when he said he wondered why he'd never seen me put money in the pot. In my opinion, at the end of the night, the programs got sold. Did it matter who did it?

The security would come out after a while as all the people walking in had our programs already and were not buying the official ones inside. I hated the selling and if I was doing a concert or football I'd graft with Dicko mostly as he loved selling tickets. I didn't mind buying them, going in and out of the pubs and car parks with my "anyone got any spares" routine, feeling like a cockney spiv!

One night took us to Middlebrough. I don't know why but I did a till and got arrested in some daft village. I got off at first but the registration had been clocked, it was a Dutch car, so stood out a bit. In the next village, just as we got out of the car, Colin said he'd just seen the old bill clocking us and with that he was off. Spud darted too and that left me getting arrested! I was slow in my defence.

After a night in the cells I was charged with burglary, my jaw dropped. "A till is a burglary, I never knew that!" I was told anywhere that's private is burglary "not theft". As I was in a Dutch car with a passport I'd be remanded! Then told I'd be going to borstal "fucking borstal, are you joking?" I said. "No, you're 20 years old. It's borstal till your 21."

The entire time I'd been growing up I'd heard horror stories about borstal. I'd been staying abroad to avoid it in a way too! Though all the stories were unfounded for me luckily, as the second I got there I got on with everyone. They were all up for a good laugh and I got the nickname Strangeways straight away! The worse part was the staff who had us all trotting round the exercise yard at mad o'clock taking silly classes like back at school. I was moved on to Durham jail the day after my 21st birthday. I went 'not guilty' on the charge arguing that I'd not gone into private property as I leant over the counter to get the money. If I wanted a burglary charge I'd go burgling, not thieving (I was young and being cocky but that's how it is) and "can I get bail if I leave my passport, your holiness god of gods then?"

"No two weeks same charge!" came the reply. I was sent back to Durham jail.

Our Colin posted me what I'd been posting to him for years, a piece of nice hash folded up the size of an Opal Fruit. The packet was simply emptied out and replaced with a piece of hash in the wrapping, drugs weren't searched for as much back then and the simplest way is usually the best way. We all used the Opal Fruit trick for each other in the jails all over England, it worked for years too, until they stopped parcels altogether. I was watching a film on the Saturday but it was really boring so I went to see the guard and asked him if I had a parcel as I knew it was due in the post. Bingo! "Nice one boss! I've got a bit of a headache too, can I go back to me cell please?" Back in the cell I was buzzing when I got the hash, a nice piece of Afghan but first I had to wait for my three pad mates to get back as they were real funny Geordies and I could only just about understand them really.

We had a laugh, playing cards and smoking all week – it was much appreciated by the three lads in the cell. I just hope they have used the Opal trick themselves since. Back at court I finally listened to my solicitor and caved in and pleaded guilty to burglary. I was let out straight away. I couldn't drive yet and had to go all the way back the next week to collect the car. I had a flat in Chorlton and with a few hand outs from mates I had a good Christmas and vowed to stay robbing abroad in future. However now I was making trips back to England every other week I couldn't drive but Greg had himself his prized BMW as did Sid and Paddy who came home with about half a kilo of top Afghan stashed inside it just in time for Christmas! Our Colin had his Ford Ghia plus a few other lads had started coming home in Dutch cars too. These cars were great with no insurance or driving licences. Drink driving all day and night wasn't a problem as it is now where everything's on computer databases. If we got pulled by the dibble we just said we worked the concerts abroad and the reason we were in Dutch cars is that they were the cheapest in Europe. Plus Holland's so flat the engines run forever; drug running and smuggling from Holland wasn't as popular or mainstream by today's standards either so our stories always matched up when we got a tug from coppers.

THE WIDE-AWAKE FIRM

Some days you would feel it would come 'on top' while on other days you just knew it would be a good day. We could go for days on end getting no results and reach the point where everyone would be getting on one another's nerves. Then just as quickly we'd turn into top mates again after getting a parcel of tom or a monster wedge!

Just going for dinner could cause hassle. We could all be eating and one of us on the way back from the loo would come out with "get back to the car lively!" It's not his fault that on the way back from having a piss he innocently falls into a safe or the waiter is quickly relieved of his takings. Sometimes we only paid so we could see what the waiter was carrying or if it was worth us returning to say we'd left something on the table. The waiter was always helpful and would go and check for us and again it's not our fault if he left his money conveniently under the counter ready for us to make a quick exit. It was always going to be a rush job as once the bag's in hand, we had to be quick to get away before the waiter served another customer and noticed we'd had them over.

Family run hotels usually meant more opportunities, as they

would always have money in the living quarters but this more often than not turned into a nightmare. Mostly we would all really try not to go mooching the living quarters as we'd be staying there but there's always one. Macca's "act first, think later" attitude toward the graft brought it on top for Colin once by grafting a hotel. Colin didn't have any part in it but ended up in a German jail, a real shady jail at that. As again someone couldn't help themselves after checking out the gaff, we would have to go mooching to see what was what anyway but that wasn't the point, the point was we were fucking sleeping there! These *nightcrawlers* never slept or stopped working, we literally had to sleep with one eye open on full alert as there was no rest for the *Wide Awake Firm*.

Winters were good for graft: the dark nights meant it was really easy to watch the shop assistant while standing outside a shop window as he counted his takings and put the cash bag into his case. Yet from inside the shop they couldn't see who was looking in, could they? We'd knock on the door and frantically point to the shop floor gesturing that I'd left a bag or something inside earlier, even though he's closed he still lets two lads into his shop. Talk about lax! Then I would blag him to the back of the shop where they sold washing machines looking for my imaginary lost item while Vinny sneaked off with a top wedge from his briefcase. Imagining the reactions on the guy's face would send us into a chuckle, wrong I know but that's how it was.

Winter was also good for being able to suss most shops from the outside. Just waiting until you had seen the takings being counted and put close by the till area or taken to the office, so between 5 and 6 o'clock was our window of opportunity. The streets would be quiet and dark and it'd more than likely be raining too. On nights like this Colin would more or less have us running down streets if we'd not had a good day *at it*, he would jog a little ahead of you and look in every single shop from outside cupping his hands to the window to see things clearer, then if he stood still for a certain amount of time, we would know he'd like to go inside one, then on passing him he'd give orders like "get that bloke to the left, I'll follow you in then slide off to his office. I've just seen him, the takings are in there, now!" Colin honestly thought every single shop keeper was thick, sometimes I'd dread it. "Just get them here then switch to the opposite side, they're fuckin daft!" Sometimes we'd find him at a tom shop where he'd be standing at a window, "Right, we could be on a right earner here, lads" while eyeing the watches, twirling his beloved bunch of keys. "I'm taking that, that and that, oh and that too if I have time", like he was buying the fucking things! "Right they're all daft let's get in there now! Then get her over to that corner, me and so and so will come after you, get her offside." If I ever thought it was a tall order and said so, he'd just reassure me with his "look, they're all daft innit!" speech. Fair's fair most were, but not all!

If we did meet anyone who was on the ball it would be murder trying to tell Colin that the staff were wary of us, he just never wanted to know, as he had to get in "that office now!" Sometimes, while blagging away, we'd have to more or less keep shouting the words "lively" and "nito" into the sentences. "Lively" meant to hurry the fuck up I'm not happy with my blag." Nito" meant drop everything and get out. This was usually ignored by whoever was mooching in the back, even though they knew the shop assistant could just walk off and find them in the back office. Either way we had to try to keep them talking or block their view. The last resort was physically holding them back to gain extra seconds. Shouting "nito" as loud as you could mid-sentence like we had fucking Tourettes was another tactic but it had to be done to confuse the staff who would be wondering why you were shouting like a loon. Finally, they'd see the dreaded sight of a shady looking guy emerging from where he shouldn't be. Then it was on top and time for them to call the cops. Then 'ding' goes their door bell and they would see two or three lads scramble out the door, one of which they didn't even know was in their shop until now! After a nice, healthy jog back to the car, we'd have to drive for an hour or so to get out of the way. "Did we get 'owt?" usually being the first question! "How much?" being the second followed by nervous laughter.

Colin started to believe he was invisible after a while. "They never see me" he'd say. Forgetting that they didn't see him because we made sure they didn't fucking see him! I don't think I ever saw him distract a member of staff, and if any shopkeepers ever spoke to him, he'd either ignore them or go under. It wasn't his skill set. He'd start mumbling to us to get them away from him like they were lepers or something. Sometimes I'd be blagging someone when he'd just appear from nowhere and come up behind them motioning me to move them to another place. Incoherently he'd cough "move her" then I'd walk off hoping the staff blindly followed.

It was all in a day's work to him though. In the morning he'd wake everyone up, then by the time you were awake and got breakfast he'd be in the car having already eaten, by the time you got in the car he'd be out with the map giving it a big wave across it announcing, "we'll graft all that today, chaps" like some man on a mission. I was map reader as the likes of Kev or McKee never knew where the fuck we were as all the towns looked the same to them. Even when we had big chases on the streets they'd never know the way back to the car half the time!

I've known many grafters put the white flag up after a week or two with Colin. Quite a few of the younger lads came out in nervous rashes! Others couldn't wait for an excuse to go home as soon as they got half a wedge, this was funny really as me and Colin would plod on and usually get a nice result, being back in Manchester the next day or not long after.

By this point, we hadn't done any real jail but after so many arrests the Dutch old bill put you into what we called the 'big bad book'. Computers weren't in general use yet so they had this book; half the grafters I knew had been arrested and then deported just for having their name in it and the phrase 'unwanted alien' next to it. Yet you only found out you were in it when it was too late. On average you would be locked up for between three days and two weeks in the police cells as they went from town to town with your mug shot gathering evidence. Although I'm not quite sure why they did this as in Dutch law it wasn't enough to convict you.

Then we were deported.

The police were getting big on spot checks in Holland at the time and it became a right pain driving round. Our Colin had arrived in Amsterdam at around eight one morning having just driven all the way from England and got stopped and deported back that same night! Just imagine all the criminals from all over the world getting arrested and deported for this! Spot checks are common on the roads nowadays so you are prepared, back then we weren't. So now most people used false passports as we had sacked squats and stayed in hotels. Amsterdam's hotels quickly grew to hate us as we went through them all, getting barred from most. Helping ourselves to the bar or letting big bills pile up, some were that big they couldn't really kick us out and just had to put up with us. It was always the same story "we're waiting on our wages to get sent to us", "one more day" etc. Then we still wouldn't pay! If we could slip the net we would, then just do the same all over again. Being on false names really helped in the hotels. The posh hotels in Switzerland were the best as they would let us run bills up in the bar and let you eat in their restaurants too! All your bills were just put down on the room key number, all we had to do was check in and pay one or two nights upfront then live it up in there until they got wary of our behaviour! Then we would do another moonlight flit across town! False 'passies' were needed for buying cars too as now the law had changed in Holland. People had to register any car that was bought, so they came in handy. We had so many names going we would all forget who we were half the time, checking in at hotels you would have to look and check out your own name!

Before going out to graft we would have to remember each other's names in case we got pulled. If we got a pull we would all say the same thing, as it rhymed…

"We all just met the night before, we're on our way to do a tour"

Sometimes we would actually follow a tour anyway just for the crack. The Iron Maiden tour was one where we met all the Mancs that worked the shows abroad and ended up getting involved in a big fight with security and we weren't even working it! We just happened to be stood by a tout from Manchester. Germany was mad for fighting. They were all massive Hell's Angel types but they would always underestimate the number of grafters outside the stadiums and try to bully them. That would just end up with them getting swamped up by a good few football/hoolie Manchester touts that would front them up in return, usually dropping whatever they had been selling and getting stuck in, leaving the security looking battered, bruised and confused and wondering who the fuck these mad Brit scallies were.

We usually met up with the other Mancs in Frankfurt in a Greek restaurant just near the train station. The owners even bought knocked off gear, which was a nice bonus for us! It was usually on our journeys to Swizzy from Holland as Frankfurt was half way there so we always picked goodies up to sell here to our Greek friends. Frankfurt was a rum town, so we fitted in well with the Germans, that is once we had convinced them we weren't in the army, as the army lads weren't much liked – the American, French and British armies were all stationed in Germany, Frankfurt being in the American sector back then. We used to avoid the pubs and clubs if we saw any army lads. They could be a right pain to get away from. We met a few squaddies on our travels through Germany in the early days. Three Brit squaddies in particular come to mind who we had a drink with one night. After seeing our parked car and half knowing we were 'at it' they told us "always park your car nose out lads, so you can get away quicker!" Their advice was duly noted we never parked 'nose in' again.

Football, concerts and Moroccans in Amsterdam - now it seemed we had to fight the fucking squaddie lads all the way to and from Swizzy and even in Spain! It seemed we always got into battles with the Italians somehow. I think it's because we were in small groups that attracted trouble plus being a stranger never helps. It wasn't always the case but we had to keep an eye on the Turks in Germany too, yet the Turks we met in Holland were alright with us. Just being English attracted nutters it seemed to me, with most Europeans 'English hooligans' was the first thing they said… so most wannabees wanted to start trouble with us to prove something, it never ended.

One minute we'd be having a friendly game of pool, the next we were involved in something over nothing and it's all hands on deck scrapping to get out of some backward club in the middle of nowhere! Once me, our Colin and Gordon had a little fight with some yanks and after it had settled down some Military Police turned up trying to arrest the three of us! Soon as they found out we weren't military they had to let us go and when the German Old Bill turned up they let us walk away from it all with shrugging gestures to the MPs that they weren't bothered about us in the slightest! It would be a relief sometimes just to get to Switzerland in one piece after a few nights in Frankfurt.

All the big cities in Germany have Reeperbahns, red light areas, which makes them a melting pot of criminality from all over Europe. I thought Germany's nightlife was a load of shit, along with their music; they were still playing catch up with Rod Stewart and 'Sailing'! There was absolutely no fashion whatsoever there, they seemed stuck in a time warp. I'd read enough war books to know I didn't want to get nicked there, with thoughts of the Gestapo it took me a few visits to get used to going there to be honest. Plus with all the sneak thieving we were doing it all felt like spy stuff to me but I never minded robbing '*zee Germans*' one bit and even used to justify robbing from them. If the owners of the place were old they were deffo Nazis, if they weren't old "then I bet their parents were!"

Germany was great for getting off - disappearing into other cities, towns and villages - it was so easy to drive away from an area when needed. The downside to driving was our bright yellow Dutch plates, so we had to try to be inconspicuous. If the car got clocked after a shady get away we just ditched it. We only ever ditched a car after a unanimous vote. I'd always go for ditching, as a car's not worth your freedom but many a time we held onto cars which I always thought would lead us into trouble. Other times they'd get ditched and someone would volunteer to go and drive the fucker back to Holland later on. I didn't drive then so that's probably why I always voted to get rid of them.

Anyway, back in Switzerland after an Iron Maiden concert,

me, our Colin and Macca, from Salford, were in a jewellers. Macca has clocked a glass display with a few women's Rolexes and the draw unlocked so he silently clears the watches just as the shop has emptied. So now it's just the manager staring wide-eyed at the pair of us – I followed his gaze and it went straight to Macca's hand! All I could see were the price tags dangling from his closed palms! "We're off mate, call the cops!"

On the street outside the whole village was out already, it seems the shop had emptied quickly for one reason – us! We managed to get back to the car while getting manhandled and shoved by the small crowd and without pushing or threatening any Joe Public (as that's an extra charge if you're nicked) we got in the car and they're all over it like a load of zombies, with some bloke nearly going for a ride with us holding onto the back of the car! He was left sprawled out on the floor in the snow – it must have been the slowest getaway ever on our part, doing ten miles an hour in thick fuckin' snow until we hit the road proper.

"Let's ditch the car, they deffo got the registration it's them Dutch plates they stand right out," I suggested.

"Nah it'll be sweet they never got the plate," Colin replies.

"For fucks sake Colin he's probably got the plates in his fuckin hands from when he fell off the car!"

After a bit of persuasion Colin agreed to ditch it about ten miles away from the shop and we jumped on a train to get out of the way. He actually went back that night and drove the car over the border and met us in Freiburg, Germany about an hour's drive away. Colin wasn't as easily fazed as me that's for sure. As for the watches, we only got two crappy little Rolex so we now had to drive to Frankfurt to sell them in the Greek gaff. But the car was saved, that's all that mattered to Colin who never gave up a car easily!

On our way back from Spain once, Greg got himself nicked because of holding on to a car. We were in a tiny village near Interlaken just half way up a Swiss mountain somewhere. We parked the car in the only place you could really and scoped out the village with no result. We were parked very close to the last shop, a tobacconists. Upon entering there was no response - nobody came out to serve us, so Greg leans right over the counter and produces the takings in the zap they used to put the money in. Still nobody was around so we just walked out, trouble was the door next to the building belonged to the owner who must have been busy doing something else, he's not happy at all and with a little frown was mumbling in German. It's obvious he wants to serve us. We're stood 20 yards from the car and we should have just jumped in and driven off but Greg played it cool and trudged back into the shop with the guy, emerging a minute later with a pack of cigarettes. The bloke must have checked his money had gone when Greg left because he was out like a shot shouting Greg to come back!

"I've slung his money back as he went round the counter," Greg explained, "so it's near where it should be, he just hasn't seen it yet." Then he walked back inside the shop!

I melted into the background and wandered along the only road out of town, knowing Greg had to drive out that way. By now I was cursing the fact Greg had gone back playing it cool. Okay the money wasn't on him but it wasn't where it should be either! Just as I reached the main road from the village I saw a cop car a distance away coming in my direction. The only place now for quick cover were the hills above the village. Without thinking I got into them after a small climb. I'd not really paid much attention to how steep these hills were until I had to run hard just to get a grip on the next tree. It took ages to walk 100 yards because of the steep slope. At least I was in cover so I decided to sweep back to the other end of the village as nothing was happening where I was. I was now sat about 50 feet above the fucking shop with the police car parked up. I was knackered but felt safe and thank fuck it was summer as I'd never have got up this far otherwise.

After ten long minutes nothing was happening below me and the police car was still there so I thought I'd concentrate on getting out of the village and had to go from tree to tree again. Just getting to the next tree was murder with the hill being so steep, I could hardly make it and kept crawling instead as it was easier. This took a good hour until I finally jumped onto a road by a junction and just in time managed to wave down a guy in a VW camper van who said he was heading to Berne, I gladly jumped in.

I told him I wasn't normally a hitch hiker but my missus had thrown me out of the car after an argument. He seemed okay with my story and I was made up as he drove down the mountain towards the traffic. After a bit of idle chat we were soon in Berne and I jibbed a train to Zurich where we had a hotel but first I thought maybe Greg had somehow got away with it as I saw no hue and cry go up earlier. I waited all night in the Pickwick pub in the old part of Zurich but he never showed and I had no intention of going to the hotel now either, so I broke into a nice looking boat on the river and went back into town to get a scran to take back. When I got back to the boat it seemed okay so I settled in for a good feed then sleep thinking that I should deffo have to start driving soon, as it wasn't the first time I had regretted not driving.

The next day I went on the mooch in and around the town and a little shoe shop saved my bacon. I had seen the assistant go downstairs to get a shoe to try on for the customers so I kept myself busy until I was last in the shop, then I sent her to get me a shoe in a certain size knowing she had to disappear downstairs. This gave me ample time to rifle the office. I soon found some takings – 1500 Swiss Francs about £700 – that will do, I thought. I waited for the assistant. I could have just walked out but it was always best to leave them sweet if you could. So I waited then when she showed me the shoes I just looked like I really didn't like them. It wasn't a great wedge but a lifesaver at the time and I got the fuck out of Swizzy and back to Manchester

Two weeks later back in MCR, Greg turned up at my flat. It had taken the police and shop assistant a few hours to find the money and Greg couldn't be charged with theft as there hadn't been one but they kept him in some strange set up that was a cell in somebody's house rather than a police station. He still had his beloved BMW and said it was staying in England from now on. As for me, it seemed the police never even knew I was there and had never even mentioned a second man. So I had been on a fucking mad hike in the Alps for nothing. I felt a right wally! Greg had a top chuckle at me for that and I had a good chuckle at Greg for going back inside the shop. He had managed to throw the zap behind the counter as the guy was walking around it but it must have landed in an unseen place somehow! He insisted that he was right to go back as he still had his BMW. In hindsight we should have just ignored the bloke, walked past the car and sneaked back to it later but still it was early days and we still had a bit to learn.

Learning to drive was actually forced on me not long after this just by chance. Me and Vinny were in Holland in a daft tom shop with nothing to thieve inside so Vinny slipped into the living quarters. Trouble was the shop was very old and after Vinny had been away for about a minute I could hear the floor creaking from where I stood. Trouble was, so could the manager who cleared the shop there and then! With little choice I went outside as the manager locked the door from the outside. Within a short time the old bill arrived and I saw them bungle Vinny into a van. There was nothing I could do to help the situation, so I made my way back to the car. I didn't know how to drive but I had watched other people before and knew the clutch came out as the accelerator went down – that was about it! It took a good while but I got it moving eventually, the noise was ear-shattering but I just ignored it and kept driving in what I now know was second gear. I managed to get on the motorway and back to Rotterdam without changing gear for about 15miles!

Later that day I got a Dutch guy I knew to drive me round and I'd learned to drive by nightfall. Then I just drove round for the next few days teaching myself until Vinny got out three days later without charge having told the police the usual story when caught, "he was only looking for a toilet." Now I could drive it was a different world and I remember thinking I'd let myself down more than once by not driving sooner! I bought myself a Citroen, the same car I'd learnt in, and drove back to Manchester feeling very pleased with myself behind the wheel - stoned and wadded.

THE GOOD, BAD AND UGLY

In 1982 the war with the Falklands was in full swing and if the Brits are good at anything, it's war. Maggie's army was on the march, England was in its element with it all. To the likes of me, it just meant not going to Los Gauchos for a while, which was a shame as we all loved eating in Argentinean steak gaffs in Europe. By now it was plain to see what Maggie was up to. She'd always seemed to be picking on people, so apart from the war she was at it with the IRA, football hoolies and the unions. I used to know people that went to picket pits - coach loads of hard drinking pub thugs would leave Manchester to back up the miners and the battles were all over the telly. At night I used to look out for them on the news, they told me it was ten times better than any football match they had been to and loved it, these were all big brawlers and very capable. The odd one or two were actual miners as it goes.

Good

On my twenty-second birthday me, Greg and Lou were on our way to Swizzy but working all the way *"Hi Ho"* hoping for a good result so we could make a U-Turn home! We were in a small town and went inside a very small tom shop. On entering we saw the guy shutting his wall safe. Then he disappeared into a back room. I just walked over, opened it and took out a big brown envelope, the only item in the safe, without being seen and covered by customers. Almost immediately me, Greg and Lou were out the door - I looked in the envelope but I wasn't impressed and threw the fucker in the street bin and carried on walking looking for other shops. Luckily Greg checked the envelope and there were three diamonds worth £6-7k each inside. With it being so easy to get to the safe, I hadn't really looked had I? Luckily Lou and Greg were there, so this was a U-Turn graft.

Bad

I got offered £4k for the £7k stone and thought I'd rather save it for the time being. Trouble with that was a few people had heard about it by now and it was stashed at our kid's. He got taxed for it from some gangsters, though I hadn't got taxed personally so I went to try and buy it back for a grand but was told to fuck off or they would tax the grand I had just offered anyway if I didn't stop mithering!

Ugly

Between the taxers and the Old Bill, you wouldn't know who would be banging at your door next - it was one big joke. There was a massive change going on in Manchester's underworld. It had now became all about drugs, drugs and more drugs. Firms sprang up everywhere and the colour divide even started up, which wasn't the Manchester I knew, it was all leading up to the gang thing which blighted the city from the late 80s onwards.

Probably the only gang that wasn't a real gang in Manchester back then was us lot; we were generally football hooligans or touts turned thieves. We weren't territorial, although it could have looked that way to some other people in town at night. On a good night there could be as many as 30 lads, like when the concerts were on or after big football matches. A few of the lads would get caught up in the troubles to come with the Moss Side, Cheetham Hill and Salford gangs. These lot were into armed robberies and the likes and they were ruthless but all in all we kept to our own pubs and clubs but even these were to get ruined by the gang thing eventually. Apart from Salford, there weren't any white lads interested in the big 'we are it' campaign that had started up. If anything it spelt the beginning of the end of the good old days. However, the night life and good tunes still went on - funk was massive in the clubs at the time and it was buzzing but you could feel it getting shady on a night out.

We still made trips abroad, calling in at the dam to see who lived there but we'd only stay for the weekend before returning home, hopefully we would be back on average within ten days with enough money for a good few weeks living it up. Tills and things took a back seat. Sometimes we just went over with a good kitty between us to last two or three days and try to be as safe as we could waiting for a bigger wad. Smaller jobs were ok but they could fuck the area up, making us drive miles away again after just getting there so we did a lot more scouting before hand. I never went without a map and I started getting small ones of particular regions so we could make out small unsuspecting villages and back roads for the get away. I used to love telling the driver "right here, straight on, left". We would remember certain shops where we missed money months earlier and we would keep going back until we got them in the end. By now we would know about 5 or 6 places to head for in any area just to kick-start ourselves. A trip could vary from the first shop we did and being back in Manchester that night or involve a week or two of preparation – you never knew what was in store!

JUST ANOTHER BRICK IN THE WALL

When Greg and I got home from our holidays we were both arrested. The Old Bill had busted my flat one morning over a false passport then found another one on the table. Greg was there and he was searched and found to be holding one as well. It's pretty hard to say it isn't you when your picture is on it! So there's not much we could say...

The night before court I checked into the Britannia Hotel with my girlfriend then in the morning told her I'd be about an hour as the courts were just the next building along. At the court the solicitor reckoned to expect a fine so I've turned up with £500 to throw at them if needed. We both got three months... On reception me and Greg were the joke from the warder's point of view "expecting a fine were we lads" – no shit Sherlock.

The night before I'd been in a top hotel with a nice girl and a nice mini bar in the room. Now I was sat in a cell with four guys looking gloomy with our sentences starting the next day. Although

I was sorted as we knew a fair few people who were locked up and we all had a laugh whenever we could. I remember two black lads were in a cell next to me and after chatting and getting to know them for a week or so I told them what we all did abroad. When I said I earned about £25K a year (based on our earnings over a week away and then a week at home) they just laughed their bollocks off. They were like two hyenas for days afterwards not believing me one bit. Funny wasn't in it! I'll never forget their reactions. These two would tax weak people on the wing and they thought I was real funny "tell us that story again", "no way did you just walk in without anyone knowing and get that amount of money?"

I got the sack just a few days after starting a job with two civil electricians; they told me to pull some cord down a little from a roof fitting, only I tugged it and half the fucking roof came down with force. I thought it was funny but they didn't. Either way I needed a shower and they promised they would tell the guard I needed one but didn't, so the next day I turned up looking the same, all soot in my hair and face, snapping at them calling them a pair of fucking twats. I'd ruined their job so they thought it was funny. Either way the next day I was told I'd been sacked, though with a promise from the screw I'd get a shower.

When I was finally allowed to get a shower everyone else was locked up. I could hardly believe the routine in there. I'll never forget the pile of socks and undies piled ten foot high getting sorted and vowed never to wear prison undies again! Sat right next to this pile of filth were inmates getting their haircut, it looked like something out of Victorian times. Strangeways was hanging. Slop out was a part of the routine as there were no toilets in the cells that were two or three handed and you had to do a number two in a shit parcel and throw them out of the windows at night.

The screws were always more stressed than the prisoners and they seemed to hate every last one of us. It seemed to me they were a load of cavemen. It was the end of their reign though to be fair. I used to ignore them as best as I could. We just laughed at every opportunity at the guards. They hated the new batch of criminal that didn't say "yes boss, no boss, please boss".

Whereas Durham jail was small, fairly clean and laid back, Strangeways was like a hive of activity when all the cells were open – everyone zigzagging up and down the landings exchanging stuff with the screws going mad. It was hard to stop everyone because of the chaotic goings on; slop out, work, food, exercise, visits – the screws were all over the place. I used to get stoned and watch them running round barking out orders and counter orders or "You again! Why aren't you in your cell! I'll put you on report lad!" Then off to bug someone else "You! Where should you be now? You laddie!" It was all like the Pink Floyd tune 'Just Another Brick in the Wall'. Strangeways was a self-explanatory name for a prison if ever there was one. I found it all a bit Victorian to be honest. It was lost in a time when Britannia ruled the waves and it was run by a load of Nazis who were living in the past.

Heroin wasn't in the past though, it was here to stay. It looked like almost everybody I knew was giving in to the shit! It had taken over big time. Until now the people I had known who were into pills hadn't really changed their character but heroin transformed people overnight. It wasn't a pretty sight. Seeing people you knew going steadily down hill was depressing. From all the lads I knew I'd say more than half sooner or later hit the smack. Many would ruin their family's lives. However this was early doors yet and it remained unforeseen that heroin would drag half a generation down with it. I personally think the UK government was to blame for letting England get flooded with smack in the late 70s, early 80s, as it quietened a disgruntled generation – the same generation that had rioted so spectacularly in 1981. Later gangs got involved in the trade and gangs plus drugs equals war on the streets. The police just sat and waited until all the criminals either killed or grassed each other up and stepped back in and took the street back ten years later. That's the way it seems to me anyway.

THE DOWNFALL

This is a story from a mate of mine who fell prey to heroin...

Fraz: *By now the brown had raised its ugly head. I wasn't tempted at first but the other lads lapped it up and after I dabbled I was sick as a dog. Next thing I knew I couldn't function without it. Working for Mr Nasty wasn't fun. I couldn't take a little stroll down to the coffee shop any more, it was off to the Zeedijk to score.*

Hundreds of Surinamese were selling on the streets. I don't know why but we got into the bars where we got better deals. Divy used to drive them mad. It was inevitable we would get deeper into this life, the more money we made, the more trouble we got into. It was around this time that lads who knew each other started falling out and double crossing each other, ripping one another off. Some got stabbed, others shot at – they had been mates two years ago but bad blood rose like a snake! Then the needles came out and that was it for me, I was off.

First off was Gordon Mac, part of the Ronnie and Reggie crew and there were many others who caught the Dam 'flu! Time for the Alps! Turned out it was rife there as well. No need to stay in the Dam for some. Right across from the hotel there was AZJ, an old warehouse turned commune full of fucked up Swiss injecting in their necks, groins or just plunging the needle in without even drawing blood. Opportunity knocks. These Swiss were using Zurich sugar, as we called it. Nowhere near the shit we smoked so 1+1 makes...

Off we popped the next day... over a bit of time we got to know the people there. We had a good little business going, on returning a week later I asked where so and so was as he owed us some dough. His girlfriend took us to see him in an apartment block in Zurich. Very nice, I thought. We got in a lift, then fucking wham we were out into a hospital ward only it wasn't. These were private flats with doctors and nurses running around and every fucker looked dead. It was a private junkie hospice. I went to see the poor fucker and took his Porsche keys off him. His bird showed us where it was for a gram - true love!

Mark: Luckily not all of us were into heroin. Nothing changed for me and my opportunistic thieving mates. With my sentence over, it was back abroad as usual, only now we tended to stay away a little longer and go to Spain with our earnings or just stay out of the way in Amsterdam soaking up the atmosphere. So it was a false passport for me from now on! These were funny as the passports were fine but we had to make our own stamps up. Not being forgers we just cut a cigarette pack up and used the edges pressed in ink then just put an imprint over the photo. They had to have a stamp too so we used a coin and pressed that too over the photo, I travelled under the name Marc King, taken from the bass guitarist from Level 42, and my old address 89 Burgin Drive, Collyhurst from when I was a kid!

I'd carry a passport in my own name for getting in and out of the UK to be safe. Once abroad, the police, hoteliers and car hire firms seldom looked closely at them. Along with passports we could still get inter rails and driving licences too. Cars would be hired with two or three day cash deposits; BMW, Mercs and the famous Golf GTI. To keep the car hire firms sweet, after getting our brand new car for next to nothing, we would phone them up after a few days with some cock and bull story saying we could be away a while but would be back in a week. We would keep it for months, like if we had driven down to Spain in one. Until eventually we would ditch it at some airport then repeat the process again in some other small town somewhere. We tended to pick on small firms that only had a few cars to rent. We would all take turns phoning the bosses, chuckling at our stories until we had them nearly crying down the phone. It wasn't a police matter and if we kept phoning then by law if we got a pull we could more than likely pay anyway but we never got pulled in all the years doing it.

With all the border crossings number plates were an issue – you couldn't drive a German car grafting in Holland as the Dutch hated the krauts and Dutch cars stood out in Germany as well. But both German and Dutch cars were okay to use in Switzerland. We were coming out from Switzerland heading to Spain one night and got stopped going into France at the border at Basel. Three English lads in a Dutch car with German and Swiss money coming out of our pockets and our bags packed with cameras, money and all on false passports. Our story that we were roadies following the big concerts wasn't getting any response at all and left us feeling like the Swiss police were about to arrive. Though still scratching their heads at us for hours, we just sat there until they let us on our way at 3am.

The only problem in Switzerland was the road system, because of the Alps it's all one road in and out, so if it's on top the car's a burden. One mad night our Col and me were forced to give it legs after being clocked doing a till over and ended up spending all night hiding from the Old Bill behind a snow bank on the side of a mountain. At around 5 am, we decided that it would be safe to emerge and drive off because we assumed that the police would have given up their search by this stage, seeing as it was only a daft Jack and Jill with the equivalent of £700 in it. Unfortunately we couldn't have been more wrong because they had a road block waiting for us and we ended up getting machine guns pressed against our necks. The Swiss dibble were a world away from the Dutch Old Bill. There was no friendly Scouse copper on hand to coax us into the back of a van; it was a case of, "Get in or we'll blow your fucking bollocks off."

The dibble drove us to the nearest police station, where we were informed that we fitted the description of a pair of lads who had carried out a string of thefts in the area. One of these was a sneak that had netted us £11,000 worth of Swiss Francs, a couple were crimes that other people had committed and one was a pickpocket that our Col had done a few weeks earlier. He had snuck into the backroom of a shop with the intention of stealing the money from the cashbox only to discover that there was nothing in it. Not wanting to return empty handed, he had then rooted about in the shopkeeper's jacket pocket and discovered the takings there.

The coppers put us through a brief question and answer session and then locked us up in a block of cells containing the loudest extractor fan that I have ever heard in my life. They occasionally turned it off but switched it straight back on again the second Colin and me attempted to strike up conversation. After a couple of weeks of suffering this subtle psychological torture, we were taken out and bundled into the back of a van. Driving uphill for ages. We were paraded about at a military firing range, where the copper and his mates stood holding shooters trying to intimidate us. It worked because I was only young at the time and genuinely believed that there was a chance that they could put a bullet in each of our heads and pretend we never existed. I was even more worried when one of the officers offered me a cigarette because I had seen enough war films to know they did this before they summoned the firing squad!

Once the Old Bill had finished putting the frighteners up us, they took us back to the station and asked us some more questions. I didn't even tell them my name because I was on a fake passport and didn't want to risk making a mistake and giving myself away. Colin fed them a load of shit, which meant that they could remand him to the local prison. I was returned to the cells so that they could interrogate me again at a later date. Fortunately they stopped the fan, which meant that at least I got a bit of peace and quiet. Two weeks later, Colin was brought back to the dibble shop and we were made to take part in an ID parade. One of the geezers that we had stolen from was told to pick out the blokes who had robbed him. The minute he laid eyes on me, he went berserk, wrapping his hands around my neck and trying to strangle me. Fortunately he was quite elderly and couldn't have choked a dead chicken. I later learned that he had had a breakdown after discovering that his money was missing, which was why he was so angry.

"Well," I thought to myself, "I think it's safe to say that he's spotted me alright."

Colin had better luck and managed to avoid being fingered despite the dibble attempting to hint to the old bloke that he was one of the thieves at every available opportunity. We were kept in the police station cells overnight, which meant another sleepless night listening to the extractor fan, and then transported to the local jail the following morning pending further enquiries. The coppers didn't want us to corroborate our stories so they instructed the guards to place us in isolation, which meant that mealtimes were the only thing that we had to look forward to each day – or at least they would have been if we weren't forced to exist upon a diet that consisted solely of dry bread and muesli. Every now and again we would be taken back to the cop shop and questioned but I would always stay silent. The police kept telling me that I would be deported if I admitted to the crimes and would be free once I got back to the UK but I didn't believe them so I kept my mouth shut. I later learnt that they were telling the truth but this made little difference because I probably wouldn't have confessed to anything anyway on principle.

One day I was sitting in my cell, going out of my mind with boredom, when the food hatch popped open and a little Swiss bloke who could have passed for Heinrich Himmler's stunt double put his face up to the gap.

"Hello, my name iz Doctor Grobb," he told me. "It iz very foolish of you not to own up to your crime. You could be back in your own country if you had just been honest wiv us, you know that don't you?" Who the fuck was this guy and what did he want with me? I thought. "I have been given ze task of investigating your case," he went on. "Now if you will accompany me to my office, I would like to conduct an interview."

This was okay by me. It wasn't going to achieve anything because I wasn't planning on saying a word but I figured it wouldn't do me any harm either. I followed him out of the cell to a small room with a table in it and plonked myself down on a chair facing him.

"Okay," said Dr Grobb. "I'm going to give you twenty minutes in which to confess. If you do not confess in this time then I will have wasted both my time and yours." With that, he set the alarm on the office clock and sat there staring at me, not saying a word. Just stirring his coffee like a real Nazi.

"Fuck me," I thought to myself, "this fella really is crackers." I remember the coffee aroma was pure torture, it smelt great. I wasn't offered one, although I could smoke.

Dr Grobb repeated this process every couple of days for the next few months. He would occasionally break the silence to ask me a question and I would say "no comment". The only time that I gave a response was when he asked me what colour the car I had been driving was. A hotel manager had made a statement indicating that we had been to the area before and he wanted to check if we had driven there in the same vehicle. "Pink with blue spots," I told him.

He failed to see the funny side of this and reverted back to staring intently into my eyes without saying anything. The Swiss police are only allowed to keep you on remand for a maximum of six months unless they are able to prove to the court that they have gathered enough evidence that you are guilty to merit holding you for longer. On the day before the date the authorities were legally obliged to release us, Dr Grobb summoned us into his office and told us that he had some news for us.

"Your fingerprints have come back from Interpol," he smiled. "It seems that you have been using false passports and that you are actually brothers."

You could tell that he thought that we were going to crack and spill the beans now that he knew our true identities. Were we fuck!

"I'm surprised you didn't get onto that earlier," I replied. "Couldn't you tell we looked alike Herr Grobb? Plus that's got nothing to do with the crime that we've been accused of, Herr Grobb!" I shrugged my shoulders as if to say "better luck next time" and Grobb signalled for the guards to return us to our cell.

The following morning, Dr Grobb came to the isolation unit to bid us farewell. He was a surprisingly good sport and held out his hand for me to shake so I extended mine back towards him only to quickly take it away at the last minute and blow him a raspberry. This evoked a chuckle from him and demonstrated a more human side to his character. In hindsight I should have just shaken his hand really.

The Old Bill ended up having to give us our car back because they were unable to prove that it was stolen. The only thing that they didn't return to us were our snide passports. This meant that we needed to get to the British Embassy in Zurich before it shut at five o'clock to sort ourselves out some emergency papers that granted us permission to leave the country. We were planning on heading to Amsterdam to watch United play Brighton in the FA Cup final on the telly with some of our mates and didn't want to miss the game.

Unfortunately we failed to make it to the embassy in time and ended up having to travel through France, Luxembourg and Belgium to get into Holland because these countries all had points where passport control was relatively lax. Worse still, we had just got onto the motorway in Holland and were driving along at around 7 am when the battery on our car went flat and we were forced to stop on the hard shoulder. We had managed to get it going again and were about to resume our journey when the Dutch Old Bill pulled up next to us in a big white Porsche that looked like the one that Penelope Pitstop drove in Wacky Races. I didn't want them to recognise us as foreigners so I attempted to convince them that we were locals by speaking some poor quality Dutch but they didn't buy it.

"Have you two got any identification on you?" the driver asked us.

The only ID that we had to show him was the papers that we had been given when we were released from the Swiss prison, which had our real names on them. The copper took them off us, quickly scanned through them and then got out a book containing Interpol's list of undesirables and started flicking through to see if we were in it. He found us straightaway and told us that he was going to have to take us down to the station to ask us a few questions. This was all we fucking needed; we had only been free for ten hours.

"You can follow us in your car but if you drive off on us then we shoot," the officer told us.

We somehow doubted that our Golf could have got away from a Porsche even if we had wanted to risk being shot at. When we got to the dibble shop, the copper asked us what we were doing in the country, so we explained to him that we were on the way to watch the Cup Final with our mates.

"I'm afraid I'm going to have to take you to the Hook of Holland and put you on a ferry to Harwich," he told us. "We can't risk allowing you to stay here because you have committed a lot of crime in Holland in the past."

I wouldn't usually have been all that arsed about getting deported but this time we wanted to watch the final.

"Why don't you fuck us off back into Belgium instead?" I asked the dibble. "I'll make it worth your while for you and sell you our car for a fraction of the price it's worth if you do it." An English copper wouldn't have considered this offer but the Dutch Old Bill were proper rum bastards. It was a decent motor with an amazing sound system so we knew that he would want it.

"But you will just come straight back across the border the minute our backs are turned," the copper told me. "I'll tell you what I can do for you though. If you sell me the car for 500 Guilders, I can take you to a police station near the Hook of Holland that my friend is in charge of and let you watch the match there before deporting you. After that you'll be escorted onto the ferry home." I just hoped it wouldn't be Etten Leur police station with Bobby Ball waiting!

The car was a 'come day, go day' anyway so we weren't massively arsed about it. The officer upheld his end of the bargain and before we knew it, Col and me were sitting in a room with a load of Dutch Old Bill watching United play Brighton. The dibble knew that we were criminals but didn't seem to give a fuck. It was one of the craziest experiences of my life and shows you what rum cunts the Cloggy coppers are.

All of the Old Bill were rooting for the underdog and supporting Brighton so it was perhaps a good thing that we drew 2–2. Shortly after the game had ended, we were driven to the ferry port and placed in the holding room with its glass window, ready to be deported. All in all, it had been a strange trip. We had done a bit of grafting, got one over on the Swiss dibble and witnessed the type of antics that no policemen in the world would ever indulge in outside of Holland. Was it worth being locked up for hours on end in a police cell with a noisy-as-fuck extractor fan whirring away right next to it, being fed so many bowls of muesli that we were worried that we were going to overdose on it and thinking that we were going to get executed on some mad army firing range for £700? Possibly not but it was something to laugh about once we arrived back in England.

It was another crazy overseas adventure to add to the collection. We later found out that the case against us in Switzerland was eventually taken up again and we were tried in absentia. We were given a six-year ban from the country and eighteen-month jail sentences to serve if we ever returned – which we obviously did time and time again. No worries though as Colin and I actually got nicked in the Geneva area and locked up for two weeks or so later on but we were on false passies. Luckily for us they couldn't hold us as no cash had been taken, we just took a security guy for a ride on our car in the snow. There's no crime if some nutter wants to try car skiing, is there? We never saw him, even though we thought we heard shouting – the stereo was on loud. Colin even protested at court and ran out as his brief hadn't arrived. I was pissing myself when he was escorted back in rubbing his shins after he had received a few digs!

Either way we were both deported the very next day by three CID who told us to escort ourselves to the check out while they hovered over us to make sure we got on the next flight to London. We both plotted up at Lincoln's house in Stockwell.

A NEW HQ - ROTTERDAM

The lads living in the dam were getting followed or photographed everywhere they went, the police were building dossiers on us all, so a few of us decided we would rag Rotterdam instead. With the surrounding towns and villages there was plenty to go at, plus we had now sussed out a certain supermarket chain that had small but very busy off licences attached to them. These stores had nice safes in their back offices, although the keys came in two separate parts, the top half was always easy to find in the back room, then we had to find the other half which was usually found just under the tills in a drawer or even in the manager's jacket hung up somewhere nearby. All we had to do was get the staff away while someone got the bottom half of the key, then with the two parts together it was job on. The first one we did netted us 25,000 guilders. We were shocked as the shops were really small, this meant they always had mega dough in them. We did every one we could find in Holland for almost a year or so until eventually the store wised up to the fact they had been battered.

We normally shared our new found thieving knowledge but this one we kept to ourselves, It was the best regular earner we had (apart from the tom shops that we knew with the keys). But on a Monday morning we would be up bright and early and down to breakfast as they averaged around the same (c.20,000 guilders) about £7,000 which was a top result for a sneak in those days.

Roufy had been dating a Dutch girl, Isabella, while he'd been a DJ in Spain, so we attached ourselves to her family who were Surinamese. Izzie's mother was a top lady called Sigrid and soon it was like a home from home. Colin moved in with his girlfriend Bev from Manchester who had moved there too. Mine and Greg's birds didn't – Greg's girlfriend Bev was pregnant at the time, the girl I'd been seeing had more or less 'Dear Johned' me when I was locked up in Swizzy so Sigrid's daughter rented us her flat, happy days we had a base in Rotterdam!

Up to now we had mainly worked north Holland or east towards Germany but now we were based in the southwest it opened up a whole new area. These came to be known as the 'dreaded islands'. On the roads it was dead with hardly any traffic to blend into when trying to get away after an earner, there were two ferries that connected these islands. Spud and me hated the islands, though nobody would graft with our Colin who hardly knew the word 'safety'. We had to kerb him half the time from doing something as we knew the roads were empty and most went on for miles without a junction or motorway and it seemed to take forever to get into a populated area again. Winter on the islands was even grimmer but we still did them all; every village, town and suburb.

Rotterdam, or 'Rotten Dam' as we soon named it, wasn't Amsterdam that's for sure, to me it felt like Salford or Liverpool. We soon found the main street to booze on called the Binninweg where we found a Surinamese club called The Tudor, a pub aptly named The Booze and one called The Three Musketeers, which was usually full of Brit workers who all had jobs at Europort, one of the biggest ports in the world. We really started getting into playing darts at the boozer. The landlord, Barry, was a United fan from the Isle of Man. It was good to find a half empty local to go to, knowing that we would always be made welcome, that is until we became a pain in the arse! But that process usually took a year or so. Nevertheless, Barry was sound and we got to know him well over the next couple of years.

Now, in most clubs they had a 'pay-when-you-leave' policy. On entry you got a card where the staff clicked a mark on it as to what you had ordered. If you lost the ticket it was 150 guilders £40 - sweet. So on one ticket it was double brandies all night plus gallons of beer leaving the other tickets with one or two daft drinks on them, then you left paying a silly 150 guilders - we went through every big club in Rotterdam like that. Even though the clubs were shit it was worth the chuckle getting drunk for peanuts! Anything we paid for wasn't really paid for either, as all our money was stolen anyway but we still had a duty to make cutbacks, "wherever and whenever" was the golden rule.

"To pay is to fail" wasn't a phrase back then but it sums it all up. We were just living for nothing really and having a good time doing it, the cost we paid was prison time and they didn't even dish that out in Holland, or couldn't with their crazy laws. It was like you had to get caught red-handed for the Dutch to prosecute and seeing as we were good at what we did, we seldom came unstuck. They seemed clueless as to what to do about us really. Opportunistic crime isn't high on the list compared to some of the other things that went on. We didn't warrant full on surveillance, we were just small fish in a large pond. We were fully aware that the police in Holland had bigger fish to fry: murderers, dealers, terrorists, kidnappings you name it. Holland was a magnet for criminals from all over the world. Most were on the run from their own countries so the Dutch dibble had their work cut out with the foreigners, that's for sure.

We soon found out we could get an international driving licence by handing over a 'UK Provisional' by saying you needed one for work – the Dutch never asked what 'Provisional' meant. Now we all had full European licences. I even went home on one and got arrested for drink driving in Moss Side one night, was fined £100 in court the next day and they didn't even know how to implement giving me points on it.

After a winter in Rotterdam we headed for Spain; me, Gordon and our Colin had arranged to meet up with Sid, Paddy and Dicko in Lloret. We drove through Germany and Swizzy on a good parcel building tour of the tom shops. We had earned pretty well in Holland so we now had a great parcel too on top of a decent wedge to blow on having a good chill out. We had been there a couple of nights and went into a club called 'St Trop' run by the Dutch. We had been fine in this place the last few years and because Roufy was the DJ we got in for nothing, without queuing up. So we were all surprised to see Dicko getting carried out by four bouncers on our second night out. It turns out Dicko had 'goofed out'. The Dutch weren't daft, they knew a smackhead when they saw one.

So Dicko goes mad when he's at the door and without us really paying attention it's got moody really quickly with Dicko getting battered by the doormen! With six of us now there was a standoff while we got Dicko in an ambulance.

They had given him a good old going over and his arm was in a sling. Battered and bruised we headed back to the hotel and went to see Roufy straight away, who was now in the 'Mont Blanc', another Dutch bar we frequented. He knew the cloggy doorman who were all kung-fu intimidators. We asked Roufy to find out where they lived, then the owner of the bar told us they were all Den Haag lads and lived at a pension above the shops. We knew they never drank anywhere outside their beloved 'St Trop'. The next morning me, Sid, Gordon and our Colin got the Spanish coshes sorted and let ourselves in the flat proper, making our way to the top floor rooms. We went in at once – whether the rooms were locked or not didn't matter, the kick-in works well as we set about getting in as many digs as we could. They were well sparko. Then we quickly ran into a few lads on the landing below who had been awakened by the noise. With four Brits heading down at them at full pelt they went down quicker than the lads upstairs. Then down the next steps there was an Indonesian guy who didn't want to know but Gordon was in a full rage and went at the guy until the blood got too much. Colin asked him to stop but he was in a different world – we finally got hold of his arm and dragged him down to the outside door. The noise had been tremendous and their girlfriends screaming from the bedrooms hadn't helped. Out on the street a crowd had built up with all the smashing and commotion, we must have looked a right sight. You forget all reason when hyped up but I bet we looked a little bit madder than the usual mad Brits abroad coming out onto that street that sunny morning!

Either way the Dutchies got a fine alarm call that day, that's for sure. So we thought it wise to get the fuck out of the way for now, after the shortest holiday ever. With the miles and hours behind us and time cracking on we found ourselves in Marseilles. By now it was night time, we were knackered and without much thought we all nodded off. Imagine two Dutch cars in the middle of some car park just glad to be out of Spain. Fuck sake! When we woke up it looked like we were in the middle of Morocco! We had driven into the shadiest part of town by the looks of it, then Colin gets a tap on his window. As we look at him another shady got his arm in through the gap in my open window like a snake – they had seen my wallet and were going for it, the fuckers! He wouldn't let go and quickly wriggled it from my grip. I'm out after him for the whole of one second until I saw what looked like Baghdad on a bad day…

I got straight back in the car chuckling to Colin "he can have the fucking passport I need a new one anyway – if the guy had tried for the toiletry bag that was right underneath my passport he would have been quids in!" That was where I kept the jewellery. I still think of that shady Moroccan's face. He didn't know what he'd missed out on that day, it could have been his best payday ever.

Dicko was now in pain, not just from the beating but now he needed some gear; we headed for the beach to get our heads round where to score smack. I always knew people on gear and to tell the truth my thoughts were clear on the matter, no one can get someone one off it, it's as simple as that really. Anyway we finally managed to track down some of the devil's powder on a right old street where we felt more like we were doing a robbery more than anything. Six of us, in twos, pretending we were not really together, the only white people on this shady street full of Arabs! Thank fuck it was real gear or else we would have had to go through it all again. We weren't impressed by Marseilles that's for sure so we drove out pronto and began the long drive back to Holland.

The parcel of tom we had we couldn't even sell in one go, it was that big. We had to split it up in the end and it all got frittered away bit by bit. It wasn't hard to do that in Amsterdam's red light area, with all its pubs and clubs open 24/7. 'Sensi' (what's now called 'skunk') had hit the coffee shops in Holland around this time. The 'Redleb' and 'Afghan' hadn't been any good since both had trouble with civil wars in their respective countries. The Sensi wasn't as strong as today but was still the best smoke around. It stank to high heaven too. I used to buy that much after a while I even got nicknamed 'skunk'!

★

England were to play a friendly in Paris. We were not the biggest England fans but as it was only a 4 hour drive me, Lou and Greg were up for it. I regretted it as the game itself was shit. When I went off to get some drinks I saw a scuffle going on and me being a nosey bastard I had to have a look. The English fans were running riot, twatting anybody really then I saw a French guy getting kicked to fuck in the head. I hate the sight of bullying and got in the middle of it "come on lads he's had enough" is all I said. Big mistake! Bish bash bosh. I don't think I'd ever had such a quick hiding. Fuck knows but it felt like a thousand punches landed on my face! "You nawvern cant" was all I heard as I took up the crab position waiting for a further beating. They were all cockneys. Talk about wrong place at the wrong time! At that point the riot police turned up flooding the place with CS gas. I'd been beaten to fuck and now I couldn't breath, the old bill were amazed when I spoke English and helped me to the first aiders. Anyway, I returned without drinks to Lou and Greg who just started chuckling at the state of my face! The game ended 2-0 to France and outside it was pure mayhem, going off left, right and centre. Even half a mile away from the stadium it was kicking off with the arabs. We ended up seeing these English fans hyped up to the max, "Fuck know's what our real army's like storming Goose Green," I thought to myself.

Later on we got near the Belgium border and thought we would get a hotel for the night. Without thinking I asked at reception for a room but was instantly blanked, no wonder when I went to the toilet and saw myself. I looked like the elephant man. Again I got back to the car where Lou and Greg were laughing their heads off at the state of me. I had to have a few days off the graft when we got back to Holland. Typical, I go to see England and ended up battered to fuck from the English fans for being a Northerner!

★

Some memorable games I had to be back for that year were Liverpool and Barcelona - one for football, the other for fighting. All the Manc grafters had to be at Old Trafford for the biggest game in years. Everybody came back to Manchester for United v Barcelona, every fan knew they had to be there and the stadium was full to the rafters with the best atmosphere I've ever heard at Old Trafford. Every character I knew was there, all the thieves living or earning abroad, the casuals were in full attendance it had gone from 30/50 lads to 3/5000 now with fashion taking over completely on the terraces in the last 5 years or so.

When the players came out that atmospheric night a chant came up from the Stretford End *"Maradona, Maradona"* the player couldn't ignore this, the fans loved him. The chant went on as he makes his way to the stand, just as he's about to wave they give it *"Maradona you're a wanker you're a wanker"* he knew he'd been had and it was a great start to the game where Robbo took full charge of Marafuckindonna all night. Utd won 3-0 on the night so went through 3-2 on aggregate, we were all on the pitch at full time.

A SCOUSER'S VISIT TO OLD TRAFFORD

I can't really remember my first visit to Old Trafford, they all morph into one, expect the September '84 game, which ended with me receiving a load of stitches in my head. It was probably the worst violence I'd been involved in following the reds and reports of the day differ depending which end of the East Lancs (or London) you come from. But this is how I remember it...

We arrived at Victoria on the ordinary and were herded onto about 7 double deckers which took us to the ground. There must have been about 3 or 400 of us and we were chomping at the bit to get involved. When we arrived at the concourse it was going off all over the place. The plod blocked the exits of the buses, so in the end we booted out all the windows and got involved in the mayhem. I can't even remember who won the battle (if anyone), but I do remember a blonde lad in glasses from Miles Platting, Binzy, scattering us everywhere with the thickest metal chain I'd ever seen. Over the years I've bumped into him and his brothers in Europe on bits of graft and also spent time in Armley with one of them.

A New HQ - Rotterdam

Anyway, I can't remember the result as I didn't get in until three-quarter time and spent the whole game having running battles up and down that road where the Lou Macari chippy is. After the game we were kept in then herded up towards Warwick Road station, but another firm broke off towards town down Chester Road. I'd been previously with Everton in a night game and knew they would be waiting at Trafford Bar station. As we pulled into Trafford Bar someone pulled the cord and at the same time we were ambushed from the opposite platform with bricks, pebbles off the track and all sorts; the windows came in and there was nowhere to run as the train was packed. We tried to barricade the windows with seats but I ended up getting knocked out with a brick. When I came round, the white cashmere crew neck I was wearing was covered in blood, by this time everyone had started getting off and tearing up the platform, as I got off one of the Mancs threw a shopping trolley off the bridge above onto the live wires and there was a big explosion to add to the mayhem.

When I got out of the station I went up to a Manc plod and told him I needed to go to hospital. He just replied, "Serves you right for coming here, you scouse bastard". We battled all the way back to Victoria that day, the plod had lost all control as there was another scouse firm on the loose heading to Market Street, I've got the newspaper cutting in front of me now, apparently they looted a branch of Ratners escaping with thousands of pounds worth of Tom, Ok... it was a Ratners, but that was like a Goldsmiths to us Mickies back in '84! Whatever the class of Tom Shop was the Manc grafters "wouldn't have been happy about that, lad."

GOODWILL TOUR

We met a couple of grafters after the game that told us their mate Stuart was locked up in Germany and that his dad was old bill and they didn't really want to get involved. Stuart had started going away a couple of years earlier, since he was fifteen they said. Being in a pub and half pissed we weren't told and forgot to ask what he was even in for.

Coincidently, Paddy had been nicked in Germany at the time at Langsburg prison, the same one Hitler had spent time in plotting the Nazi state. I told them that I'd go visit him as I was heading off to see Paddy anyway. "What's his full name and age? I'll kill two birds with one stone."

Our Colin then said he'd come, as he was up for grafting with us up there. The next thing, we had Spud's girlfriend's brother piping in, could he go abroad with us? As we knew him anyway and took the odd apprentice on missions he was told to get a passie. Spud wasn't too happy but everyone needs to get out of Manchester some time.

Würzburg was our first stop so we only needed to graft expenses on the way knowing it would be better to at least "get there first" without incident plus with this new 'kid' onboard it was for the best. We had to see a prosecutor to get permission to see Stuart, it was a real Germanic atmosphere with him getting arrested for a jewellery theft. After going through what felt like a court appearance we got permission, in grunted broken English, to visit the next day. The woman in charge looked like she wanted to put me and Colin in there with this young guy we'd never met.

The next day up at the prison it went smoothly enough, I passed him a nice chunk of hash on our hand shake while Colin shouted loudly about getting coffee. Stuart looked sixteen at best but was wise enough to plug his much needed smoke. He told us his story in the twenty minutes visiting time; that his mate had been locked up and Stuart had tried to bail him out, only to end up getting arrested when he came to visit, "just like you now, only I didn't leave."

Now we knew that he got arrested while trying to visit his mate we were more than happy to see the back of that prison, I can tell you.

We were satisfied knowing that we'd made a young grafter happy with a fine chunk to get stoned on for the next few weeks. We knew that a visit's a visit, they mean a lot to everyone and we always visited who we could, when we could. Next on the list was Langsburg to visit Paddy who was doing two years, he'd been sussed out in some office but by simply pushing the assistant on the way out of the gaff, it got him a charge of aggravated theft.

We went through the same interrogation as before to get a visiting order, then saw Paddy who again got a nice piece of hash passed to him. Visits were far easier back then, nothing like today, so with our good will tour over we headed into Swizzy glad to be away from jails and visits for now. Our new recruit Tommy hadn't seen much yet apart from a good few shops we had grafted along the way and two prison visits!

We grafted the North end of Swizzy, working down to Basel picking up our necessary items and a fair amount of tom. I remember on this trip we came across a shop giving away a nice amount of Dupont and Dunhill lighters that were real flash ones and could be sold to any one, we had around forty of the fuckers, and enough cash from the generous shop keepers of Switzerland to carry on our journey to Lloret. Tommy couldn't believe it, he'd never been away before and ten days after leaving Manchester he'd done his 'first tour of duty' and he was in Spain loving it. We didn't spend a penny of our own on that trip and the three of us stayed in Lloret on just the money from the fuckin lighters we had brought with us! The jewellery was taken back to Holland with us as it was too good of a parcel and would keep us in with our buyers back in Amsterdam. That holiday was essentially paid for with a box of lighters, which says it all really.

FRANKFURT

Stuart: *I guess the saying "like father, like son" didn't apply to me. The fact that my old man was a copper meant that he was big on discipline and would come down on me like a ton of bricks whenever I did anything wrong*

Ironically, it was an attempt by my old man to steer me away from crime that made me decide once and for all to fleece the shops on the continent. He had repeatedly warned me not to "shit in my own backyard" when he suspected I was up to no good in Failsworth, this made thieving in a foreign country seem like an even better idea; if it all came out on top then at least I would be able to say I had taken his advice.

I was still only fifteen the first time I went abroad with criminal intent. It might seem bizarre to the average law-abiding citizen that a kid of that age would set off overseas to rob shops simply because he had heard other lads were doing it, but I was craving excitement and the thieves who crossed the channel got a tremendous amount of respect. They were viewed as modern-day pirates, braving unknown territory and coming back with riches from all over Europe. The continent represented freedom and adventure; I couldn't wait to experience what it had to offer. In the late 70's, the sneak-thieves knew there were richer pickings to be had in continental Europe and started targeting shops over there while their teams were playing abroad. Tales of their adventures overseas circulated around estates all over Greater Manchester, causing other lads to join the hordes that flocked abroad in search of easy pickings and word quickly spread to Failsworth. I had already gained an aptitude for doing sneaks on clothes shops by that stage and was immediately captivated by the idea of expanding my operation to mainland Europe.

I had been going away about a year or more mostly in south of France, but now knew enough lads to hit the rest of what Europe had to offer. I had arrived in Frankfurt to meet two brothers from my town called Big B and Little B. The B's had been grafting with a tall black lad from East London called Lloyd.

The other lads were Scouse J, Little Stu, Paul M, and an ex-Para trooper straight out of the forces called Dean from Oldham. I wanted to get involved with this crew because they were all older than me and on the ball, a lot of them were Bernado's friends so I knew if I could show them how game I was, maybe I would eventually be accepted. Each day me and the team; Dave, Budgie, Mick and Little Tiny, would split up, arranging to meet up at the bar near the Bahnhoff. We'd be in a two-man and a three-man team, one of us setting off south and one going north.

Each night we would meet at Wendy's burger shop and whatever we copped for we would sell to the sex kinos or the person that would work at the brass houses.

The gear we had off at the start was top notch and easy to sell; we'd load up the lockers at Frankfurt station. After about five days the lockers were filling up fast with bits of odd jewellery. I would always leave the key with a person I trusted and that was Dave. One day we didn't leave Frankfurt, instead deciding to stay in the city and possibly have a pop at some watches we had been casing. We got there and on this occasion decided it was good to go. Me and Mick distracted the lone shop keeper, asking him certain prices on watches as Little Tiny snuck around the corner, jibbed inside and got to work. As me and Mick were blagging the guy, Little Tiny appeared with that cheeky Chappie face, mouthing that he'd had a top cop so let's make a move. We said we'd be back to look further at the watches and the guy didn't have a jar of glue that Tiny had hit it hard, so we knew we could walk away without breaking sweat.

The next morning we decided to put the watches in one of those boxes you get from the post office and sent all twelve back home, knowing that we'd have a nice little earner waiting for us when we got back. While we had been getting all sorts of equipment someone had said we should get some Coco Channel and No. 5 and we could get a shag from the prostitutes, who had signs up to say they had weekly screenings against STDs, which was good to know! The brasses were fit as fuck, you could take your pick and they all wanted big name perfumes; they'd obviously caught on to what we were up to. I think they thought we each had a proper pair of balls nicking all this stuff and only looking about 16. The guys that protected the girls would always let us in, and if not you'd just slip them 20 marks; it was a big adventure in them whorehouses.

After a successful day's work having off some nice watches, we waited *for the others. The hours passed by and Budgie and Dave weren't back, so we started to think the worst had happened. Eventually around 10 o'clock Budgie appeared looking like he'd seen a ghost. "We got nicked" he said, "for three attempted thefts." Dave had got behind the counter in a shoe shop and saw the peter (safe), so started looking in the draws for the safe key. No luck, the manager must have had it, so they moved on. They had been grafting in Würzburg, the Bavarian part of Germany, where they are a lot stricter on handing out sentences. They carried on grafting and came to a toy store, but by this time the police had been called out for them acting suspiciously in the shoe shop. The police had followed them and Dave was seen going in to jib a private room that read 'Nein Ausgang', meaning 'No Entry to the public'. So now the police had well scoped them out as they went into an electrical shop. They were flagged up to the police for acting suspiciously and as they exited the shop the police were told there'd been a theft from a cash box.*

So all in all they had been seen acting sketchy in three separate shops and fitted a description, not the most flawless grafting but no one's perfect. The police pounced on them in the busy street, cuffed and carted them off to Police HQ. They searched them and found a couple of expensive watches and 900 Marks. As Budgie was telling me this it looked like they were going nowhere. The police said they wanted to know where this key had come from, more precisely which train station, but because they all looked the same Dave refused to tell them and Budgie denied knowing about it. The police said they wanted around 4,300 DM back as a fine but weren't letting Dave go as he had done all the jibbing. They let Budgie go to get the money for the fine or Dave would go to Würzburg prison until the full amount was paid. Back at the hotel and after a spliff everyone started to get paranoid in case Dave might give our location away. I said Dave wouldn't do that, we had become very close friends and he was like an older brother to me, so I said we can all get that out of our heads, and that I would go and retrieve our stash from the station.

This wasn't going to be a case of slipping a wad of cash into my jacket, this locker had some shady looking stuff in it. It was going to be nerve-wracking considering the transport police had to open my locker, and they said I must identify at least four items in the locker. I was bricking it that they might see the jewellery. I described a Martinique shirt, Liberto jeans and a couple of other clothes. Luckily the expensive bit of gold was hidden under all the clothes. Thank fuck. I told the other three to keep up a conversation with the police to keep them from rooting through the locker. I handed over my real passport and paid the 25 DM for the key I lost and so it was documented and logged by the transport police the time and date that I'd gone into the station. "We've got to get this wedge back to get Dave out" I said, and so an early night was needed, but first we had to sell as much of the stuff off as possible. So we rallied around the kinos, brothels and kebab shops with our jewels and came out with 2,500 DM. Budgie and Mark Cooney, however, decided they wanted to go home, which was a shock, but Tiny I could always rely on, he loved grafting. So Tiny and me decided we would keep 1,500 DM and they could have 1,000 to go home. There was no way I was going to let my friend, someone who had become like a brother to me, rot in a Bavarian jail.

The next morning, after being kept waiting by the staff for what seemed like an eternity, we were informed that for some unknown reason we weren't allowed to hand the bail money in just yet and had to return the following day. This was a little bit annoying but provided us with the opportunity to do a few of the local jewellers over whilst we were in town. We should really have kept a low profile until our friend was free but if you leave a load of criminally-minded lads in a strange town with nothing to do then realistically they're going to go thieving whether it's a sensible thing for them to do or not.

The following day we made our way to the jail, which looked like something from the war, as it was built inside a pine forest. We sat down in the waiting room and again were left in limbo for ages but this time for good reason because after hours of sitting there idly twiddling our thumbs, an ugly German copper came in to inform us that three lads fitting our description had stolen rings and eighteen-carat gold chains from two city-centre jewellers. The officer knew my real name, which didn't bode well because I was on a snide passport. He had obviously been in touch with the Old Bill in England. The German dibble were very clued up and seemed to know every shop that we had been looking for a graft in. We all ended up getting charged with theft and I got locked up in the adult prison despite the fact that I was still only sixteen. To make matters even worse, they sent

Tiny to a different nick so I was the only Brit in the jail.

The prison that they sent me out to was called JVA Aschaffenburg and was very different to an English jail because there was no taboo on grassing. Inmates who had testified against their co-defendants were placed on the same wings as the people that they had stuck in there, which seemed bizarre to me. The mad thing was that nobody dared to lay a finger on the informers because they knew that if they did then they would be likely to become the next person who got snitched on to the screws.

The guards housed me on a wing that was mainly populated by alcoholics, vagabonds and vagrants who had been locked up for making a nuisance of themselves. In hindsight, I think that this was because the authorities thought that I was too young to be thrown in with some of the more hardened criminals and wanted to protect me. I was a little bit nervous because it was my first stint inside but soon became good mates with an American and a top dog Dutchman, who both assured me that they would look after me. It was a relief to know that there were other people there who spoke English because a lot of the German prisoners were quite hostile and would slag me off, thinking that I couldn't tell that they were taking the piss out of me because I didn't speak their language. Little did they know that I was merely biding my time before I made my move!

Everybody in the prison was given a job to do to keep them occupied and the pay was okay. So I worked on a production line, making parts for extension leads. It was quite repetitive but paid well and life wouldn't have been that bad if the pair of Germans in front of me hadn't always been talking shit about me and sniggering away to one another. I might not have been able to understand German but the word 'Englishman' was clear enough and the fact that it was always followed by loud laughter made it blindingly obvious that those two cunts were cracking jokes at my expense, I just wasn't having it. The ugliest of the piss-taking Krauts had been issued with the task of fastening parts into a component using a screwdriver. Nothing was automated back then in prison workshops so things like that had to be done manually. This was handy because it provided me with the perfect means of getting back at him. All I had to do was get hold of a similar screwdriver to the one that he was using, heat the plastic handle up until it was boiling hot and then swap it for his.

My plan worked even better than I had expected because the red-hot

The Collyhurst Flats where my family lived from 1959 to 1970

Left: The much beloved 112 bus which Colin and I virtually lived on having to commute the 8 miles from Collyhurst to Sale every day.

Above: Outside Auntie Patsy's, Moss Side 1964
Right: A Collyhurst Cowboy mesmerised by the new tower blocks, 1965.

Me (in my Rupert pants) getting stuck in at Pontins Holiday camp, Blackpool 1971

My one and only job! Here I am off to work at Cleanwalls, although it didn't last long, 1977.

Me, my younger brother James and Colin, 1978

John McKee, King of the Grafters, with Luchein his dealer, Amsterdam 1976

A rare photo of the Zeedijk in the 70s. Shady doesn't begin to describe it!

*Co-Co shou
Roufy and Colin
jazz funk mc
Lloret de Mar, 1*

*Spud and Dicko in
Berne, 1979*

OPPOSITE PAGE: A FEW OF THE LADS
*(top left) Me skinning up in Roufys DJ box Lloret De Mar, 1979;
(top right) Terry Corrigan; (middle left) Fraz (who was taking the first picture
Amsterdam 1983; (centre) Kevin; (middle right) Diller;
(bottom) Donnie, Kev, some Dutch guy, Essy (on his bike).*

I'm in there somewhere! Amsterdam's Queens Day Riots, 1980.

I missed the riots in England in 1981 but we caught up with the news on the telly as city by city violence swept the country. Here Moss Side is ablaze, as told in Spud's story.

Our pride and joy: Our Colin and Spud standing by our first VW Golf, 1981. It wasn't a turbo but it felt like it.

Spud, Lou myself and Colin in Swizzy, 1981

I'm looking pretty pleased with myself here as I've just been released in time for Christmas, 1981.

United captain Bryan Robson is chaired off the Old Trafford pitch after our sensational 3-0 win over Maradona's Barcelona in 1984. It was a hard jib to get on that pitch as we were up at the back of K Stand and dropped down into the scoreboard and over the fence. A great night!

Gems looted by fans on rampage

A SOCCER mob looted a jeweller's shop yesterday after smashing in the windows with bricks.

Fans ran riot after the big match between Manchester United and Liverpool.

Worst hit was Market Street in Manchester's city centre.

Terrified shoppers, many with young children, ran for cover in the rampage.

The windows of a pub were smashed in as Liverpool supporters made their way to Victoria Station to catch trains home.

News of the World Reporter

Then came the attack on the jeweller's, Ratners. Three plate glass windows were smashed and rings and watches snatched.

Later police searched fans at the railway station in a bid to find stolen jewellery.

A member of the jewellery shop staff said:

"There were hundreds pouring down the street, with police trying to control them.

"Suddenly the bricks started flying and glass flew into the shop.

"We do not know yet how much stock has been stolen."

Police said later that two Liverpool men were helping with inquiries into the incident.

Nine fans were arrested at the match.

Newspaper reports of Jockey's story of Scousers robbing a jewellers in Manchester, 1985.

(left to right) Me, Roufy, Colin with his Basque bird, Divy with his Cockney Reenie and our James, 1985

Cockney Tim and I with a couple of girls and Pedro, Lloret 1986

With Irish Tommy in Girona and you can tell by the state of the green Nissan that I still haven't got the hang of driving. It was Tommy's first trip abroad when we went to visit Stuart.

Gibbo, James, Colin and Jan the Man, our top Cloggy mate, Barcelona 1988.

More happy faces on the Wacko Jacko tour in Sunny Spain. Ecstasy had just landed as had huge profits, happy days!

Our kid and Toby working the Korean Olympics in 1988

Bobby G's calling the cops, Amsterdam 1990

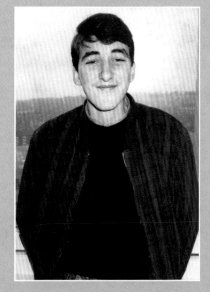

Salford's most prolific jibber Stephen McEvoy at Leeds University on the Madchester tour with The Happy Mondays, 1989

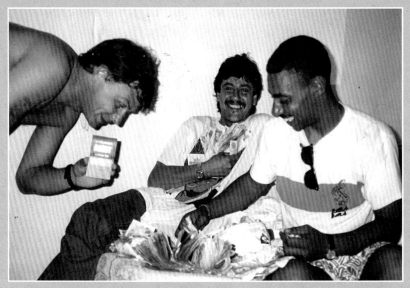

Colin, Roufy and Dave Lawrence with the profits from a night on Michael Jackson's BAD Tour, 1988 - Colin is holding one of our fake guest passes.

In Barcelona on the Ramblas just before the Champions League final against Bayern Munich, 1999. Greg (second from the right) and me (centre stage) take in the atmosphere.

Helping Colin set up his computer after saying he feels confident enough to attempt writing a book Oldenburg 1998

END OF AN ERA City's last ever game at Maine Road (left to right) Dicko, Me, Kevin O'Brien and Renno.

Left to right: West Ham's Cass Pennant, Stuart C, Marcus and Colin at the film premiere for "The Casuals" National Football Museum, 2012 in which Colin featured.

Taking my daughter Jasmine to her first bingo session in Salford, where she won £50!

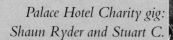

Palace Hotel Charity gig: Shaun Ryder and Stuart C.

Stuart Campbell, Hot Shot, Bez (it was his 50th)
and Colin in China Town.

BACK TO OUR ROOTS: *Me and our kid on Bengal Street, Ancoats,*
where the famous Scuttlers used to roam.

molten plastic on the handle stuck to the geezer's palm, causing him to shriek in agony like a hound dog the minute that he picked it up. Next second he screamed his lungs out and started waving his hand to try and get it off. The guards ran over and, thinking he was about to use it as a weapon, tore it from his grasp. This ripped the top layer of skin from the palm of his hand and left him wailing even louder than before - he learnt a valuable lesson that day: don't fuck with the English.

Apart from that one minor incident, my first time inside was relatively hassle-free. Working on the production line made the time pass quicker and we were allowed out on the yard every day, which helped me to avoid developing prison pallor. The food was sorted; schnitzels, curry-wurst sausages to die for, black-bread, plenty of sauerkraut and homemade soups that always had plenty of Smokey-pork with kidney beans thrown in the pot. I started pumping weights and felt like I was getting there, a couple of moons down the road I switched to thinking about the pumping sessions them ladies were due once I got back home.

Part way through my stint, a guard came to my cell to tell me that my girlfriend and my mum were coming to visit me, which gave me something to look forward to. All things considered, my first time inside could have been a damned sight worse than it was. On the day of my visit, I woke up thinking, "Fucking hell, it's going to be good to see my mam after all this time. I can't wait to get a nice warm cuddle off her." Imagine my surprise when I sat down in the visit room and my old man Campbell came striding up to the table with a face like a smacked arse.

"You've caused me a whole heap of bother this time son. Were English jails not good enough for you or something?" I was in for a right bollocking. "I've had to travel all the way down to Dover, then overnight being seasick on that fucking rocky ferry, all day on a slow train through France and Belgium without any decent food to see you here in the Land of Sauerkrauts all because your team of petty tealeaves believe they can make a fortune! More like the Goon Squad I'd say, son."

"Hold your horses here now Dad," I protested. "You told me not to shit in my own backyard!"

This did little to placate him and he continued to lay into me, telling me that I was a disgrace to the family and that I had brought shame upon myself. I had been expecting my visit to be the highlight of my time inside but instead it had turned into the lowest point of my sentence. I think part of the reason that I turned to crime in the first place was to rebel against my Old Man. The fact that he was so strict made me want to do the opposite to what he told me to do and transformed me from a law-abiding young kid into a hardened teenage criminal.

I ended up being held in Aschaffenburg for a total of six months before my case went to trial. I was settled in when right out of the blue I'm called out of the workshop to be told there's a visitor and low and behold there was Marcus B with a cheerful grin across his kipper plus Colin his brother, both I would get to know well over the next few years, what a pair of stand-up guys! They heard on the Manc grapevine what had gone down with us getting nicked and, as they were passing, the good fellas took time out to visit someone they'd never met and give him a chunk of hash, knowing that when you're inside visits can be few and far between.

A few months later, prior to my court hearing, my solicitor told me that I was going to be given a choice of either pleading not guilty and risking more porridge or admitting to my crimes and being deported back to England with a five-year ban. It was a no brainer: I chose option B and before I knew it, I was making my way home on the very welcome rocky ferry eating pie and chips and drinking bottles of beer. I even copped for a couple of spliffs via some students on the windy deck. My first taste of incarceration did little to deter me from my life of crime; if anything it made me try even harder to avoid getting caught.

CALL THE COPS

Back in Rotterdam, our Colin started grafting with Tommy, who got one of his mates over called Darren Campbell. On their first major wedge Daz went and spent his share on a BMW to take him with him. The only trouble was the engine set on fire and blew up on his first drive out on the motorway. He'd only had it a few hours and had just thrown 5000 guilders down the drain, about £1500. Almost all the lads I knew would only ever spend a thousand guilders max on a personal motor but Daz, whose old man was 'Shine' a famous DJ back in Manc, was Moss Side and he wanted a Beamer, innit!

Our Jay now came over as it was summer school holidays. Dicko was to take him to do all the concerts as there was a cloggy ticket tout called Rinus who let the Mancs work for him. Holland was the only country to have a firm of touts at the concerts so the Mancs didn't have to fight security here as they had been paid off by Rinus.

With that I just went to graft with an English girl I was seeing at the time and I started taking Dutch Isabella out with me too, just taking our time, getting them to walk around shops that I'd never normally go into. We were on the outskirts one day when we came across these shops I knew well from previous visits. There was one shop I'd been in before, I knew the layout before going in and that two people worked inside. "Right girls, all you have to do is you go in first – Issie get the assistant to this window area inside the shop, I'll come in with Trace and you do the same with the other assistant, yeah" both nodded. Issie had the women where I wanted them and the bloke wasn't concerned with me leading Trace to a convenient spot when I could slip out of view 'bish bash bosh' sweet as a nut. It took 5 seconds behind the counter then I just went back so the girls could wrap it up and get the fuck out. We got 14,000 guilders and the girls couldn't believe it. We were back in the flat counting it out within twenty minutes, it was so near to where we lived.

The next time I took them out we got picked up by the police in some little village, luckily I was on a false passie or else I don't think we'd have been let out so quickly. The girls were twitchy at best and it obviously knocked them back a little getting arrested, but I asked them to plod on until we copped a good enough wedge so Trace could go back to UK with some money as we had spent the last of the previous wedge by this time. They couldn't have hoped for an easier answer for their poor nerves. We drove into a sleepy little village in the middle of nowhere. Villages were always good at dinnertime as people usually let their guard down as happened in the very first shop we went into. It was a very small shop with nobody around and I just shouted for help. Still nobody around, I went to the office and lightly tapped on the door. No answer.

So I let myself in, and the first thing I saw was a fuckoff sized Alsatian sat in the corner behind the office desk. "Hello fella" I said. The dog was fine and never budged! I slid open the drawers while stroking this fucking dog and I found a good enough amount in the drawer, around 4-5,000 guilders, which I was more than happy with. Then right next to the dog on the floor was a strange out of place shoulder bag, the kind that men carry around. The bag was full of notes, it must have been the month's takings. Either this or the shop owner's a drug dealer, we were in Holland after all. So I'm back in the shop now looking a bit gobsmacked really. It felt strange that there was no assistant, just the owner's not very good guard dog. I probably should have taken the dog too, I thought, just to make it a complete head twatter for the owner!

Money from desk gone - Money from bag gone - Dog looking after money gone!

The girls were too nervous with the graft though, and even felt sorry for the people I was taking money from. Yet the money in the bag was a great result especially as nobody even knew we had been in the place anyway. Tracey went back to England. I wouldn't really see her after that. She had always known what I did but witnessing it and then doing it certainly wasn't for her, that's for sure, though she didn't mind spending it all in the years I was seeing her. I even made a short trip to Manchester two weeks later and walked into the Reno; she's sat there larking about with her mates, tanning the money on coke, brandy and spliffs. One minute she's almost crying in a shop feeling guilty robbing folk, the next it's all laugh a minute down the Reno!

Either way, it would be a while till I grafted with any girls again, the only real girl grafters I knew at this time came from the north side of Manchester, I'd grafted with Mary Flynn before and she knew how it played out. Eddie Beef's sister was rummer than half the blokes I knew and got up to all kinds. We had the Terrorhawks too, they were a bunch a no-nonsense girls from Miles Platting that would probably knock most blokes to the ground in a street fight! They got their name because they swooped down on their prey as if from nowhere dipping in town and at the festivals. Three girls playfully hugging a guy meant only one thing in their company "you're getting dipped mate, call the cops!"

By the way, we all used the phrase "call the cops" at this time. If I was chatting away to some assistant and there was a commotion with whoever was darting out of the door with the takings, I'd say "Right, call the police I'll go and see where he runs", then I'd be out too, like a good fellow citizen looking for somebody, who I knew would be in the car by now.

Sometimes you ended up working solo for whatever reason, which was fine with me, it just took more patience and cunning. One good thing about going solo was that you hardly got noticed by the shop assistants. They would just nod and let you be really, then after finding the office I'd just wait for my chance, when they left to go about their daily chores. I've had times when I have sat out of view for an hour or more and more often than not it would pay off. The only thing was you couldn't mooch about for ages as you had to pop in and out from the office to see everything was clear outside. If the money was where it should be, which was usually by the calculator, or in a safe where, after finding the key, you would then get a bit nervy being alone. It always felt like somebody could just walk in on you but normally I wouldn't go in unless I was pretty sure I had at least a minute, as that was all it would take.

One time, grafting by myself, I was hung over after a night out in Rotterdam with no money or car so I had to jib a train going anywhere. After a few short stops I jumped off the rattler and walked to a village. Being on your own, it was always best to walk around and see what was what first, telling yourself to come back to this or that business, factory or shop – it didn't matter, they all took money. All that mattered was not getting noticed really. This particular village I'd ended up in wasn't happening so I nicked a pedal bike and just went cycling out of the gaff and after a few kilometres I came upon a massive cycling outlet in the middle of nowhere. Not really a shop as such because it had offices. So I went in to have a peek, as you do. There were three offices all linked up but the manager was inside chatting with some guy. I walked past, went upstairs and looked around the office but without success, so I went to go back down again. The manager passed me on the stairs and let on to me while chatting to the customer he was with. Now all I could see as I crouched down was a woman by the till two offices away so I slipped inside quickly, then lo and behold there's only a safe on the floor half open and I'm all over it like a rash. I quickly grabbed all the hundreds leaving the rest as I had no time as it was, then as I popped my head up I clocked the woman was heading towards me so I ducked right down and headed through the offices leading to the till, then I was just near the door. The woman walked right past where I'd been, she didn't even know I was in the place, you could tell. I was out of the place and back on my bike, buzzing to fuck as this wedge felt decent and was all new notes, which was always a good sign, I peddled like hell until I ran out of steam. Reaching the next village I'd had enough and thought my lungs were bursting.

It could only happen in Holland that there was a coffee shop and I fell into it ordering a coke and a bag of weed! I was only two kilometres away now so I stayed where I was until I'd calmed down, then had a quick look at the money. Bingo! I thought it was one hundred notes but all I saw now were thousand notes. I had a quick count hiding my hands under the table - 30 one thousand notes plus all the 100 notes - I was on to a winner and ordered a taxi pronto. Then went and double-checked in the toilet. I had six thousand in hundreds 36,000 guilders in all. I took the taxi back to the village I had nicked the bike from 2 hours earlier, then caught the train back to Rotterdam. That night Pink Floyd were playing at Feyenoord's ground and when they played that tune *Money* it put a nice smile on my kipper, I can tell yer! Even at today's rate nobody would refuse £10,000 – thirty odd years later I still buzz off that wedge!

I was out one night not long after this with Sigrid and got pulled over and breathalysed. Being over the limit I was taken to the dibble shop but after a night in the cells I was told that I was wanted for a robbery somewhere. I was driven all the way to Etten-Leur where I was placed in an interview room with the same bubbly little Mickey from a few years back. He didn't recognise me but I remembered his kipper straight away. Bobby told me that I was being charged with carrying out a sneak thief at an Etten-Leur supermarket. Two lads had dipped the keys from the manager's jacket before helping themselves to the contents of the safe. One of them supposedly fitted my description, which did my head in a bit because I genuinely hadn't done it, or if I had I'd forgotten about it.

"All Brits look the same, especially in The North," I joked. "But nah, you've got the wrong guy for this one."

I could tell that Bobby still thought that I was the culprit; he was a Scouser (kind of) so he was obviously clued up and knew that I would never spill the beans even if I was guilty. I was kept in the cells for two full weeks whilst the Dutch Old Bill had me on ID parade where it's not a line up as such but you are made to stand by a small glass window. It just means it's probably you. If I had been picked out I knew it meant fuck all in a Dutch court as they had no more evidence to tie me to the theft. They then sent me to court in Breda, where I told the judge that it was a case of mistaken identity and that I wasn't even in Holland at the time of the crime. This was enough to secure my release. Again it was strange, they seemed fucked unless you were caught red-handed which didn't happen that often.

Bobby shook my hand and bade me farewell, at which point I sprang it on him that he had arrested me a couple of years earlier. He was gutted to hear this because it confirmed that I was a thief, which made him think that I had avoided being sent down for the supermarket even though I hadn't done it. Fair play to him though because despite clearly feeling as if he had been had over, he still chuckled as I was being set free. I suppose he must have thought, "You win some, you lose some."

Walking out of the cop shop, as anyone knows, is the best feeling in the world. Though now the problem was that whenever I got pulled for drink driving my passengers, being Dutch, gave the police an address to watch us from. They started calling at their homes asking about us every other day, then the police started turning up at the pubs we drank in. They would tell the owners of the bars to give us a wide berth telling them we were trouble and would rip them off as soon as we had the chance – so after little less than a year we left Rotterdam.

BACK TO BASE

We headed back to the Dam where we found out Terry Corrigan was in hospital getting a pacemaker fitted, he was only 24! He had collapsed in town just getting something to eat in a café and now he was fitted up with wires and electronic equipment all over his chest. We all thought he was a goner for sure although he pulled through and was back on the mend in no time. Then we heard that Essay, a lad we all knew from Manchester, a solo grafter who had been coming over for a while now, had got himself into a fight with two Moroccans and ended up stabbing one who later died – he got 4 years! After he was released he got heavily into cocaine and died not long after.

Paddy was the first of our lot to get the big one – 100,000 guilders and he was by himself too! That was £30k back then, enough to set a person up for life but with good news comes bad. He had only gone and got into heroin after resisting it for so long. We all begged him to give it up but as everyone knows, druggies (like drinkers) don't want to listen. So after two years Paddy had managed to spend the money and was skint and back in Amsterdam. Terry Corrigan and Paddy were rare in that they were best grafting solo and they both had a gift for finding the biggest wedges. It was as if they tripped over money. Some people have that in life, call it Devil's Luck, I don't know, both were steady heroin users by now along with countless others.

As if Mancunians hadn't caused enough trouble in Amsterdam over the last few years, Skinny Vinny was on the loose now. He had become a monster crack cocaine head and was freaking everyone out wanting guns and armed robberies done and would never shut up about them. People started to give him the cold shoulder - we all knew he was ready to flip his lid and when he did a year or so down the line it would be for something unmentionable. He ended up branded and was out of the circle for good.

Donnie had turned into a full time street gangster and was on the pipe himself now, living it up in a world of guns and coke – he'd even started sending skunk home regularly via some Manc girl grafters. They had it all strapped to their legs so that they could hardly fucking walk and looked like they had just jumped from a fucking horse but they all got home, luckily for them.

For the rest of us who didn't do gear, it was all as we sadly expected, believe it or not you were gutted when you found out so and so had started using or had died from drug use but from an early age I'd seen it all before and it just bounced off me. My response was typically, "oh well, what can yer do?" How the lads grafted on heroin I have no idea. And how they never looked like users was amazing – it seemed they had to have enough left to toot as they told me they got straight that way! They left the big toot till after the graft where they would all start the gargled voices on the way home in the car. It used to sicken me but we grafted with each other from time to time. We could go out with whoever had a car or was up and ready at Barney's having breakfast. There were that many Mancs in town it didn't matter who went out grafting, everyone came from the same streets back home in sunny Mancland.

In hindsight we should have put our money together and bought a coffee shop, but one thing I learnt early on was that with Mancs it was every man for himself. Everybody had their own missions, with a missus and kids to support back home. Then there were some that liked nothing more than going back to count their money and jib into our flats without chipping in. These guys were the ones who were never there when rent day came at the end of every month and thought it well funny when pulled about it later on, laughing about it to themselves. Even having a kitty was too much for these people, as this meant they were putting towards all the booze, food and drugs.

"I don't smoke or drink and I'm not that hungry."

"Well you still gotta put in the kitty, yer skin flint!"

We would have a few flats between us all over Amsterdam changing addresses every three months or so. One flat we had in the Liedesplein just had a kitchen and a shower. In between the two were six beds all in a row leading to the shower, it was more like living in a dormitory and a case of first up best dressed applied here. Divy and most of the lads from Sale lived here and we always wound each other up, as lads do. One night after a full day's graft I got back and jumped in the shower. My socks stunk so just for a laugh I put my sweaty socks in the Div's pillow case. Every time he lay down he said he could smell something "can anyone smell that?" With no answers from the lads, who were all trying to keep straight faces, he actually picked up the case more than once and looked under it and around the bed, everywhere but inside the pillowcase. It took him three nights before I told him, plus the others were getting fed up with the smell too by then. Straight away the Div threw a punch at me, missing as usual.

There were a few of us going out one night from Dicko's flat but when we had all squeezed in the car there was no room and just the Div stood there. Dicko picked on Div at times "get in the boot if you want, Div". The Div then proceeded to get into the boot, which is at the front of a VW Beetle. Dicko was in stitches, as we all were. Dicko got to driving up and down kerbs followed by braking real hard after going fast and all we could hear were the Div's complaints coming through the fucking dashboard. Finally, after getting let out, he was licking his wounds moaning about his treatment "funny, always me innit" who else would get into the boot of a Beetle! He even managed to disappear down a trap door once in the Tamaso coffee shop, which had us all howling with laughter. If nothing else he was an entertaining, rum fucker who lived up to his name, The Div.

Going out in groups could get too much, especially if you were the one carrying the exes. At night, the bar staff would be loaded with orders "five toasties please and 7 beers and two cokes" then just as they have started pouring them, "oh no, sorry, it's 7 toasties, 5 cokes and two beers instead now" then from the back another change in the order, "I'll have a brandy in my coke now" then everyone wants fucking brandy and coke now, "no beer and forget them toasties now as well, here as it happens, it's shit in here, shall we fuck off!" - more than likely leaving some bird behind the counter dizzy and gobsmacked holding half finished drinks.

Colin, who was always very demanding, went overboard about ham and eggs, which by the way the Dutch are famous for. Trouble is they were never done to his liking. He wanted his eggs flipped over. The owner, who was not amused by three mad shouting Brits in his gaff, tries to work out Colin's request, so flips two eggs over, then walks away. Colin's now shouting him back to re-flip his egg but the moment's gone. Mine and Spud's are okay so we start eating, leaving Colin paying for the eggs then reordering again! The bloke's face said it all. Either way the bloke's paid then breaks two eggs and walks away again. So Colin, instead of waiting, decides to walk behind the counter going straight over to the eggs and just as he's flipped them the bloke appears bewildered at the pure cheek with Colin trying to stop him in his tracks like you would the traffic. The guy was having none of it and lands Colin a cracking dig to the jaw, the bloke's now taken off his wooden clog too and started trying to belt our Colin with it! I just thought it was funny until Spud sprang from his chair picking up a big tub of something heavy and swung it onto the Dutchman's napper giving Colin time to get off from this nutter who wasn't really happy from the moment we walked in.

Now the guy's outside in full anger - all pumped up to the max and it was time for diplomacy. I thought then blurted out "Manier, we never wanted or intended any problem. Will 100 guilders do it for you?" The interruption from me went well. He seemed to listen. Thank fuck as this guy was massive and livid, plus it had to be stopped as we were in the middle of nowhere. Fair play the guy took the hundred, albeit in a very moody way, crinkling the hundred up in his hands he headed back inside his shop where Colin's eggs were probably in flames by now. We fucked off a good few miles to pass the dinner time with us all chuckling knowing this was why we seldom ate in the day.

THE INTER-CITY JIBBERS

Despite Liverpool's football dominance in the 1980s, two problems just wouldn't go away: their continued failure in the FA Cup (then the glamour competition) and their record against Manchester United. Their run to the 1985 semi-final was their best since 1980, and they had not won the competition for 11 years, an anomaly for a team so dominant and ruthless in the other major competitions. Even stranger was their inability to beat their Manchester rivals in the league during the decade (although Liverpool fans can quite rightly point to a League Cup final win in 1983 for some solace). In the 20 league games contested between the two clubs, Liverpool only won two during the 1980s. If there was one team that the red machine would have wanted to avoid, it was Ron Atkinson's United. And so it would prove in two bona fide classic Cup ties

The United v Liverpool semi-final replay at Maine Road, where United won 2-1 with two of the best goals I've ever seen from Robbo and Hughsie, saw some of my mates go fighting, while I'd be all laid back, spliffed-up. Our Colin ended up on the field celebrating. I just sat back stoned watching it all go on. Outside a big battle went on - no change there then, yet a hundred or so scousers gave United a run for their money until United's numbers inevitably took their toll. To make matters better we had a good bit of banter having stopped an all-Merseyside final. Then we went on to beat Everton with Big Norman Whiteside's blinding finish in extra-time at Wembley.

To be fair, English hoolies had taken the piss when on their ventures abroad and all the English teams got themselves barred from playing in Europe, which didn't help any of us that stayed abroad. Being young and English we were given the hooligan tag. Those of us that were in Amsterdam one week were waiting for a bunch of Manchester lads to arrive, although a ban on English fans didn't include the pre-season warm up games. The next we know our mates hadn't arrived, the reason being that it had gone off on the ferry, it was all over the Dutch news that night.

News report

About 150 rival English soccer fans battled with knives and broken bottles aboard a North Sea ferry early Friday in a bloody brawl that left four people seriously injured.

After the ferry, bound for the Netherlands, was forced to turn back to England, dozens of police were waiting at the English port of Harwich and made 14 arrests. Another 110 soccer fans were put on a train for London with a police escort.

The incident came at a time when English clubs were under suspension from competition in Europe after a riot at the 1985 European Champions Cup final between Liverpool and Juventus Brussels in which 39 fans, mostly Italians, were killed.

British Sports Minister, Neil McFarlane, said the brawl on the ferry is likely to add years to the ban on English teams.

"The people who were involved in this are absolute idiots. They have probably set back for years the time when English clubs can resume full-scale competition with European teams".

The brawl broke out on the Dutch ferry Koningin Beatrix when Manchester United and West Ham fans began trading insults in one of the ferry's crowded duty-free bars.

The Koningin Beatrix left for the Hook of Holland at 10:30 p.m. local time Thursday. But the captain ordered his crew to lock the rioters in the bar, and he turned the ship around at about 1 a.m. Friday when the fighting became fierce.

About 2,000 terrified vacationers aboard the ferry locked themselves in their cabins during the brawl.

A member of United's ICJ later said "We threw everything we could get our hands on - glasses, bottles, ashtrays and even fire extinguishers. It was great."

After the ICJ and West Ham's ICF had the infamous rumble on the Beatrix sailing over to Hook Van Holland there was a real effort from Maggie and the government over the next few years to stamp out the core of most football firms. Operation Omega with Man City's lads, along with a similar operation against Chelsea's Head-hunters were the only Crown Court cases of note to hand out stiff prison sentences. The Mars operation against United's firm was a joke; the daft dibble who operated undercover wanted to come in court wearing balaclavas. The judge said "you're not turning my court into a pantomime" and after a few days the case just collapsed; we all celebrated in the court room as though we'd just beat the Mickeys at Wembley.

Man City's Guvnors came on strong, just after United's lads all got offside after the kick off on the Ferry. Many of the Jibbers ended up in crown court and most got jail, my mate Brunsie got eight years for just grabbing a megaphone and singing a United song while shouting to the lads "let's give it to them I.C.F. fuckers" (a Japanese tourist filmed his actions). So then from 1986 to 1990 City's Guvnors took a firm grip on the city centre every weekend. We saw mobs fighting and believe it or not City's boys had bigger numbers back then until around '90/91. Our lads had named themselves ICJ as a piss-take as we knew full well West Ham paid for their tickets. Some even travelled first class. The name stuck as United's Inter City Jibbers paid for fuck all from leaving Manchester to getting back.

THE LAND OF THE ANTS

FRAZ

We had it all, we were invincible, nothing would stop us! That's what we thought rampaging round Europe like a little army from a little place in England - Manchester, well Sale to be exact. Football was the root of this - away games, banging tills, smash and grabs on the Seven Sisters Road! 1980s Britain, Thatcher, yuppies... We were the casuals as some might say. Europe was our work place, Inter rails were a thing of the past. It was first class travel these days, Swiss Air used to reserve us seats. Fly out Monday morning, car hire all on the swipe, sometimes we didn't even get out of the airports before we had a wedge down our pants. Then it would be off to the Dam for a bit of R&R.

Chilling down at Lake Konstanz or up in Kloisters. Well not for long, something would go west; a jewellers, a safe (bonus) we couldn't get a bite to eat without one of us nicking a waiter's zap. Nothing was safe, we were good — we didn't make a mess or harm anyone. Not like today's sneak thieves. That's why we got tagged from St Mortiz to St Tropez. I was asked once by a police officer, while being deported, "Do you people from Manchester think money grows on trees, here in Switzerland". I just gave him a blank stare! Where else could a scruffy council estate kid earn over a grand a week or more?

The Dam. Everyone's bolt hole, if you could earn there, the world was yours, as Scarface once said. We got into everything and I mean everything. That was our University of Life (or death for some) God rest their souls, too many good lads to mention. We were wise to most things but dumb where drugs were concerned. The flat with the seven beds! Yes that was a place, we just graduated from Greg's disco in Sale to the flat with the seven beds. Fagin's lair... the starting point for grafting Liedersplein way before the Bulldog.

There was a police station down the road and Blaney and his 40 thieves living round the corner. Out on the graft, over to the American

Hotel; wash, shave, shit and off for breakfast. Barney's Bar used to be the ideal starting point; good fry up, then trains, planes and automobiles. Some on bikes… off to graft. The good times… always a yin to the yang! The bad times.. getting to Barney's and there would be loads from different parts of Manchester all infamous in their own right, nicknames you wouldn't believe but it was good to have a nickname it stopped you from getting nicked!

It was all good… sunny days outside the Tomaso bar, today it's the Doors bar. Sat there planning your next trip to the Land of the Ants sending someone off to drive Yankee Bob mad cos we all had motors off him that ended up dumped all over Europe. Greg normally got stuck with the task. Him, Sid, me and the other two in our little clique, were persona non grata at Bob's after a couple of BMWs that didn't get paid for! Twat started off selling cars from a bridge. Now he's got a showroom! Another story that…

Anyway we were sat there chilling; Essy, me and a few others. A police car pulls up, an old Herbie – white, no computers on board like these days just two big daft cloggy cops. Essy got a bit uneasy - the day before he'd spiked the owner with a load of acid who then jumped out of a window and ran down the canal naked, crazy as shit. Next thing Ronnie and Reggie from Wythenshawe are singled out. "Don't run!" cries the cloggy cop. Yeah, right. A pair of snatchers and they ain't going to run!

Off they went, the cloggy cops took out their guns. Bang! Fuck it's for real, a bit of a sobering thought these fucks have guns and will use them! It was like a cold bucket of water being poured over me! But that didn't last. Some nurses turned up with a copious bag of Charlie. Good times. Chunks of weed. The full menu was just left on the table for anyone to build up. Popping bottles of Grolsch like champers long before it arrived in Blighty.

Then off to a night club or night drive - most of the time it was the latter, waking up in some mad place in the Alps overlooking the border. We made it our mission to find sneaky little jibs over from Holland in Germany then Swizzy. No zolls for us, we were under the radar. The other firms wanted to get on board, so it expanded. Whoever was around got into the motors. It wasn't only the Dam. Everywhere we went we bumped into little firms grafting. Maddest was in Hamburg. It wasn't arranged but by the end of the night there must have been a dozen lads from Manchester all on the graft. Needless to say there was high jinks abound... Call the cops!

Anyway, not to be side-tracked. Overlooking the Swiss border with the sun just coming up and there sparkling the Rhine was just appearing out of the morning mist - Stein am Rhein. We crossed over the little bridge and the customs weren't even awake. We drove into what looked like a Hollywood movie set like Willy Wonka, Chitty Chitty Bang Bang and Baron Münchausen all rolled into one. I've seen many more places like it but this was the first time – a proper chocolate box cuckoo clock.

I got lost in its old world buildings. Creeping through the attics was like going back in time. I was day-dreaming about Willy Wonka when I heard a whistle! Yes a whistle! Like a meercat I pricked up my ears and headed back to the car. I got there the same time as Essy but where's the Don? We got in the car and Essy opened his coat – there was thousands and he'd even filled his socks. Then all of a sudden the Don appeared with the biggest grin on his face. "Drive" he says so off I go. He opens his pants and it was full of ants, a massive wad of ants - Pink 1000, purple 500. I looked over then BANG! I wasn't watching and had hit a car. Money is flying all over the car, then... thud! A large metal object hits the dash - it's a fucking gun! Panic stations! Abandon ship! Head for the hills! As we tried to the money's all over the car watched by a red faced farmer! He was one lucky fucker that farmer, although a few years down the line he might not have been... Anyway we gave him some money - he was happy, we were very happy.

IT'S LIKE A JUNGLE SOMETIMES...

TAXING

ie. People taking money from dealers or fellow criminals who couldn't or wouldn't report it to the police.

Taxing was becoming big business. One grafter even got taxed going home when four hooded guys jumped out and demanded his Rolex! Although in fairness he shouldn't have been wearing it really as hardly any of the other grafters did, we sold ours as soon as we got back to England. These taxers were the scum of the underworld, we now had to watch ourselves as it was well known that the lads that went abroad had money stashed somewhere at home, so I moved flat just to be careful.

Donnie had the taxers at his house one night, where he had to lock himself in the toilet while they were trying to hatchet the door in to get at him, they found a bit of cash and fucked off after ransacking the place. These taxers were to change Manchester for the bad, and the trouble would soon start over Cheetham Hill/Moss Side that would be the ruin of Manchester's criminals.

Gang culture was now rife in Manchester, which had been going downhill since the riots, and it was now getting too much to even go to Moss Side. In the Reno one night spud and our Colin had gone down just to get a scran, then Colin got followed into the toilets by three guys who were about to stab him up over 'nothing' until Fonzo and Junior luckily put two and two together and followed the guys into the karzee and stopped them.

The mad thing about this Moss Side/Cheetham Hill thing was that half the people from both areas knew the other half. It was just the same at the football, with City and United fans really but that was only fisty cuffs where you could be steaming into each other only subconsciously looking to see you didn't end up scrapping with a mate who supported the other team! This new shit was shootings and stabbings even kidnappings; it all got too much for most grafters when a good mate of all the lads got shot in the legs while sitting in his car on Princesses Parkway. This made the headlines in most of the newspapers and showed us all how sinister it was about to go or had got.

Things got so bad that Donnie had to run a bloke over with his motor outside the Reno one night as he was surrounded and it was his only way out of the situation. Ritchie the cat was being hounded left, right and centre and it came to a head when three blokes wearing boiler suits and crash helmets smashed their way in to his gaff using his front window to gain access while he was watching telly with his daughter. They gave him a top going over, stabbing him several times and taxing him for a few bob too. The Gallery, our grafter hang out, had extended into a bigger club and that was infiltrated and would get ruined slowly but surely by the visiting Salford lads or the 'Cheetham Hillbillies' as they were called.

All in all it was the beginning of the end for sunny Mancland. It all became very sinister not knowing who was friend or foe. We had all been to and fro from Holland to Manchester regularly but now it was time to leave for good as its own criminals were ruining good old Manchester.

Almost all the grafters decided enough was enough and we seldom came back to the UK after '85/86. It's a shame to say this but we felt more than a few times that being white in Moss Side wasn't cool anymore, which saddens me as Manny was never about race. Also 90% of the white lads going to Moss Side to score were looking for heroin, so this made the new generation of black lads look down on the white junkies, and who could blame them? I even got a blade pulled on me outside the Reno but just laughed him away.

I brought a Surinamese girl back with me around this time. Thinking she would like the Reno, I took her there. She was freaking out as soon as we went in through a back alley full of people waiting to get in. After ten minutes she wanted to leave, saying it was the roughest place she'd ever seen, and after a week of seeing the goings on in Manchester she promptly flew back to Holland saying we were all mad. Given she was a 'working girl' from Amsterdam, I assumed she would be pretty streetwise. She was but while Holland was lawless in one sense, Manny at that time was on another level, like the Wild West.

The only white firm around at that time was Salford who would stand up for themselves yet they luckily had the numbers and wouldn't be fucked around by the Hillbillies who were almost all black lads. They were real gangster types but Manchester isn't that big so they managed to drag the town into an abyss of out an out violence lasting five years or more, people were getting beaten up, shot up and grassed up and there were absolutely no rules anymore. It was fucking sad!

I had a Scouse mate who once said to me while Manchester was at war with itself, Liverpool lads picked up the loose ends and started making fortunes between themselves laughing at the Manc's stupidity. When all said and done, criminals should stick together, not go all Chicago with guns shooting each other up.

Manchester was morphing into something different from the place I knew. The Reno finally closed its doors in 1986/87; it was one of the best clubs I've ever been to and was our playground where we grew into young men but nothing lasts forever.

In life, as in crime, there's always someone worse or better off than you, everyone can't be a gangster, you are what you are, you do what you do, we were happy grafters, living the Life of Riley doing what we did abroad. We weren't on any copper's radar yet but we were known to the gangsters in Manchester who would tax us if they had half a chance.

We were more than happy with our neutral position in the underworld, but it was looking more fragile by the day. We'd become strangers in our own town and there were very few friendly faces anymore; the friendliest place in England had just become the moodiest, especially since one of the guys we knew had been shot!

GOOD RESULTS

We were in the middle of nowhere one night knowing the next day we were going for some Rolex as they were on our 'to do' list. It was a fair drive to reach the gaff for dinner the following day, so we stayed in a little village the night before. Knowing we couldn't get too pissed by going out clubbing, after a few drinks in the local Colin wanted us to leave saying that we had to be 'clear headed' for tomorrow. Fair enough we thought so we went back to our hotel rooms to play cards with a crate of beer. We had a few games for money to make the night a bit interesting plus the usual spliffs. We were having breakfast waiting for him the next morning and in he walks looking like he'd been out all night, the fucker hadn't even shaved!

When I asked what about 'looking smart', he just coolly replied, "Yea but they don't actually see me, do they" with a top grin, adding he would kip in the car anyway as it was a long drive! It seems Colin and K'ob had gone out anyway and not got back until 4! John drove and we made it for lunchtime as planned. We had seen and knew the set up of the place, there should only be three staff on at dinnertime and we had sussed out the best time as they had fewer staff. There were two ways into the shop - front and back, it was a big jewellers in quite a well-to-do town. The old cobbled streets were half empty, which is good as we would be running round the fucker real soon! After a quick scout, it looked half full so me and K'ob went in one way, it looked nice and packed for dinner time. One of the staff approached us so I gave her the nod and smile that I wanted serving and led her out of the shop to waffle on about some tacky item on display outside, meanwhile the other two staff were busy serving. We were lucky - inside had enough customers milling around that helped block and cover Colin and John. It went real sweet. John, who was big and wide, just blocked while Kev also took up position a yard away ready to blag any staff that approached – it wasn't needed, Colin just got his key ready knowing it would fit the window lock and slide it open. From inside the shop you would never notice it was open if you looked. Colin emptied all the Rolexes and gold Omegas from the main display into his trusted briefcase, closed the window and put his priceless keys away!

Nobody, it seemed, had even known they had been in the place, as the three of them hadn't even had to talk to anybody! I'd kept yapping away facing the shop door, until I saw K'ob come out and with a quick glance I got the thumbs up. I knew it had gone and swiftly got rid of the staff I'd been chatting to.

There is an art to walking fast without appearing to be running, while at the same time not attracting attention. Nipping in and out of shoppers that are getting in the way, the four of us zig-zagged past them together but separately, if you know what I mean. I could see by their faces it had gone well, sometimes you don't get the full window, this one "had been cleared" Colin declared. With a full tank of petrol we didn't stop until we got out of whichever province we were in. As it happens we actually broke down on the motorway, but luckily were well clear of the area. John started flapping, making everyone nervous "what if the police stop with us just sat here". Luckily the breakdown van arrived first, this was a result in itself as the Old Bill would often stop to help people broken down on the motorway. Luckily it was a fixable job and the bloke even fixed the heater too. We paid him gladly plus a wee tip, as we weren't members. We had driven there and all the way back with no heating, just doing a 10 hour drive for one minute's work. That day I still think we were all just as made up that the fucking heater was fixed, as we still had a little drive yet to Amsterdam! With the border to get over you never knew if you would get a tug, especially on a motorway so we soon slipped off it and went through one of our little sneaky crossing points sussed out through our time in Europe, we had used them for years. Soon as we got back to Holland we stopped for a beer, some smoke and a good look at our kettles, lovely jubbly!

★

Not long after this the three of us had another jewellers on our shopping list. It was the same again, we had sussed out it had to be done at lunch time. It always amazed us that jewellers seemed to have an insane lack of security at that time. On the street outside the shop there were two big, wide jewellery displays - one being full of the good old Rolexes and Omegas. In between the windows there was a 4 or 5 metre walk down a little display passage leading to the entrance. On entry you would face the counter about 3 metres into the shop, with the shop inside now leading all the way back on itself back to the watches. We all stood off a bit outside until we could time it right. There were only two daft staff, Colin wasn't using a key though as he insisted it would 'pop' with a screwy. This made me cringe a little as that can be loud as fuck. Colin and me were going in together, Colin with his briefcase looking like a businessman. We saw that a few people had gone inside so we floated in, one staff was serving at the counter and so straight away I got the other staff to the side and sat down so I could face the counter. She sat opposite and I started my usual crap that I wanted to buy something for my wife. This way I knew she didn't have to show me any items, just talk. I then see Colin slide out of sight just as the door dings open and in walk Kev and John.

Kev stays at the counter while John floats off to cover Colin looking in the cabinets while walking down to his window. The counter was still shielded by a few customers plus K'ob started a daft false cough then within ten seconds I hear 'CRACK', it sounded like ice breaking up - the whole shop must surely have heard it! It certainly made me shudder at the time but there were no reactions to the noise at all. The twenty or so seconds after felt like ten minutes. I soon saw Kev signalling me to stop the blag, which is so easy when you know you've got to get out of the place pronto. Inside the shop was sweet, so we were back out of the passage only to see John looking all around him on the street, like he was looking for somebody. Me and Kev soon realised he was in his 'Old Bill Mode', pretending to be a do-gooder. This blag was often used and was a good bit of acting from John; it seemed everyone on the street had seen Colin from the outside scooping up a whopping amount of Rolexes. We saw John do his bit and Colin was away without the crowd getting involved, John was gesturing to the crowd that he was following Colin. We just clocked the faces of a group of gobsmacked bystanders. We knew the staff would soon be out to see what the commotion was all about, only to be told they had been robbed. Back at the car Colin and John were flustered a bit by people seeing it happen. Kev told them it was okay as we were all back at the car now but we'd better get a move on. Driving off Colin told us that as he got his arms in the window there were a group of people that had approached the display just in time to see him take it all away. Although he looked smart and as "you never know" was his motto, he just carried on as it's over in seconds anyway. By the time the shoppers outside had taken in what they had just seen, Colin was walking away out and down the road.

Back on the drive though Colin and John started a big daft row about John freezing after being clocked and failing to take all the gold Tissots. It got that heated we had to stop, and me and Kev wisely got a taxi to the train station then back to the Dam as it's no good four guys rowing in a car with 20 odd kettles is it? Again, even at scrap prices, it was an amount we were happy with when clearing a window, no point taking just the best if we could we take it all.

Even though tom shops had been battered for years it seems there were always new ones with gullible staff waiting to accommodate us in our work. How they never heard the noises we made still baffles me to this day!

Stuart was now out and about and had been hanging around Amsterdam for a while now...

RIGHT ROYAL RESULTS
AT THE CASINO ROYALE

Stuart C.: *I flew to the Dam to meet Colin B, we had a few weeks banging jacks (tills) and having over a good few travel agents, with me wearing suits, smart shirts and ties. It was a pleasure to be able to graft looking like the King of coolio, it's something I really miss as they were the days when looking good on the jib brought us not only decent wedges but the good life.*

One of our most lucrative results in The Dam was on a brand new top jolly casino. In the main entrance hall facing the reception area was a glass cabinet displaying watches, diamond rings and bracelets and we worked out that the punters usually handed their coats to the staff at the main counter at around 8.30 to 9 pm, this provided the perfect distraction. The clientele tended to only spend a couple of minutes at the counter, which meant that we had to work quickly and quietly. Within the blink of an eye Colin had opened a cabinet up and filled his beanie hat to the top with a lovely parcel of tom. We left the case slightly open because we were hurrying but did have time to pull a nearby set of net curtains around it so that there was a good chance nobody would get onto it. We were safely tucked away in the Bull Dog coffee shop, downing a few Heinekens and smoking ready-made joints of Thai weed, to celebrate our nice tickle.

We were both proper made up with what we had managed to come away with a sweet parcel. The combined value of the tom added up to the equivalent of just over £100,000, which isn't bad for half an hour's work. In our haste to get away, we had left a fair few items of jewellery so I phoned up a couple of the lads and told them that the case in the casino was still slightly open if they wanted an easy earner. I was trying to put my mates onto a raise but the response from everybody that I talked to was the same: "Why didn't you just empty the fucker?" Then right out the blue we saw Stoke's top Jibber Gizmo, I hadn't seen him for over a year.

We pulled Gizmo in and gave him the script. We got the tom offside at a safe gaff, then ran it over with Gizmo telling him how the punters usually collected their coats from the counter at around midnight, meaning that there was another window of opportunity in which we could help ourselves to the remaining jewellery if the scream with the Casino staff had not already gone up. He was up for it, so we went back and finished off what we had started by clearing the fucking lot. It was a good job well executed.

Later that week we sold the parcel at the Thieves market, then we sent half of the bees and honey that we got for it back home and went out on a 'Beano' with the rest of it. We thought we'd performed the perfect jib, but unfortunately a few days down the line Colin was coming out of a rave when he got swooped on by the Old Bill and taken in for questioning. This should have put the wind up me but had the opposite effect. It got me thinking that I should put some money on the roulette wheel at the casino the following night and have a sly look about on the top floor to see if there was anything worth robbing up there.

Sure enough, after frittering a bit of cash away and taking advantage of the complimentary drinks I spotted a small display case with about six gold Cartier watches in it. I used a small penknife to open the lock and quickly copped for the lot of them. This not only provided me with another tasty earner but was also good news for Colin, because the fact that the place had been had off whilst he was locked up raised doubts as to whether he had done the first two sneaks. Col was quick to take advantage of this and told the judge that a firm of Cockneys, who had lost a lot of money at the craps tables in the casino, spotted the jewellery on the way out and helped themselves to it because they considered it to be an easy graft. He said the Cockneys had shown him what they had stolen in a coffee shop and told him where they'd got it, so he'd gone in afterwards and helped himself to a single gold ring worth £1,300 from the open display case. We had stolen jewellery that was worth many times that, so he was understandably made up. The ring that he had confessed to taking was the cheapest item from the list of missing jewellery. Col, not for the first time, was just deported.

The casino incident just shows you how lenient the Dutch legal system was back then; if Col had been caught in England he'd have almost certainly been landed with a lengthy jail sentence. It was clear as the blue sky he was telling porkies, no Brit judge in living memory would have allowed him to walk free. Perhaps His Dutch High Honour thought that the casino deserved to be robbed for having such lax security because the ease with which we were able to fleece it was remarkable for such a big, posh-looking place. The fact that we were able to have it over on three separate occasions within the space of ten days speaks volumes. Not every graft was like that though; the staff at other places were bang on it. For every top theft that went smoothly, there was always the odd one that fucked up...

GOING UNDER IN GHENT

Me and Kisby were grafting one day, checking this woman who was on the fifth floor in a massive department store. She'd been counting up the takings for fifteen minutes; they were long, long minutes, I can tell you. At last she put them in the safe and slipped out to a small kitchen to brew up. If she heard any noise it was sure to be game over. However, I'd sussed that the room had one-way glass; she couldn't see in but we could see out. We were in quick as a flash; I heard it clear in my head, "In one: Bully's special prize!" We tucked our shirts and socks in and stuffed as many wads as possible down there, it was done and dusted in a minute. Unfortunately she saw the back of me as we went out the door and started howling "Thief! Thief! Thief!" With the chance of a stealthy sneak down the shitter, we both bolted down the escalator, barging away plenty of shoppers. We still had three more floors to get down!

I half-turned around to see her chasing after us like an Olympian, leaping and vaulting over everybody and making us really work for this Pot of Gold. On the very last escalator I skidded down the black handrail like Bart fucking Simpson and she was still on my back! Kisby was away, good luck to him. I came bursting out of the main doors like a wild hog, knocking over punters onto the old cobbled side street. I ran across the main roundabout and I was fucking knackered by this point. An oncoming car was coming too fast my way and I ran thinking "This car might just hit me on purpose as everyone can see the women's really closing in on me", I had about £20,000 down my grundies and stuffed up inside my shirt, I'm sweating buckets, the nerves were now kicking in. I missed the car by a millimetre and kept running but then I heard a loud crash and turned around to see this other car smack into my pursuer sending her rolling over the bonnet. Call it shock or whatever but she got up off the deck and was now looking like the bird in The Terminator; bolting up and screaming after me again. I ran down an alley towards a group of local big guys who'd obviously seen the accident. They cornered me in the doorway of a shop and despite trying my best to get past in one last bid for freedom, I was fucked.

They marched me back up to the fifth floor and demanded the money back, all in perfect English. "The other lad's the one who's got all the money, I was just his look out" I protested, trying my best to play it like I'm stupid. Knowing that obviously the boys in blue were due any minute I started looking about for an escape route. I saw a three foot drop to the next building, so jumped out of the window, landing on the next building, looked up at them and maybe pushed my luck too much by sticking up two fingers to them all and shouting out, "Fuck off you Gobshites!" My celebrations were a bit premature to say the least, as the slates on the very spot where I'd landed were wet. I slipped but thank fuck ended up on the gutter and got my right hand onto a drainpipe. I had a nice firm grip then my left hand swung into action, climbing down to about the second floor I was in motion and them silly cunts took the stairs (boring bastards) and followed me down. Seeing them all with gaping looks on their kippers I gave them the classic Brit two fingers again, "Fuck you and Tin Tin the ugly twat". By now I could hear the sirens in the distance as I clambered down with about 60 feet left to freedom with that wedge stuck to me like glue. I was buzzing my bollocks off and felt a new surge of energy followed by the sound that soon brought me back down to planet earth - the drainpipe was cracking and in a split second gave way on me. Smack! It was like the sound of a grand piano rattling round my head, my legs just crumbled under me. Still conscious, somehow I managed to drag myself into a nearby barbers and I remember even asking him to make it a quick trim and then blacked out with the pain.

I woke up chained to a hospital bed with the police looming over me, asking, "Who's the other person that was with you?" So I asked for my phone call. "Mum" I whispered down the phone, "When you come to Amsterdam, don't bring Kisby with you because they're after him" because I'd blagged them about being bullied into doing sneaks thefts by a Moroccan who was feeding me bits of smack getting me hooked.

The two big operations that followed wiped me out, I was totally shattered every day and night struggling with just no energy at all. I suppose after the first MRI scan when they told me I may never walk again

I lost all positivity regarding my future. Fuck it, I thought, I'll have to go on the jib in a wheelchair! After a month in there I got talking to Leoni, an Italian Yank with a French mother living in Gent. He was a mercenary, he smoked a bit of weed as well as a bit of smack, soon we smoked a bit of smack together, and the pain all over my aching body vanished instantly. He was wheeling me round one day telling me how the robbery and the chase had been on the news and also the front pages of the newspaper; it was big news because of the bravery of this bionic woman. I thought fair does really; she should've taken a cut for her troubles. So I made a phone call to my Afro-Caribbean girlfriend Trisha from Ardwick Green, a right good looker and well on the ball to say the least. "Come and see me, darling" so she turned up, and she brought my mate Gary Kitney. He brought out bags of brown, rocks and all the rest and started dishing it out like a nurse on afternoon rounds, "Here's a bit of crack for you, some sensi for you" - sorting everybody out. After all the patients had been seen to, the head nurse walked in, unaware that Gary's a walking pharmacy and smacked off his tits.

Later the mercenary said "Look, I know how to get you out of here. If you can get in a wheelchair, we'll have your girlfriend park you and her on an outside visit in the bay outside and get her to bring in flowers for you" so over the next couple of days I prepared to jib the fuck out of there. The head doctor had also told me that soon the crown court prosecution would be on my case. I knew I'd be ok to stay on the hospital waiting for my case to get to the high court, which takes about eight to ten months before sentencing anyway. I was expecting three to four years, which was about right, and at least I'd be going to the big new prison up near the Dutch border, which I knew held about twenty-odd Brits on the same landing, so it'd be like a sitcom compared to doing porridge in Strangeways. The head doc said he had no problem letting me recover here as I was in need of lots of treatment that would take up to six months, and I would need my legs in traction to have any chance of recovery and being able to walk normally in the future. That probably sounds like a good deal, but it wasn't as attractive as the mercenary's offer.

So the next week Marcus came down with my cut from the parcel - happy days. Trish landed and went to buy food and brought a huge bunch of flowers in for me and I started getting bits of clothes together, she said

Right Royal Results

"What you doing that for?" I said "Look, I know a way out, and it's where the ambulances come in, there's no CCTV in that corner, you're wheeling me out" and she started laughing, saying "No, no I can't do that" and all that bollocks, Marcus had a few words with her, putting her at ease and she ended up doing a good job. She wheeled me with the flowers across my groin area straight past the office and staff waving over to them in a jolly manner, striking up ciggie's blowing big clouds of smoke about, waiting for the right time to strike when an ambulance entered inside via the electric doors. She timed it perfectly, pushing me past everyone with ease across the main road and straight into a smoky bar with local piss heads all playing cards. We got some beers in whilst waiting for Marcus with a taxi, when it turned up we all climbed in, and I couldn't believe what was playing on the radio, "Should I stay or should I go". A classic Clash tune!

CASHBACK

As Stuart says, you win some you lose some. I've a few examples here...

Sometimes we had little option but to cut our losses and run... Paddy and me were working in a tourist area out in the sticks one sunny day, when we came across a picturesque little village; the only thing that stuck out was this small department store, the kind of place we wouldn't ever graft normally but we decided to have a gander anyway. Inside was just like any other old department store with the offices being upstairs; the store was busy so we didn't get noticed. We flew up the stairs and soon found ourselves inside the first office, this was a canteen room for staff breaks but we were well hidden, phase one done. Paddy carried on crouching along a narrow hallway past a second office while I stayed where I was, just to block or blag any staff if they came up the stairs or out of the middle room. After what always seemed to be an hour, but in reality was only a minute or less, Paddy came back towards me looking flustered and gesturing that I should follow him. He led me down the hall to the end office and darted over towards a massive wall cabinet and opened the fucker up; the main cash strongbox still had the key in the lock. We gladly emptied the cash out of the fucker and just about managed to get the wedge down our keks. Most of the lads always wore two pairs of pants or tracksuit bottoms underneath tucked into your socks, that way the money's always safe, even if it goes down your legs. These were the largest notes – we were both looking at a hundred or so brown window envelopes so we worked out that they would be the floats for the tills downstairs or something. Normally we would leave little notes but there were too many to ignore. Either way, we had to think quickly. I found a bin and empted a bin liner and put as many of the envelopes into it. Sweet! We were offmans...

To get downstairs we had to crouch past the middle office

where staff could be heard chatting away, then we found ourselves back in the tea room where we had started. We were both peeking down looking at the situation when a women *we hadn't even seen* was drinking coffee and watching us both from the side as we crouched down with me holding a bin bag full of cash! "Verboten here!" she pipes up, "what do you here?" Then she put two and two together and started *that* scream that all women have that penetrates through your fucking head, just like an air raid siren!

HELP!

With no option we headed for the stairs, half way down and she's at the top shouting down to all the other staff on the shop floor. With the exit so far away I had to make the drastic decision to *abandon the cash* which I did promptly, throwing the fucker sky high behind me. The bag gave way with a hundred or so envelopes raining down from the steps – it was either that or knock out five or six staff and Joe Public. Being sneak thieves we would seldom turned to violence. Plus Paddy had already done two years just for pushing a staff member out of the way a few years before. So if it came on top we tended to sling it and do a runner, if you threw the cash back, the owners would be more than happy to see the back of you, most of the time. On this occasion I half wished I'd kept the bin liner, as the staff down stairs or Joe public didn't even respond to us flying past them out of the store. I felt I'd let us down but we got outside which was the priority but it could have gone either way. If I'd ran out with the bag, would their reactions have been any different?

Police had been called by now, so we had to get out of the area. We knew we had a great wedge between us anyway, like I said we had the big notes so we weren't arsed at the time – freedom being the better option than an all out battle in a fucking department store in the middle of nowhere.

Back at the car, the map was quickly out and so were we. We were flapping at that point as it really was rolling countryside. We decided to ditch the car a couple of miles away, as we saw an area of dense woods and decided to hide in there until we'd figured out a plan. Half the village had enjoyed our little spectacle and surely the registration of the car had been seen. We knew there was a small town with a train station within a few hours walk so taking the map we set off. It was stiflingly hot and took five fucking hours but we finally reached the outskirts of a little town and we could easily see the station.

This is when you go into spy mode. I was an avid reader of war books, I just loved the cat and mouse side of things. We still had to be careful as we had stolen money and although we had lost a wedge and a car, we were within touching distance of safety and being able to melt back into the crowd. We were out of sight here and could easily see everything in and around the station. There was no sign of the Old Bill. We were too far into the country to get a taxi, they usually wanted long conversations too, so safely onto the rattler it was and back to the nearest biggest city. There we checked into a posh hotel, as we knew we had a good wedge. At the end of the day we got the equivalent of around six grand each meaning plenty to go on a quick few days to España!

★

Another time, Greg, Colin and myself left Amsterdam for "a week on the map". This could mean going over borders and back or just doing a hundred or so kilometres full circle back to the dam. This meant we could do both reconnaissance or, if a good enough parcel could be taken there and then, then obviously it would be librated into our grateful custody. We'd already had a good few gold chains away from working a full week just doing tom shops, we did this regularly if we had good ex's.

Either way, on this occasion we were just saving up for a break. Instead of hiding the tom in the car as normal, we decided to wear our ill-gotten gains around our necks, just for a laugh really as they were thick gold rope chains with pure weight so we all resembled Mr T on a good day. We ended up in a tobacco/book shop, inside the place it was split into two parts and the assistant was already near the book section and not at her till where she should have been. I got the whisper from Greg to get her offside, and Colin must have flown into action the minute her back was turned. I got her into the next room and there on the wall was a huge window looking through into the book shop. Me and this woman got a widescreen, HD view of Colin blatantly stuffing cash down his kecks with a wedge clamped between his teeth as well. She could only look at me gobsmacked, and I could only return her gaze with the same astonished look.

Colin disappeared from sight, then in no time at all I heard the shop bell go, so it was time to join them, no point hanging round. By the time I caught the door, Colin had some six foot thug looking at the three of us a little confused until his wife came out of the shop body popping while shrieking and wailing, like they do. Well we didn't have to speak a foreign language to know what she was saying. Without any hesitation the money was thrown sky high for them to pick up from the floor and scattered everywhere, leaving us to get off. Only this guy wasn't playing our game and decides he's going to give chase instead. This meant we had to run past our own car, as we were in a small village and didn't want the registration plate clocked, but after running a few hundred yards we were in the fucking country, diving over massive hedges onto the only field available until we came to a river. I was for swimming the fucker until Colin threw the remainder of the money in the air but this guy wasn't having it one bit and the chase was back on. So now we had to run in a massive U-turn and lose this guy who was getting closer to me all the time, probably because I was the smallest among us. With the weight from the fuckin chains we all had on, having to grip them to stop them slapping our faces, we weren't making much progress at getting away from this beast. He had half gripped me twice already and I could almost feel his fucking breath on my neck. He had been pestering me non-stop then Colin turns round, heading for me, then BANG!

"I'm getting fed up with you now mister, stay down yer mad cunt" Col says as he sparks the guy out. Then he turns to me saying "He nearly had you then, Marcus. Plus I can't run anymore I'm fucked!"

If you could run, we always did. We wouldn't want to get banged up for assault. It was always better to get away without violence and live to thieve another day. The saving grace for this type of situation is that there's hardly ever a police presence in such villages, with not much of a choice now, we had to run past the fucking shop again but this time with an audience outside it. They didn't flinch, just let us on our way looking gobsmacked and probably wondering where their hero had gone! Having given a dig to the beast we now had to get out of the area but we were so fucked we didn't look back to see if anyone was noting the plates. We felt like we had just run a marathon and we were coughing and spewing up in the car, gasping for breath. We were only so healthy after all, this wasn't the Loneliness of the Long Distance Runner, that's for sure. So we gave the car full throttle until we felt safe enough to relax a little but we needed a drink fast as I for one couldn't breath after all that running. The only thing in sight was a small airport. We went in without thinking but in hindsight it's obvious that when we entered the airport we must have looked dodgy, as we were gasping for breath and sweating it looked like we'd just survived the Sahara and fallen into an oasis.

Just our luck! Straight away there's two Old Bill really scrutinizing us from 20 yards away but quick as a flash and almost instinctively we start pointing at the departure board and play-acting and blaming each other for missing a flight. Without making eye contact with them again or purchasing the needed drinks we were offmans, back to the car and the nearest big city - out of sight, out of mind.

That night we booked into a hotel/brothel, the sort of place where ID isn't required and paid three women to remove what felt like a thousand prickly thorns that we'd collected during the hedge-hopping. At the time we didn't even feel them going in, even though they were stinging to fuck now. Yet we were all chuckling and smoking spliffs and drinking beer with the three darlings. They were laughing their heads off at us, while we chuckled at the thought of the hero hulk going through the same procedure, only not with three gorgeous birds (now wearing three gold chains) that they had *successfully* persuaded us to part with.

★

One rule we had was that if it came on top we would have to run past our own car, so the registration wasn't taken down by Joe public. On this day there were four of us grafting. We had just been through the village and nothing was happening, but as we drove out we clocked a timber yard. Two stayed in the car while me and Diller went inside for a quick mooch. Nobody was around so we proceeded to the office. The only problem was it was a big office, so instead of one of us looking out, we both started to look for the money. It seemed to take ages but we eventually found a nice enough wedge that was looking lumpy inside them brown window envelopes. Just as I grabbed hold of them, two customers came in waiting for us to serve them. I didn't speak the lingo but managed to say that I'd go and get the chief as they often called the gaffer, although these two guys were well suspicious and the moment we left the office all hell broke loose. We had walked straight into three staff who were looking at us, as we were looking at them. It meant one thing – it was time to do-one!

I tried in vain to speak a bit of lingo to throw them off the scent but to no avail. One bloke grabbed me and I wriggled free not realizing I quite visibly had the envelopes in my hand. Then another bloke had a go at grabbing me, this time Diller got in between us getting me out from his grip. Our car was right outside this wood yard, so as we had done before we both ran past the car knowing we would get rescued by Kev and Pete around the next corner. The only thing we failed to notice was that there weren't any fucking corners or streets in which to run down and lose ourselves. We were in the middle of nowhere and we had jogged on a fair bit.

At last we heard a car revving and, thinking it was ours, we stopped then nearly got taken out by it – it was the two customers with a member of staff that had grabbed me earlier. The bastards had tried to run us both over! As they got out I ripped an envelope open and slung the fucker into the air. Nine times out of ten this was usually enough to stop people but these three weren't interested and gave chase. Unbeknown to us at the time Kev and Pete had been surrounded and blocked in so couldn't get to us. It seemed one minute there's no fucker around yet now they were mob handed with no rescue in sight for us. I ripped open another envelope and did the same thing with the money again but still didn't get the reaction I'd hoped for...

So me and Dill ran through a primary school with all the kids in class and us running down a long hallway until we reached the fire exit door via the gym. For some strange reason these guys never gave chase through the school but they knew the area and were on us again as we were soon spotted. I now had one envelope left and obviously didn't wanna part with it but there's always a time to start negotiations. In my broken translation I told them this was all the money I had taken, and even though me and Diller were small and bollocksed from running we both picked a log up and showed that if they followed any further we'd be fighting them instead. This was the last ditch as we had nowhere to run other than the big woods behind us. Luckily the guys got the message and let us slip away into the woods.

When we got our breath back we were slagging Kev and Pete off for not picking us up, but knew something must have happened to them and after what seemed like hours later we finally came into a small village. We walked into a café hoping to get a taxi but the assistant was looking us up and down like we were aliens or something so we decided to get out of the place and hid close to a bus stop. It's strange when it's a bit on top how time stands still. It felt like a full day until a bus arrived, Sod's Law (and it certainly didn't surprise either of us one bit) that after just a few stops we were driving past the fucking wood yard again! Everything was quiet now, leaving us wondering where our mates were as the car wasn't outside either and the store was closed.

The bus carried on through the village and we got off at the next town. We were getting that paranoid feeling that you give yourself once it's all over but with all the adrenaline pumping through you still, we managed to get ourselves to a train station and head back to the city we had arranged to meet up in. We always made the same plan everyday, that if it came on top and we lost each other, we could meet up at a specific bar. We booked a room and went to find Kev and Pete in the nearest bar to the city's train station. We booked one more night but after two days it was obvious something had happened to them so we decided to hire a new car and graft our way back to Amsterdam.

We found out later that as we had ran past the car, all the people in the yard had seen them both fumbling and looking suspicious and put two and two together. So while the three guys had jumped into a car to follow us, the rest of the wood-cutters had proceeded in blocking Kev from driving off, smashing the windows in and dragging them out until the plod arrived to arrest them both. Kev and Pete did a couple of weeks in the cells giving the story they never knew us and were only innocently watching the proceedings happening around them. They couldn't be charged for just sitting in a car outside a wood yard, even though the car just happened to be a well over due hire-car that we had been driving for months without keeping up the payments. As that was a civil offence they just let them go in the end and we all met up in Amsterdam where both were gutted to find out that I had thrown the cash back. However, it didn't matter too much, as we had a little money from a few garages that we had robbed on our way back to the dam. Diller's *forte* always got him a good few earners, he enjoyed driving around the countryside looking for garages where they only had a bell on the forecourt so when a car drove in it would alert the staff that a customer had driven in. So all he had to do was park the car a hundred metres or so away and just walk in and help himself to the takings. It was always a good earner but hardly ever a real wedge.

We were just happy to be back together again and with our new car we headed off to the Black Forest where Greg (who was now called Spandau Greg) had got himself a six berth caravan and plotted it on a site about 30 miles from the Swiss border. As usual we attracted the wrong kind of attention – this time it was the Italians. We were out one night, just Greg and me, and we had been waiting ages for some bloke to turn up with a smoke we had ordered. He turned up with a piece of hash worth about 20 Deutschmarks. Greg just twatted him, landing a cracking dig although we hadn't thought it through and we were well outnumbered. We managed to get back to our car and told a German girl we were with to do the driving. She couldn't even get the car into gear meaning we were sitting ducks just sat there. Soon the eyeties arrived in numbers and started to surround the car.

We couldn't just sit there, so without even planning it we broke out the Spanish coshes – they always went down well. I swear, we were outnumbered and about a dozen Italians were gobsmacked as to how or why we should carry the fight to them. It was either that or a smashed up car that was needed for graft, so out we got. None of us could believe how quickly they got on their toes and started backing off. This is a moment all Brits love – having a firm on the back foot. We managed to twat them almost at will, then chased them down the street back to the club where they disappeared inside. We weren't daft enough to follow them in. We ran back to the motor and fucked off lively as they were bound to get more numbers together and would surely be tooled up when they returned.

A year later this little episode was repeated… we were driving through the same little town on the German/Swiss border and it went off again. Our Colin, me and Greg found ourselves chasing two lads right in front of a load of locals who just looked on. Colin and Greg were beating up this Italian lad, there was no way we could actually go through the village after that so we sacked graft that day and got back to the caravan to plot up and have a rethink on the situation. We had burst the bubble again. A few nights later we were sat in a car at some traffic lights and as happens in life, who is in the car right beside us but two Italians. Just looking Italian was enough for me and Greg so I gestured for them to wind down the car window. The daft twat did so and I spat out the biggest gob I could muster, he got a face load of goz dripping down his face, then Greg drove off at high speed. The car was speeding behind us now but I had clocked two cars following us. We knew the area a little so pulled up in a small car park belonging to a small club in the middle of nowhere. We made a quick stop and both jumped out – the best form of defence being attack. As we reached the first car the driver hit reverse. It was a bit confusing but the car we were about to fight had Germans inside it "who the fuck are you guys?" "Oh we see you at the lights" the driver said, "we know the Italians. We hate them too we will fight them with you!" Laughs all round! After a few beers with them we decided to front the twats at their club.

Greg, me and these four Germans headed over to the club that night but the manager came out saying the guys inside didn't wanna know. We had won, albeit with a little help from the locals. Now we had them behind us, we were free to relax again. The Black Forest was very different from the rest of Germany where it's all built up areas. This was all villages and trouble never really happened, so it ended there. We could now buy our smoke from a group of hippies we were introduced to. Things went okay for a while until a Manc lad called Jenks paid the caravan a visit. He was AWOL from the army, or prison can't remember which.

We said sure, we'll put him up. Talk about army – he was a one man army this guy! He managed to ruin our hide out attracting the attention of the local police as unbeknown to us he had gone burgling the local hotels and clubs. One night the police came to arrest him and he wasn't having any of it and started a big car chase over hills going off road, anything to try and get away but he got stuck and got off on foot. Still, this now meant the police knew about the caravan site. It was time to move on. Yet again we'd been scuppered by helping some one out. We were all gutted as we loved the black forest but what can yer do...

MAGIC MUSHROOMS

<u>FRAZ</u>

Now you may laugh or think I'm telling pork-pies but one year passports weren't exactly fool proof! Let's say I'm on a passport - Steve James DOB 25/10/1958. The Don is on a passport Steve Jameson DOB 25/10/1958. Hmm, you might think this would raise some suspicions at passport control but this was the 1980s. We got a hire car with the moody briefs and set off towards Stuttgart. At Freiburg we stopped for something to eat. No sooner had we finished paying than a safe in the back office had been ragged and had off. Someone snagged the keys halfway through dinner.

As we got near Munich the temperature started to drop. Fuck, what were we thinking? It was about 3 feet deep with snow and the campsite was shut. We really didn't think it through. We were up in the forest when G had a brainwave; the last time we were there Jenks got left behind. He was now living with some Germans and when we found his place we knocked on. The Germans weren't having any of it at first, saying Jenks wasn't there. We weren't going anywhere - it was cold as fuck and we were in jeans and t-shirts, hardly dressed for the Alps. Anyway we pulled the 'German guilt' card about what their fathers had done in the war and it worked. A little mean I know but they let us in.

So, when we got in there was Jenks, sat like King Dick! He'd been speaking German telling them he isn't here. We gave Jenks a couple of digs and he had a few bruises forming round the eyes. He had a German bird as well, an absolute stunner for Jenks. So there we were, a cosy little bunch. I was handed a cup of tea and after a few sips I started to feel like The Cheshire Cat or the Mad Hatter, I was tripping off my nut! I didn't find it funny that Jenks' Fräulein had paid me back for slapping her boyfriend by spiking my cuppa with mushrooms.

The next morning we were off to work, "Hi Ho!" only I didn't really want to, as we had plenty of bees from the night before, a few ton each. We came across this little town, a nice gaff (I'm not a travel writer). It was like

Magic Mushrooms

Winter Wonderland, had a Christmas Market type vibe about it. I had cold feet (literally), so our first priority was getting some snow boots and snow gear, so we could get kitted out and blend in. We just went into some shops, got dressed in their sheepskin coats, fleeces and ski pants and off we went!

We were in a bookshop, and I saw G go up the dancing bears, so I hung around to make sure no one went up after him. Five minutes felt like a year, then suddenly the scream went up, "'Ello 'Ello". I stood there trying to look inconspicuous but it was obvious I wasn't one of the locals. A stormtrooper grabbed me as I was scurrying out of the door. I spotted The Don across the road, he'd heard the cry as well. It was on top, enough to send shivers down a grafter's back. Two cops appeared, and I started to protest and thank them, saying "I thought they were going to eat me!", any old nonsense. They put me in the car anyway, and fifteen minutes later I'm off to the bizzy shop 5km out of town. I spied our car following, "Crazy fucks" I thought, but it felt good that I wasn't alone. In the bizzy shop they questioned me; I made up some blag about how I was working on a site in Stuttgart and threw in a few porkies and half-truths, "My missus has left me". To cut a long story short these cops went off duty at 6pm. They had no proper cells so I was taken outside and locked up in a garage with a bed, toilet and a sink. It was right beside the dog kennels. I was told to stay there until morning, when an inspector would be round to see me. So I got my head down, fucked from the previous night's shenanigans.

It must have been a couple of hours later that I heard a whistle, the Manc grafter's whistle. I replied, then heard G's voice before "Bang!", he jemmied the door off, it was The Great Escape from the kennels! I found out later that it was some kid and a granny upstairs who put the scream up. G locked them in a cupboard and watched as the cops drove off with me. He said he couldn't let me take the wrap for that, and it was good they were going to break me out no matter what. All this and the Swiss border was looming at Schaffhausen. We plotted up in a hostel-type hotel, laughed about the dog kennels and fell asleep.

The next morning it was business as usual. We were down the street having a mooch in a hotel when I came across a cabinet full of kettles, and not the tea making type. Out came the Manchester key and "Bang" I opened the cabinet. They weren't Rolexes, but just as good, Longines - the best Swiss watches going. I collected about a dozen and scurried back to the motor, then we were off. G was going on about getting some weed, I personally wasn't that interested. So off we popped to Zurich. Down by the lake there was a fair in the middle of the street, all Christmassy – this was the middle of October but the Swiss have a festival every other week about something. G started chatting to these two Swiss guys who he'd done a bit of business with in the past, and they said for us to go with them, so we jumped in the back of a 7 series. They were doing wheel spins up busy streets, then down through the old town driving like cunts. They arrived at their place, by the zoo, which was suitable for this pair of animals. They returned to the car with a slab of hash that must've weighed a kilo and started hacking at it in the car. They gave G a chunk, and kept hacking into it with pieces flying all over the car. Of course the charlie came out and that was it, guns on the dashboard. "Fuck sake" I thought, sat in the back while there's an ounce of charlie on the console and this Swiss fuck is chatting on, snorting and swinging his gun on his finger like a cowboy. I just wanted to punch the twat in the head.

So there we are: us three sat in the back with John Wayne and Stirling Moss up front, loads of lines, G building a spliff that could choke a horse, and hot rocks falling all over the seats. Stirling Moss decides to pull doughnuts in the snow, giving it hand brake turns. Sure enough, like a cold shower, a set of double headlights come on, the Polizei. Remember, dear reader, that I started this tale by noting our fake passports. Well it was okay jibbing through customs separately, but Steve James and Steve Jameson sharing not only a birthday but a car full of drugs was a different story. I just grabbed a chunk of hash that had landed near me, thinking "If I'm getting jail..."

These cops weren't your usual gun-toting Swiss dibble, they were like military, SAS, machine gun fucks. We had a hire car back in Zurich full of tom, about a grand each, and another car came alongside us. This was it, no Christmas. We were carted off to separate jails. The Swiss fucks tried to put the blame on us. The best of luck was that Mr Jameson was taken to a different gaff to me, and we were both released. G, however, had been nicked a couple of months before so was getting deported. I couldn't believe it, it was good job we didn't have the car keys on us, we left them in the cig tray. It must have been the fastest trip back over the border from Zurich to Schaffhausen. The next day we decided not to push our luck and got off *back to Dam, "If in doubt, get the 5 o'clock out!"*

WACKO JACKO

We all got word that Wacko Jacko was doing his BAD tour, and it'd be a great opportunity for earning. I flew to England to meet Colin and Roufy and we all chipped in and got thousands of programmes and T-shirts copied from his official one. We got stopped entering Spain as the luggage we had looked too large for three. They pulled us aside but before anything was said I just got a hundred programmes out plus about twenty shirts and handed them to the head man. He gave me a grateful wink, took the programmes and let us through with a top smile. We had back stage VIP cards too that we could go through security with. It was no problem taking punters inside three or four handed for good money. As usual I didn't sell a single programme and got stoned instead, just shuffling my programmes on to the other Mancs that were working the concert. Back in Lloret, Gibbo, a lad from Moss Side, had brought with him some tablets that were the new drug on the scene from America. He had managed to get hold of them from a yank he knew. They are now known as ecstasy but back then they had no name as yet, "they're something like acid" we were told.

When we took our very first one I tried to be sick as I decided I didn't really fancy how I felt. After 20 minutes I felt low and was shaking to fuck but then had a total turn around. I suddenly felt fucking great – this is where the saying 'can you feel it' came from, as that's all we kept saying to each other for the next couple of hours. We were all pretty clueless about what to expect from them, the next thing we knew we were all in the St Trop. Jan, a Dutchman we had known for years from Amsterdam, was with us too. He was a top armed robber, a real hard nut too, all of a sudden he's up doing some mad dance followed by Roufy, who was usually a cool dude, doing the biggest maddest pogo I'd ever seen.

"What the fuck you doing Steve?" I asked him.

"I don't know Marcus but I feel fucking great" he replied.

Without thinking this tablet had taken over and all I really recall was that all the tunes that we had heard before seemed to sound 50 times better! We were going for it now doing mad dances. Jan came up to me "wow what the fuck are them tablets" while he did a crazy dance. The next day while we were all still out of our nappers when these strangers started letting on to us. Gibbo started a big story that we were all professional dancers from London! I remember I had my walkman on listening to OMD. I'd heard it a million times before but now I'm dancing in front of a beach full of people. I couldn't help myself. This new drug deffo had something to do with dancing that's for sure plus the fact that I and most of the lads had never danced before in our lives, that said it all!

Gibbo had about 20 tablets left and started handing a few out to the lads that worked the bars that we all knew. We gave one to Geoff, a 'socialite' that we knew. He was working that night but knowing he'd love to feel like us, we dragged him out of his bar. After he dropped his pill, he locked himself inside a small room at the back of the pub and freaked out. I had to kick the door in to get him out. We took him for a walk on the beach until he was on our wavelength. After that he was happy and took over as leader that night. He started doing a mad dance, we must have looked like a pack of weirdoes to be honest, even the St Trop doorman wanted us to leave until Gibbo gave him a tablet too. He came back after a short while grinning and shuffling a little dance too! All that week we fucking tanned them and went on a real beano. We would have danced to fuckin Mozart the way we all felt.

Back in Amsterdam these new tablets had already hit town before we'd left for Spain but as we'd been away in the Black Forest we hadn't taken much notice. Up until then I'd been a spliff head. I wasn't into class A drugs but this drug just put you on top of the world and Amsterdam was gonna have a great rave scene to come with these fuckers. It took off big time! The new music coming out of the US was made for the drug and vice-versa. Within weeks a new club scene had been born and was already taking off, flyers started appearing advertising venues; House music was born!

With all the goings on in Amsterdam's raves we needed a break.

A few of us got a shit load of E's and high-tailed it back to Ibiza. We were taking that many that I never knew if I had already taken one or not half the time. I don't think we sold many as we all decided to stay for the summer living on a diet of E's and booze, hardly ever going back to our hotel and sleeping on the beach in San Antonio with all the other revellers. It was like how you imagined the 60's during flower power – just pure partying 24/7. As was the case wherever we went, it seemed half of Manchester was there too!

After a few days I met up with a French girl called Sylvia, she had been seeing a lad from Manchester, Bernard, a good friend of Stuart's. She soon sacked him off, preferring me instead. I'd met a few female criminals in my time but this girl was a real gangster's moll. On my first night at hers I found a handgun while she was out of the room. What was this bird up to? Then after further rummaging I found a fuck off bag of white powder - cocaine, about half a key's worth. Me not really being a dealer or taker I was gonna fuck off, but the villa was out in the middle of nowhere, I thought I'd stay the night and do one the next day as I'd always stayed away from the drug world as best I could. Turns out she had been on Ibiza a few years and knew almost everyone on the island, although she normally only trusted her own contacts who were all Spanish and Italians. As usually happened after a week with Sylvia, there were 5 lads staying at her luxury gaff. She loved the Mancs she met because she said we were all crazy and right up her strasse. The E's we had taken over were gone pretty soon, as was our money. It was time to get back to the graft, but she convinced me that I should come to her house in the South of France. I didn't really wanna bother but had no choice as my return flight had long since departed, plus I was now skint.

By this time there was just me and a great lad from north Manchester called Docker who decided to tag along. She paid for our flight to Nice where she had a top gaff with a swimming pool, the works, but after living off her for a week it was time for us to slip off and graft. I asked Docker if he fancied a trip to Swizzy. He was up for it but it baffled Sylvia, who told us she had pure money and would look after us. We weren't into going cap in hand, so borrowed our fare for the train to Basel.

We were just near the Swiss border and Docker pipes up "Shit Marc, I've not brought my fuckin passie."

Now I'd been to this border control a good few times and knew when you got off the customs were waiting at the end of the platform for the tourists, "No worries mate, all you need to do is get off the train the opposite side to everyone else, cross the tracks and you're in!" Docker's face said it all but he had no option. It worked a treat and I met up with him soon enough. I now found out Docker wasn't really a jibber and he didn't adapt to blagging the staff that well plus we were now grafting on public transport which didn't help things but after a few days we finally got half a wedge.

Pink Floyd were playing Lausanne that night so I made my way to the concert. As usual, all the Manc ticket touts were there and we soon got given back stage passes and met up with our Colin and John McKee. I was sat by myself having a spliff when I saw a girl trying to gain access to where I was sitting. No problem, I helped her climb a small partition but just as I had got her in, I could see a security guy heading my way, you could see by his body language that he wasn't happy that I'd helped a girl get backstage. BANG! I just smacked him, a belting sucker punch, before I knew it there were another firm of security workers heading for me. They then got a bit confused as I was wearing a pass just like them yet they knew I wasn't really a worker and tried manhandling me towards the exits. All hell broke loose when I got backup from our Colin and a lad called Daffy. It was three on three now. The real security saw it all and came bowling over, it was plain to see the fight as it was in an empty part of the arena. We were now battling with them; going down the stairs to where the entrances were and by now they outnumbered us. From nowhere John McKee arrived, he rammed in between us and the security with a metal barrier. It was a sight to see as when John goes, he goes. He looked wild, with his eyes bulging and roaring like a fucking Viking.

Then some English bloke from nowhere came over to us "you fuckin Mancs are always the same, always starting trouble." BANG!

I twatted him too and it all erupted again. By now the police had turned up and didn't know what to do or who to grab, as we all had security passes on. They thought it was a domestic between grafters, and by now we were well and truly outnumbered. Plus we were knackered and couldn't fight anymore. We took stock of ourselves, we looked a right sight and the stewards were shell shocked at what had gone on. I don't know who but somebody must have got the first aiders in and three of us were whisked off to the local hospital. It was strange but me and our Colin received stitches in the same place, our left eyes were opened up. Poor John had had his balls kicked up into his abdomen and was in pure pain although we were still buzzing and knew we had given a great account of ourselves. It was some battle. The Swiss old bill weren't bothered although we were asked to make statements. Suffice to say we did one and got back to the hotel, the next day we looked like right twats, so headed back to Holland to recuperate.

The train stopped at Maastricht, a small town just over the Dutch border. John was in real pain with his injury by now so we decided to get back to Manchester from there. Everyone got through customs but me, I got pulled and put in a cell. Ten minutes after the flight left they came to my cell and said I was now free to leave! This was a typical Dutch manoeuvre, they thought it was really funny that they had made me miss my flight. I now had to buy a new ticket and wait for the next flight later that night and that only went to London. I didn't find it so funny as I was in pain now too and I knew I looked a right state.

After a bad ass journey I finally reached my mother's house, only to find that the French bird Sylvia was already there! This girl wasn't fucking around, I remember thinking. I'd genuinely forgotten about her, though obviously she hadn't forgotten me. It seemed we were now going out with each other. The last thing I was looking for was a relationship plus I hated the French. Oh well, she was here now so after a few days my face looked nearly normal again. I took her out around Manchester. She loved the town and everyone we met and made the comment, "I love Manchester it's full of criminals." After a week she again got confused with me when I told her I had to get back grafting.

"Marc, I have plenty money you come live with me in France."

I wasn't having any of it and she wasn't happy but agreed, plus I wasn't into pimping from some bird I barely knew. As promised I did go back to see her but she was a full on dealer and I didn't fit in on the French Riviera, it was too poncey for me. After a few weeks I fucked off back to Holland.

A right old firm of Mancs arrived in the Dam, over a hundred or so, though normally it would be for football match, these were here for a major weekend rave. The Hacienda had arranged a party to be held at our local club, the Roxy. It was where those of us that lived in Amsterdam had gone regularly for the past year. It was a real buzz seeing people I hadn't seen in ages all raving and sweating their nappers off. I remember Fonzo getting hoisted in the air by the doormen, as they'd had enough asking him to stop blowing his whistle and clanking beer bottles together, and they kicked him out. We tried to keep him in but to no avail, other than that it was a top night, one of the best from the rave days and that's saying something as every night was a top night to us lot.

At the end of the party all these t-shirts were getting thrown around all over the floor, on closer examination I found out they were the fuckin T- shirts I had put my money into from when we had worked the Wacko Jacko tour, oh well, talk about throwing money away, the shirts were shit quality anyway. I remember thinking to myself not to invest anymore money in the swag game as a few lads were intent on making rave commercial back in UK.

Meanwhile it was rocking in Ibiza. As told by Stuart, by the now socialite criminal...

BALEARIC BEACH BUMS AND BEATNIKS

IBIZA

Stuart C.: *We started serving up these new pills and they flew out. Instead of selling about fifty to a hundred E's a night at £40 each, which was alright in '87, a year later we were selling thousands and making a small fortune. Most of the punters at first were from mainland Spain, Scandinavians, Italians, a few Yanks and of course plenty of English Bulldogs. A lot of the girls would be working outside the bars trying to get people in the West End and San Antonio, and we'd be in there selling our E's one by one, as well as our weed and coke, basically whatever drugs we had we'd sell there. We'd go down to the Café del Mar to watch the sun go down, this was before we'd go out. The Garda were always hanging around the café but we'd get a warning from the owner because he liked the amount of business we brought in, so he just turned a blind eye to it all. So in the Café del Mar they had a proper chill out room with big bean bags and we'd just crash out on them, stoned as you like, even stoned from the night before. Then we'd go to Paradiso where at three o'clock in the morning before it closes, the water comes on and that's part of the dance floor. So everyone would be jumping around in the water, I did it once and I thought it was a stupid thing to do because you still had the rest of the night walking around piss wet through. Not the best move for a style guru!*

Then we'd jump over to Amnesia for a bit, head to Pacha for a while and then go back to Amnesia until it closed, which was about six in the morning. After that we'd finally go home, and you saw all the shops opening. On one occasion we went into this video shop on our way back, Kisby snuck up the stairs and came back down with a grand and a half, after that we just headed back down to Café del Mar where everyone would be dossing, because even though everyone had their own apartment they'd still be down there smoking weed and getting the beers in. We were drinking 24/7, so we really were '24 Hour Party People'.

Balearic Beach Bums and Beatniks

Everything we wanted, we had; we always had cars, I had my motorbike, and then there'd be people there like Max, little Casey and Olivia's sister. We also had the odd celebrity coming down. After sitting around until about ten, eleven o'clock we'd retire back to our apartments to see what drugs we had left and count our proceeds. I mostly did this with Tony Cannetti, a lad I was living with at the time; he was a pretty hard person to live with, but a very funny guy in his own way. He was a proper babe magnet as well, as soon as he walked into a club there were girls all over him, he even got offered modelling deals but he never took them up on it, he'd just tell them to "fuck off and get out of the way". That's just how he was, quite full of himself. He'd done Borstal and he'd had a rough upbringing. Mick Medley, who was a top lad, was the leader out of the Sheffield lot, the one who'd calm situations down and say "Do this a certain way" both were proper Sheffield boys. Tony at the time had become my grafting partner and whilst he wasn't the best grafter, if it was there then he'd have it.

In Ibiza we never had to pay in to any clubs because they knew who we were, they knew we weren't the type of people who would take a slap and get away with it, nobody got away with anything because there were thirty or forty of us there when we were out in force. We stuck together because we had people trying to muscle in on our business, and we wouldn't let them do it, it was our turf. Later on in the mid 90's it was the Scousers who ran it, with Amnesia being changed into Cream and what have you but you can't keep an empire forever.

Whilst I was out there I met a really nice girl, she was a carnival queen and her name was Snowy. I told her I'd be back in the winter but I didn't end up going back. The following year when I did go back I found out that she'd had an abortion, so when I saw her she was crying, saying "why weren't you here, you promised me, you scumbag". I didn't know what to do, didn't know what to say or anything, lads at that age don't know how to handle adult shit like that. Obviously it's a bit hazy now due to all the Gary Abblets.

One night I met a mob of sound Middleton lads; Leon, Dessi and Docker. They were three tall blonde lads and their mate, Carl Platt, approached me wondering if I could sort them some decent weed, which obviously wasn't a problem. I went and got them a bigger weight than they asked for and of course they were buzzing about it. Later that night I saw

*them hanging around the West End so went up and asked them, "Do you
fancy trying this new drug?" Plattey was right on it, he'd just come out
of jail in Australia and had heard about this new rave pill going round
the clubs down under. Soon the lads had all necked a little fella and were
coming up; buzzing, dancing, and bouncing around in time to the tunes.
We went up to Amnesia with all the girls, you only really needed to take
one back then as they were pure and very, very strong, we deffo took too
many just being greedy bastards really. Docker said to me he just couldn't
believe how our firm stuck together and kept under the radar from everyone
else. If he asked me now I guess I'd say "Make sure they're your mates"
because someone will always have your back, and they won't be looking to
stab you in it either.*

*I did get mistaken for being a Sheffield lad on a few occasions because
of the amount of Sheffield boys I hung around with. I remember M Blaney
was always telling people I was Sheffield Steel just for a laugh. Blaney was
a proper grafter who came to visit me when I was locked up waiting to get
deported.*

*Respect I say to lads who go out of their way to keep in touch with
each other when banged up abroad. When you're locked up abroad and you
have the warden come to tell you you've got a visitor, you don't expect that
visit to be from a Manc, it was bang on. It's especially top when they bring
you some money or a wee chunk of hash that goes up where the sun don't
shine, it's just what proper stand up guys do for you. We were all streetwise,
you know, obviously I'm not comparing us to 'Goodfellas' or anything, but
I'd say we had a few sayings that summed us up pretty well.*

*The one within the firm I liked was "No Problems for No-Problem
People"; if you're not a nightmare and keep your head, you shouldn't have
any issues, and for the time being we didn't. We were just typical tough,
Northern, Working-class boys with an edge and a knack for a top jib.*

*Back in London. I'd met this girl Laverne who was in a house with
seven or eight lads and a couple of girls all chilling out and that.*

*Eventually I asked her to come abroad with me to San Antonio, Ibiza,
and she said yeah. When she came over, there was about forty of us; some
from London, Sheffield, Huddersfield, Stoke, all different areas, and we all
got on well. You'd think with forty grafters there we'd have everything we
needed but she brought something else to the party as well; she knew people*

like Steve Strange, Boy George and Mick Jones from The Clash, so we got to selling them this and that.

Being a massive fan of The Clash it was a result to not only finally get to meet my idol Mick Jones but the cherry on the cake was I ended up partying with him in Ibiza, having a great time in the big clubs as we strolled into all the VIP areas day and night over a three day binge. We'd go to Dave's Bar off our heads and Dave would never charge us for a drink. Mick would knock about with us in Ibiza every now and then. We met up again in Amsterdam in 1991.

As you can imagine this made us a fair few quid over that summer but all the money we made was easy-come easy-go; whatever money we made in the day went out with us that night, sometimes morning would creep around and we'd have just enough money to buy a few coffees. Soon after we started knocking about with DJ's like Nancy Noise, Lisa Loud, lots of girls from London, Joanne and Lisa McCoy, a few girls from Sheffield and this stunning Italian girl called Uri that I ended up going out with for a while. We'd had a good summer then had a trip back to London and what became clear when we were back in London was MDMA (called X's) were huge on the gay scene. Soon we started to distribute them in Spectre and back to Ibiza and smashed them at the same price mainly to the Italian DJs, gays and lesbians. We had a few weeks soaking up the sun and then Laverne had to fly back because her old man was ill.

THE DEMISE OF THE SNEAK THIEF

Stuart might have been doing ok with the E's but in our case things were a wee bit different. Graft-wise, ecstasy was a disaster. We couldn't go out jibbing anymore as we were up all night which left us all waking up at mad o'clock most days, with about an hour to get to the shops before they closed. This had a knock on effect as all grafters want is to earn money, we naturally started getting lazy choosing to just snatch the takings we saw, as and when. We weren't sneaking any more, just taking instead. This led to doing snatches outside banks and the police got involved. They had always known about the Brit grafters but opportunist crime wasn't on their list of priorities. Bank snatches were, however, and there was an inevitable clamp down.

The Dutch Old Bill had set up a squad aimed at taking us off the streets. They followed us around Amsterdam but we weren't particularly fussed because they were easy to slip. Occasionally they would haul us in for something. One night, me and Bobby G had just left a club after a night out and were about to drive away when a load of Dutch policemen surrounded the car. We were E'd up to the max and refused to unlock the doors, choosing instead to do rave-style dances and chuckle to ourselves as the dibble tried to force their way into the vehicle. The Old Bill eventually managed to smash the window in and dragged us to the station for questioning.

When we got to the dibble shop we were told that the car that we were in had been linked to a bank snatch. The Old Bill behind the desk gave us a funny look, as if to say, "You don't exactly fit the description of bank robbers." You expect people who do those types of crimes to be huge, hulking guys and I'm only five foot six. The looks that we received were probably also partly due to the fact that we were off our nappers. I was then stuck in a cell and left to stew until 9 am when I was told that Bobby had been set free but the police in Leiden would like to see me over another offence that had been committed there. I'd already been to the police station in Leiden three months earlier for allegedly snatching the takings from a bakery but I managed to get off. I hoped it would be a repeat of last time.

There wasn't too much cause for concern because the fact that I was in a car that had been used in a robbery didn't mean shit. My plan was to give the dibble my usual sophisticated response of, "It wasn't me". When I got to Leiden, I did exactly that and ended up walking free again. Witnesses had stated that a mixed-race guy was responsible for the Tony, which shed doubt on my guilt. I was chuffed to bits that I had got away with the snatch. The Old Bill were fuming when they saw that there was a right old wedge of cash among my belongings when they were handed back to me.

When I got back to Amsterdam I went for some food at Barney's to celebrate. Barney's was where all the grafters used to go to smoke spliffs, eat breakfast and discuss their plans during the heyday. In days gone by, the dibble had a place directly above the gaff and would take surveillance pictures of us, which was funny. After spending the morning debating the best spots to go jibbing in and co-ordinating our activities, we would stick the Vs up at the Old Bill on the way out to let them know that we were on to them. Now that everyone had moved on to greener pastures, the place wasn't the same any more. The era of the sneak thief was nearly over.

A few weeks later, I was getting out of my car with two of my mates to do a snatch in Vlaardingen when a copper pulled up next to us and told us that he was taking the motor because it didn't have any insurance. The weather was cold, wet and dank; being left without a set of wheels was the last thing we needed. Getting pulled wasn't particularly surprising given the fact that there wasn't a soul on the streets. We stood out like sore thumbs and had been asking for a pull.

After confiscating our car, the Dutch Old Bill dropped us off at the local train station. We got a rattler to the Hook of Holland, where I wanted to hop aboard a ferry home but unfortunately the dibble in the Hook were also on my case. This time it was a division known as the Queen's Police, who were a no-nonsense outfit. They told me that I was wanted for another crime and ushered me into the back of a police car. The Old Bill completely ignored the speed limit as usual and drove to Leiden at well over 200kph (120mph). By this stage it was midnight and I was so knackered that I fell asleep partway through the journey. There aren't too many people who can say that they've nodded off whilst travelling at that speed; it was testament to what a long, tiring, disaster-filled day I'd had!

I arrived at the dibble shop in Leiden and was taken straight to the cells. The next morning I was greeted at my cell door by the same two coppers who had interrogated me the last time I was there. They looked proper made up with themselves and assured me that they had all the evidence that they needed to have me put away.

"We've got proof that you were involved in snatching jewellery from a shopkeeper here last November," the officer-in-charge told me, giving me a wry smile. "That isn't the only thing either." The copper unfurled a map of Manchester with little photos of lads stuck to it. "Yes, we've been to Moss Side, Miles Platting, Collyhurst, Wythenshawe and even Sale where *you* are from I believe?" This had to be a fucking wind up. "I've even been to the famous Hacienda and visited Strangeways Prison," the copper carried on. "I am now extremely familiar with your home city. You see Mr Blaney, my colleagues and I are a team that was put together to bring an end to your trips to our country. Operation Bullseye has been going on for some time now."

Operation Bullseye? Was this fella having a laugh or what?

"We have traced a vehicle that was used in crimes here to an American car dealer in Amsterdam. We have obtained a witness statement from the dealer saying that he sold it to you. We also found your fingerprints in the car. What do you have to say about that?"

"It's fucking rubbish," I scoffed back at him. "I do remember getting a car from a Canadian but I didn't even get the papers for it. I sold it on to some Geordie lads who said they wanted to drive to Germany in it to do some building work there."

I thought that this was as good a story as any. The dibble didn't seem convinced and locked me in a cell where I spent the remainder of the night. The following morning I was told that I was being charged with robbery. Somebody had popped the tires on a jeweller's car whilst he was paying at the counter in a gas station. They had proceeded to relieve him of a load of tom that he had placed on the backseat of his vehicle. Popping people's tires was a common technique that Manc grafters used for preventing the victim of a crime from following the getaway car. The motor that we drove off in was apparently found 10 km away from the scene of the crime.

"The jewellery that was taken was sold on for 33,000 guilders," the Dutch copper told me. "I know this because we know who you sold it to."

"I've never even seen that amount of money," I chuckled. "Besides, I was in the South of France when the fella got robbed."

Unfortunately, I had actually been living with a girl in Holland and she had accidentally let it slip to the Old Bill that I was staying at her place at the time the jeweller had got his tom snatched. I ended up being taken to The Hague and held in custody for three months before receiving an eighteen-month sentence. This was a massive relief because I had been expecting a much longer stint inside based on the amount of effort the dibble had gone to in order to secure a conviction. It was a bit of a joke really.

★

If you've seen the film *One Flew over the Cuckoo's Nest* then you will have a good idea of what it's like in Dutch prisons. Most Dutch inmates have drug problems and are either permanently off their heads on methadone or strung out on sleeping pills. The prisoners were always moaning about their sentences despite the fact that the legal system in Holland is incredibly lenient. I was once in with a fella who got eight years for kidnapping and torturing two people. He would have almost certainly got life if he had committed the same offence in England.

Luckily I wasn't the only Englishman on the wing, as there were two Scousers in with me who had been done for cheque fraud. One of them was called Geoff and was always happy and upbeat, which the Dutch inmates found baffling. He would sing away to himself as if he didn't have a care in the world. There were also two lads from Fallowfield in South Manchester on another wing who were in for the same thing as the Mickeys. Thank fuck it wasn't just me and a load of miserable methadone prisoners.

Although most of the other cons were serving their time for drugs, it was weird because nobody seemed to have any. This meant that I had to get Sylvia to smuggle me in some weed from outside. During her first visit, she plonked down eight bags of weed on the table without even bothering to try and disguise what she was doing. It was blatant as fuck. I'm sure the warders looked the other way and pretended they hadn't got onto it to avoid having to do anything about it. That's Dutch prison guards for you!

Smoking weed made my sentence pass a lot quicker. There is nothing like blazing a spliff in front of the telly to while away the hours. One night, I lit a joint and turned on the box to see the Happy Mondays partway through a set at Liverpool University on the BBC's *Arena* program. This was a buzz because I've always been into the Mondays. Better still, our Colin was on stage with them! He had got to know the band through a group of Salford grafters who were mates with Bez and Shaun Ryder and had been hanging about in their dressing room when Bez had invited him on stage for the final song. It was the last thing that I had expected to see on telly in Holland and brought an immediate smile to my face.

"The lucky bastard" I thought to myself, "I'm stuck in a Dutch jail and he's having the time of his life."

I went out on the wing the next day buzzing to myself at what I had seen. My mood was further elevated by the sound of Geoff singing a Dean Martin type tune. It made a change from hearing the locals' incessant complaining about every element of prison life. Geoff and me got talking about his singing and he told me that he had performed on stage before.

The months flew by and it was soon Christmas. To celebrate

the occasion the screws allowed Geoff to do a show in the gym during our time out of the cells. Everyone was proper into it and Geoff was in his element. It goes to show you that prison life doesn't consist entirely of doom and gloom; there are good times as well as bad in there.

Shortly after Geoff's performance, I asked the screws if I could be moved to the wing that the Fallowfield lads were on. They agreed and I was transferred. I settled in well, partly due to the fact that the regime was relatively lax. We had table tennis equipment and tellies in there and got to play sports every other day. The locals still weren't satisfied though and one cunt in particular was constantly making out that the jail was hell on earth. He was six foot tall and built like a stallion but acted like a soft, sulky child. So one day, at my wits end, I put a battery in a sock and and flew into his cell with it to give him a crack. Unfortunately I ended up striking his head with the middle of the sock as opposed to the part with the battery in it and the battery end somehow managed to bounce back up and twat me in the bridge of the nose! I started bleeding pretty badly and I began to wish that I had used my fists instead. The screws turned up at my cell door a couple of minutes later to ask what had happened. They thought the Cloggy had hit me and wouldn't believe that I was the aggressor because I was so much smaller than the other guy. In order to ensure that there were no further confrontations, I was moved onto another wing, which suited me fine because there was a more relaxed atmosphere on the unit that they placed me on.

The Strangeways riots coincided with my move to the new wing, which was great because the news reports gave me something to watch. The Dutch cons couldn't believe how bad the English prisons were and were taken aback by the fact that the prisoners didn't have coffee pots and all of the latest mod cons and weren't out of their cells smoking spliffs all day like the inmates in Holland.

I was now free from soft-arse whining bastards but that didn't mean that the rest of my sentence would be easy because partway through my stint, I received the news that the French bird that was bringing me in weed had got arrested in France. She was looking at seven years for a gun and a kilo of coke. I had first met her in Ibiza whilst soaking up the sun, sea and little fellas over there. She was a female gangster with connections to Columbian cartels, which made her a valuable asset to the lads. One guy I know made use of her connections and earned himself a right few bob. He ended up getting twenty-five years for it though and to make matters even worse, he escaped partway through his sentence, got nicked in Holland after a couple of years on the run and was then deported back to England to do the rest of his bird.

I was now left with nobody to smuggle weed in for me so I got in touch with our Colin and asked him if he could help me out. Col told me that Little Brian was working with a Dutch girl behind the counter in a coffee shop in the Dam so I arranged for Brian to send this lady on a visit with some pollen. Going on a visit with a woman you've never met before is pretty nerve-wracking but fortunately it went well and a few visits down the line, we became a couple. I eventually moved in with her and we had a child together, although sadly our relationship didn't stand the test of time. Lots of other lads wanted sorting out with weed so I got Little Bri to pass it on to their birds so that they could smuggle it in. The wing was soon awash with the stuff but the guards didn't seem to mind too much, I guess it kept everyone quiet – well, everybody except one person. I was walking to the library one day when I saw two guards escorting a familiar-looking mixed race guy across the wing. As he drew closer, I realised that it was a lad called Paul who was in the ICJ.

"Alright, mate!" I shouted over. "What are you in for?"

"Doing a snatch but to get away, I ended up twatting some have-a-go hero with a brick," he told me. "'Ere Mark. These Dutch prisons are mad. They're full of nonces and grasses. I keep getting shifted around from one jail to another for battering them. You don't get time added on to your sentence for kicking off over here though."

I couldn't help but laugh. Paul must have been the guards' worst nightmare. Later that day I was sitting in my cell when a screw opened the door and asked if he could have a word with me.

"It's about Paul, the other Englishman," the guard explained. "He is a loose cannon, my friend. Do you think there's a chance that you could calm him down if I move him onto the same wing as you?"

"No worries, sure" I told him, laughing as I spoke.

Having another Manc in with me made the time go faster. In return for the move, Paul promised the screws that he would tone down his behaviour. He kept his word and stopped raging against the system for a while. We had a right laugh together. Unfortunately, just as things are going well in prison, something always fucks it up. This time it was a transfer. In Holland, you spend the first six months of your sentence in a remand prison before being shipped out to the gaff that you will be serving the majority of your sentence in. I was off to De Schie, which was the biggest, newest jail in Rotterdam.

There was a lot more tension in De Schie than there had been in the remand prison. The staff didn't know how to control the inmates. The situation wasn't made any better by the fact that people's sports sessions, doctor's appointments and visits kept getting moved about and delayed. Shortly after I had arrived one of the prisoners that I had got to know a bit joked to me that we should start a riot like the one in Manchester. I took the fella's words with a pinch of salt and didn't give them a second thought.

Later that day I heard raised voices so I looked out of my cell window and saw people lobbing burning toilet rolls around the place. For a split second I thought that somebody really had started a riot but then I realised that this was as intense as it was going to get. Some of the locals were shouting 'Blaney' and 'Strangeways' which again, I thought very little of – that is until the door banged open and six huge riot officers with helmets and shields came running into my cell. They lifted me clean off my feet and held me up against the wall. The head prison guard was at the back of the pack and took great delight in telling the officers that the so-called riot had been my fault. I had only been in the prison for a matter of days so I've got no idea what his logic was for thinking that.

The riot screws dragged me out of the cell and I was shipped out to Noordsingel prison, which is also in Rotterdam. I was still in my boxers because I hadn't been fully dressed when they had burst into the cell. Noordsingel is quite an old, rundown prison so I wasn't best pleased. The Dutch prison authorities were on pins because of what had happened in Strangeways. I guess they didn't want anything to take place that could possibly cause the Cloggies to follow the Manc's example.

No one in Noordsingel would give me a shirt to wear so I was forced to remain in my undies until my belongings were sent on from De Schie a few days later. It was a good job it was summertime! Shortly after arriving at the jail, I put in for a visit with my missus-to-be. Later that week, she smuggled me in some of the strongest hash I've ever smoked in my life. I was getting mashed one day when a prison welfare officer came to my door to tell me that I had been found innocent of being involved in the riot in De Schie and would be getting moved back there. I was so out of it that her words didn't even register. The minute she was gone, I closed my eyes and drifted back off into space.

By the time I arrived back in De Schie, the staff had got their act together and the prison was a lot more organised as they had managed to get some experienced guards from elsewhere to assist. It wasn't actually that bad a nick now that everything was running smoothly; they even had an Astroturf pitch for playing football on. A couple of weeks after my return, a screw came to my door and asked me if I would mind having a chat with some officials who had come over from England. I said yeah sure, because anything that gets you out from behind your door is a good thing when you're locked up. The guard escorted me to a little office where Lord Justice Harry Woolf was sitting waiting for me. I'd seen him on TV before so I recognised him instantly.

"If I knew you were coming, I'd have baked a cake," I joked to Woolfy. He laughed and told me to take a seat.

"I'm here to ask you some questions about British jails," the Lord Chief Justice said. "Have you been in prison in England?"

"Yeah, Strangeways and Durham," I told him.

"Okay, what was the disturbance here that I was told about? It seems as if you have everything in Dutch prisons."

"It wasn't even a riot," I answered honestly.

"Well if the riot police turned up then it must have been a riot," Woolfy replied. "Anyway, as you will undoubtedly know, there has been a disturbance in Manchester so I would like to know what you would change about prisons in the UK if you were given the chance to improve them, as here in Holland the prisoners have everything it seems."

"That's an easy one," I said. "Firstly, I'd demilitarise them. Get rid of them peaked caps that you have to wear and all that 'yes sir' and 'yes boss' stuff so the cons wouldn't resent the guards as much. As for Holland, the guards are cool and call you by your first name, not howling rank numbers and surnames like you were scum, as happens in England. That system is Victorian at best. Oh and you could give everyone a single cell and a bag of weed a week as well. They turn a blind eye to smoke here, it helps calm things and the so called riot here was really about the prison not being ready because there was no gym, doctors were few and all the visits were getting messed around with. In my honest opinion, Strangeways need burning to the ground – it was a shit hole where all the guards were bullies in military disguise."

Woolfy chortled to himself again. He seemed to be a really relaxed, down to earth guy. After a brief chat, he thanked me for my time and I went back to my cell thinking that it had been the strangest conversation that I had ever had. The only thing that's changed since is no slop out – that's it! Cheers Woolfy !

While I was in jail things were still buzzing in Amsterdam and Manchester with the Ecstasy scene still in full flow. One weekend Stuart got a call off legendary Clash guitarist Mick Jones...

1988 AND ALL THAT

PHONE CALL

Stuart C.: *So I said, "Mick, just go into town and ask for directions to Barney's Breakfast Bar, you can buy top weed in there as well." Barney's did a proper English breakfast. I told Mick all about our exploits from here; Barney's was our base camp for years, and where we'd have a full English while plotting up before hitting the road. It was a good place to chat about upcoming grafts, usually to fellow Mancs, and was a pretty safe place to discuss all things criminal. This suited us down to a tee, as Interpol, GMP and the local police had Operation Bullseye in full swing at this point. They came up with that name after infiltrating us in the Flying Dutchman whilst playing darts, as we were all dab hands at the arrows. The undercover Dutch and Manc dibble had spent over a year getting bits and bobs from mingling in with us all, it worked well for them to just have us all off their patch and they had disbanded the firm by the mid 90's.*

I took Mick and his wife on a boat tour around Amsterdam's sleazy canals; we passed the new jail, saw Anne Frank's house, had a few free beers in the Heineken brewery, poked our heads in a few museums and chilled out in the Last Water Hole. It was actually nice to take in the other side of Amsterdam's culture. We probably visited a dozen other places but I kind of lost count.

"Right, have a kip, I'll come and get you later and take you and your Rene out for a lively night on the tiles." So about 8 o'clock I picked them up, Rene was a stunningly beautiful lady, they were a very nice couple to have the pleasure of spending the night on the tiles with. First it was The Flying Dutchman for a few, next was the new Bulldog up west and then straight on to The Milky Way. By the time we get there the E's had come up so we were flying. I'd have probably been flying anyway as I was a massive fan of his new band Big Audio Dynamite and now I was with the

guy, obviously people were coming up to him now and then but he seemed the sort of guy who didn't mind signing things or having a quick word. He'd no doubt met his heroes in the past, people like Keith Richards and Rod the Mod, so understood the urge. Eventually it was getting a bit too much though; he couldn't hold a conversation without someone interrupting him, so I said "Come on we'll get off in a minute."

I decided to head off to Mazzo's, a top venue as was the Roxy but that's a very high profile gaff so I thought a much smaller club would be coolio. Mazzo's wasn't a high-octane flashy sweatbox, it had a long bar with well-dressed barmen, very pretty girls knocking around, some nights you'd get the staff all buzzing about on roller-skates. Mick and his missus loved it in there and what a night it turned out to be, as luck had it all the chaps from separate firms had just landed at the same time, we ended up taking over half of the dance floor without any malice at all. You see many times we would pull in the in-crowd, even if the lads were a bit rough round the edges, we'd learnt our trade after many years on the jib and most had spent time in jail that must leave its presence on the Jibbers.

Anyway in the area that mega Mazzo night were the Middleton mumblers: Big Bird, Captain Chaos, Bernardo and Fraz, Kevin O'Brien was passing the coke around in them classy snow-seal wraps, Bobby G was wolf-whistling, shouting out, snapping his fingers letting the full club know the lads have landed so his best advice to everyone was to 'Call the Cops'. We'd all say "Better you call the FBI or Interpol" even the Mondays used that line... Next lot in were the Salford Snappers; Time –Bomb Paul, his brother Jay, Eddie B and the Devils Head McAvoy, last in after midnight were the Moss side lads Ozzie Sadie, Cotts, Paul Adams, Fonzo, Amid, Junior, Melvin and co. The timing was perfect, soon lots of women were tucking in tight, the whole club got on it, and greedy-bollocks over here popped another pill (not that I needed another but hey, what a rush).

The next day we meet up again in the train station at the Bistro on number 1 platform, Mick said excitedly "Hey Stu-Pot, got to say it's some facking firm you lads have got here in the Dam."

Then he blurted out, "Hey, Stupot Jet Set-Scallies in the area.

"Is right fella!"

See he'd heard the catchphrase "in the area" a few times over the night, it must have stuck with him, I openly admit I was as proud as a peacock to hear that coming from one of my biggest idols.

★

I joined the Mondays as they toured the Universities – twenty-four hour partying in Lancaster, Liverpool and Leeds. They then invited me over to Holland on their quality coach to the Pink Pop Festival, just south of Eindhoven. It was red hot weather for the next week, we'd timed it perfectly, and I also got a pass that was the bollocks: VIP - Access All Areas. I was having a ball backstage, mixing with people like Lenny Kravitz, Annie Lennox and Bryan Ferry. This wasn't someone's back yard, it was the real thing. Once we'd booked into the hotel we headed over in a mini bus and obviously I'd brought pills, coke, weed, and bit of the other for Shaun and me. The Mondays were brilliant that night, I remember Shaun looking over at me and gesturing me to roll him a spliff, twisting his fingers at me, not his melon but his fingers, shouting "Build us a spliff Stu". So I rolled him a big fat fuck-off one, nice big cone and all that. After lighting it I walked onstage to give it Paul to pass over, and ended up tripping on the main cables, the lights, the sound system, the whole fucking tea party went black.

The stage was in total darkness expect for the big glowing joint, which made me piss myself. Then out of nowhere I felt a hammer blow into my face. I swear it nearly knocked me out cold as I fell on my back. It turned out to be their head of security, an ex-boxer called Pat Barret, better known as The Black Flash. I soon twigged why they called him that, I never saw it coming.

I managed to pull myself together, I was lucky that once I got back up I couldn't feel a thing I was so off my head, I thought it was a hit off one of the pills I'd taken, so I ended up turning round to him and said "Who the fuck are you?" What a plonker eh? He hits just me again but even harder. After ten minutes on my back not being able to hear a thing I decided a few lines of Charlie may clear my head.

Later, when we were all back in the dressing room, he came over and said "Stuart, seriously sorry about that fella". I said "Look, I can't hear you", which I couldn't after being twatted really hard, so he repeated, "Stuart, really sorry about that". I still couldn't hear him, so he ends up hollering like fuck the same thing over and over again, and the Mondays' crew were in bits cracking up. Nowadays he's a legend back home looking after the kids on the north side of Manchester, coaching them the noble art of boxing at the Collyhurst and Moston boxing academy run by a proper old school gent who's even got a MBE for his services to boxing, Brian Hughes. Anyway, thank fuck that we never had a falling out over it. I bumped into him in the Copenhagen Pub on Oldham Road a year later, when I was with a new girlfriend. He walked in with a big gold chunky chain on and all that, bought us both a drink, then he said "Do you fancy a game of pool, Stuart?" I thought "Fucking hell he's going to crack me with this pool cue!" but it was all cool. We got chatting about us being in the green room with Annie Lennox as well as lots of Dutch press, we had a ball. I'd met the new bird before in Lyon with Bernardo who could really pull the women, only that time to gain entrance we scaled the fence but once inside it had a great atmosphere everybody having a good time dancing and good times back in their tents and no one giving us hassle. I ended up dancing at the side of the stage, obviously not stealing Bez's thunder but still having a riot. The lot of us had a blast; there must have been about thirty of our lot there, one of those Festivals that'll stay with me forever, even if it's still a bit hazy at times.

Once back home I was finally put on the guest list at the now world famous Hacienda. Fact was the queue was the trendy place to be at times, it even had its own fanzine but you really needed to look sharp and make the effort as they knocked back top people all the time. If you wore a suit it was risky even if it was Savile Row cut, cost you a fortune making you look on par with Bond, yet if you had a loose zoot suit on looking like Kid Creole, even if it was second hand, you had a good chance. Getting knocked back happened at times to almost everyone, so now I was able to get in without hassle which was as good as an E itself. It was the first super-club in the UK, but sadly it took about four years before it really took off. Before then it was mostly bleak, half-empty, with rain leaking down from the skylights. The only decent nights in the early days were the live bands, and that was the only time you'd get at least 500 in. Everyone knows that Madonna played her first UK gig there in January 1984; brought over the pond for 'The Tube' by Jelly Bean the DJ. The best gig I ever saw there was Grand Master Flash and the Furious Five, they also had a young kid called Coolio messing about in the background on the decks. I just loved that name and still use it to this day. I remember Gregory Isaacs playing to a decent crowd after he'd just got a 'not guilty' in Jamaica over a gun charge. He wrote 'Night Nurse' while locked up on remand, and that was the name of his tour, what a guy. Other bands of note that I saw were Frankie Goes To Hollywood, A Certain Ratio, Thomas Dolby and The Ruthless Assassins on Zumbar night. The only time the place really hit max capacity, 2,000, was if The Smiths or New Order played.

Then came Acid House. This was to change the North of England for the better, with everyone off their heads, lifting their hands to the ceiling; if you didn't know that everyone bar the doormen had necked a pill you'd think the whole place was having some religious experience. Obviously we'd all soon got selling in there, not me specifically but lots did come through me. Having a half decent business going for our selves was a rush but it had nothing on the actual drug itself. We'd drop just half a pill before we went in, once in and up on the floor you'd drop the other half. Ecstasy was like nothing anyone had ever tried, it gave you some of the familiar kicks from things like coke but it made everything around you seem brighter and it seems like everything you did went off without a hitch, the universe seemed alright. The lights look brighter and everything looks a little bit different, it is a bit trippy but not the sort of trip you have on LSD. After about fifteen minutes you get flushes through your heart and butterflies in your stomach, and even if you've not danced all night suddenly your legs are moving. Then your arms are going, in rhythm with whoever's nearby, and soon enough you're bouncing off each other's vibes, so before you know it you're up on stage or at the edge of the podium having the time of your life.

As DJ and Journalist John McCready told The Observer Newspaper, "At the Hacienda it was almost as if a generation breathed a sigh of relief, having been relieved of the pressure of the chase. The Baggy clothes desexualised the whole environment. The rising heat from 2,000 people dancing, even at the bar, in the queue for the toilets, damped down everyone. We all looked crap. If you held on to the handrail on the balcony above the dance floor, your palms would be dripping in accumulated human sweat. You could feel down when the music was over. The huge room quickly went cold as all the exit doors were thrown open and we were herded out. Back to reality, until next Friday. The whole experience was always far more addictive than the drugs. You started wanting it all to go on forever."

A great sight to behold at those nights was seeing lots of players I knew from the grafting game and the media bouncing around in the alcoves, everyone getting the same feelings. They'd head straight for the dancefloor and have a blast with loads of women tucking close. You just had to hope their gats never slipped out the back of their sweaty trousers. I got in one situation where this guy came up to me and said "Do you know such-a-person?" Because we were both E'ing I was open to conversation, so I said "Yeah I do", and he says "He killed my mate". Now, if it had been a normal night and we weren't on E he'd have probably gunned me down, but he put his arms around me (and I definitely thought I was in trouble) and said "Nah, I love you really North-Sider". That's what everyone was saying to each other, "I love you really"; it was a love drug. These were the guys who you'd normally find round a pool table, cue in hand looking like they were going to crack your skull open. Everyone getting on with each other was the understatement of the century I know, but there were long-standing problems between all sorts of groups, and they disappeared while everyone was on it. One major PR move that got the punters in came about soon as it was known Dave Haslam's Temperance night every Thursday had a mega offer - a pound for a pint and it was Uri Geller (Stella) but hardly anyone, even the beer monsters, could sink a beer once them bumble bees were doing their thing. Ice-cold water became the only drink for the dancing masses.

The club had never sold so much bottled water, and the best place to get it was definitely not the bar; packed in tight in a queue could send you under, and waiting in unbearable heat for the bar staff to charge you £2. Everyone knew you had to keep hydrated other you'd overheat and fry in no time. Unfortunately Claire Leighton in '89 took ill whilst outside in the queue and was the first person to die from the drug. This was very sad news because you want everyone to enjoy themselves and come out the other end looking as happy as their Smiley t-shirts. I don't advise people to take drugs but if they want to and understand what they're inflicting on themselves then it's their body. I've had a long history with drugs, been through every one you can name, and many of them I've definitely regretted.

Experiencing the very first raves held in the open-air in '89 with fantastic sunshine was amazing, the flyers said 'North Meets South', 'thank fuck' we all thought as finally the Watford Gap syndrome was about to be forgotten and a truce came about with fellow ravers, see anyone back in the day who came from the north were seen as wearing a flat caps, owned a whippet, smoked woodbines, drank dark mild and all spoke with a funny accent. At last that went right out the window first with Blast Off in huge tents near Blackpool with 4,000 locals and another 1,000 from down south. Next was the much bigger Joy organized by the Donnelly's held on a farm in Rochdale and around 12.000 turned up; it had fairground rides, fruit, food and beverage stalls and was open until the morning. Last was Live the Dream near Blackburn in a clean green open dry field with two massive tents holding about 5,000.

The best rave of them all for me was up at the Donnelly's family home in the leafy Cheshire country side, the DJ got the tunes going about 9ish in the converted barn, it had been cleaned up and had 4 dance areas, easy long back seats, strobe lights and dry ice flowing down, it was pumping down like every five minutes keeping everyone chilled all night long, everyone was on one and there was no sign of any hassle. Then about five in the morning I went outside for a spot to piss and skin up. So I went around the back and down a dip when I heard thumping and pumping and what sounded like sex noises, but what I saw was more impressive than any game of hanky panky. The sun was coming up and I saw this stunning Thai lady battering the shit out of this punchbag that hung from a beautiful tree, giving it a proper rinsing while singing to the tunes coming from the tent. At first I had her down as a working maid (showing my ignorance), but bloody hell it only turned out to be Beaner's wife, a Thai boxer back in Chang-Mai. She'd even trained with Manchester's iconic Master Toddie at his gym.

The cheesiest night for everyone was mid-January '89 when Pete Waterman and Michaela Strachan aka "The Hit Man and Her" brought their cameras and silly ideas to the Hacienda - they planned an evening with them chatting with people up on stage that they had picked out from the dance floor, it was the same script every week on the hit show at the time at cheesy 'Sharon and Tracy' clubs as they were known back then.

Getting them all to dance in time and in line to the light-hearted dance tunes that you would hear now and then in the Hassie, nothing too wild. If you've ever got a spare hour just check out the show on youtube - it tells a lot about the scene and how naïve they were as you'll buzz yer bollocks off when you view how good the vibe was that night. The crowd takes over the show, soft lad and his side kick weren't able to leave the safety of the downstairs bar. They picked out a winner half way into the night who was dancing her tits off on the podium and tried to present her with the winner's trophy, she just placed it next to her bottle of water and carried on regardless, classic. I jibbed round the back of the main bar and sneaked into the small private lift that took me downstairs into the VIP area, as luck would have it as soon as I entered the party Barney from New Order said "Now Then Stu". Is right my man, he was chatting away to Neil Tenant about their upcoming joint venture Electronic, Hooky was chatting to Mick Hucknall who had the blond bombshell Brigitte Nielsen all over him like a rash (lucky fucker). I'm sure she'd be a top ride, I was even hoping there might be some adult fun in the area, was a few spare Cockney babes enjoying the vibes, sadly everyone being high as kites it wasn't on the cards in the Kinky Afro department so I just jibbed a VSOP bottle of Remy Brandy offside, see that would do nicely in the morning when coming down. In the meantime I ended up on that same podium next to the chick who, god bless her, never stopped dancing proper house style all night.

When the lights finally came on, them whistles got the whole club on a massive high demanding the last tune of the night normally 'Talking all that Jazz', 'Work to the Bone' or 'Voodoo Ray'. Meanwhile a few of the TV crew went under, mainly from the heat. An ambulance was called, that was good news for Michaela as she had been spiked and was having a wobbler, just look at that night's show on youtube and you'll see her downstairs asking a trendy hairdresser what he thinks about the club "It's the only place in Manchester to go" he says being genuine, she's all over the place and blurts back "Well I feel sorry for Manchester then" it turns out the whole of the Hit Man and Her team never had a clue about the E Scene that had been going on for seven to eight months by that time and fuck me did it show when it got aired.

Dickhead Waterman is in the DJ booth trying to make sense interviewing Mike Pickering and Jon Da Silva whilst on the decks, soft cunt's hardly able to breath complaining about the heat, no wonder as he's got a woolly black Polo neck jumper looking like he's ready to go on an SAS Mission. After a few minutes he melted and retired downstairs chilling out in the empty swimming pool chatting shite to the other half, it got worse for her as she had to go up into the club to present the prize to the best dancer who's up on the stage giving it plenty and had totally no idea.

Silly Strachan and her camera crew were coming her way again, she isn't happy when confronted with the prize, but fair do's to her out of kindness she takes the small plaque places in next to a bottle of water, then gets back to her funky moves. Next clip you get Michaela slurring her words yet still trying to copy the Jack Dancing she'd seen all night, then she ended up lounging all over Peter Pan, turns out after the smart comment she made about Manchester a little fella found its way into her drink, luv it.

Factory had filmed most big nights for years but never got round to it once house arrived (I suppose everyone was on one!) so the video from Hit Man and Her is the only good quality film to look over if you would like to go back in time to when we had the coolest club in the world at one of the most important time periods in music.

As with all great things, it couldn't last...

The start of the troubles began when Moss Side and Cheetham Hill went to war. The Hill-Billies' HQ in town was The Gallery, just round the corner on Deansgate where my mate Roufy was DJ. He'd been in Lloret with Marc B taking their first E's together. Roufy soon twigged soul related tunes like Sade's 'Paradise', T McCoy's 'I Like to Listen' Raze 'Break 4 love' and Keicha Jenkins 'I Need Somebody' - went down really well with the black soul heads who were just ready to start dropping E themselves as it was mainly the white lads who were selling. After only a year, just as it was hitting, the dibble shut down the club. So the Hill-Billies just breezed past the doormen at the Hac showing them shooters tucked under their coats and took over a corner. The dibble were on it but shit themselves, same with all the drugs that the police had demanded, the doorman handed back what was found in searches. All these went into the safe overnight waiting for PC Plod to pick them up. In the end the Factory staff were then expected to drop the parcels off at Bootle Street, no surprise the doorman ended up running it their own way...

After another year the gang war for control of the doors came to a head. I remember one night when the DJs upstairs and downstairs both had guns pulled on them and the same night a few bouncers got stabbed; students were taxed outside so we could see the decline was in the post.

Back in the day though, the buzz you got when finally outside after another mega night was that cool fresh air and another rush. Most times everyone was asking about where the after party was going down. Was it in one of the many tower blocks in Angry Ancoats, Miles Platting or up to the Kitchen in Hulme - this was a recording studio originally run by a former university student whose mother was a top barrister. The lad tried putting on shebeens playing reggae but they bombed, when the occupant next door moved out the wall was knocked through by the Spin masters, they painted it black put two lights in the corner and bingo - another mega gaff to rave in. So after a few puffs on a joint we'd be jolly well off in a convoy and the madness went for another few hours.

One afternoon, right out of the blue, I bumped into Captain Chaos, Colin. He was eating like a Viking in Liverpool's Chinatown. He got his nickname within Manchester United's Inter-City Jibbers as he just loved the madness and mayhem that came with the chaotic lifestyle following the Devils, fighting, fucking and robbing the locals. I had to admit it has a certain appeal. He said to call over later in the night and have a drink in a top old school boozer next to Lime Street called Mar Edge, full of vibrant Scousers and out-of-towners like myself. I'd just got my new passport and was chilling out in a jolly hotel on the sniff for a loose lady. Most Mancs wanting to get away from all that Gunchester shite had the same mindset as us two. See the best move was to leave the Hacienda about 1.30 and get to Quadrant Park in Liverpool about an hour later. In December 1989 local DJ Mike Knowler held a bash here for students over the Christmas and soon he was on every Thursday night playing house and rave. This soon turned into full weekenders having 5,000 plus in there, all on one buzzing their bollocks off. It was a warehouse downstairs and a huge snooker hall upstairs; these were soon converted into the first legal Warehouse raves. Every now and then when the DJ dropped a mega tune it was on par with Liverpool scoring a goal against Man Utd and being in the middle of that bursting Spion Kop! I swear it was a rush.

Around 7 o'clock in the morning the last tune went down then straight after there'd be another almighty noise with clapping and cheering, this went on for a good ten minutes, them nights were mint. Normally we'd end up back in Mar Edge in need of a few jars to take the edge off all that buzzing before jumping the rattler back home to Manc. I'd say later Cream would take the super club tag to another level but if you ask most Mickeys, I'm sure they'd all say Quadrant Park was a better night's raving.

It really reminded me a club that was hard-core back then. The Osborne Irish club on Oldham Road had been converted into The Scally-Dome (actually known as The Thunderdome) for six months it was a heavy metal club until the owner Alan Evans smelt the coffee and got involved with a lad called Muffin who knew the Madchester scene was about to hit home. The Dome had more street cred on all the inner-city council estates in Manchester and Salford than the Hacienda ever could. The DJs were local lads known as the Spin Masters, who went on to form 808 State and have that world-changing tune, 'Pacific State'. I remember it getting played in the Stretford End before a big game. Bank Holidays were awesome, they had proper hard core all-nighters rocking till seven or eight bells, the most important things to all the kids was being able to afford the five pounds entrance fee and not having to face any dress code nonsense to gain entrance.

I loved both the Hacienda and The Thunderdome and call me vain if you want but I personally enjoy dressing up and trying to pull a nice sexy lady. For me it was part of the package and worth every penny. Twenty-five years later I'm still the same. But after a few months checking the Dome out I soon twigged it wasn't worth making any real effort, in fact I started to dress down with just simple lightweight materials for my tops, baggy Armani shorts and army issue leather sandals a must - everyone was trying to control the heat and keep coolio. You see once inside it was impossible to even think about trying to mix and mingle with the birds.

And at £20 each for a Bumble Bee not many ladies could afford it so they'd share acid tabs called windowpanes and maybe a bottle of poppers then all get on one so to speak.

The heat in there was worse than the Hac, and that's saying something. It was one huge square room with two long bars on each side, all the seating areas had been ripped out so now they'd get around 1,300 inside and around one hundred jibbers tucked in tight. The stage was a touch bigger than the Hac, its huge speakers near to the stage on both sides looked like they belonged in a shebeen and became podiums, the water in the toilets was turned off after an hour, making sure you bought it at one of the two long bars. The ceiling was very low and the dry ice would mix in with the clouds of sweat that drifted up and big dollops of hot water dropped down all over you. Hotshot said it was like dropping down into the belly of an active volcano and having a dance with the devil himself. Whatever's said about the Dome it lives on - I have it down as a musical orgy of togetherness, without doubt a unique experience in a unique venue. All the pubs on Oldham Road reported that their beer towels had been stolen from the tables and bars, the kids were now using them through the night to keep sweat under control, next week they'd all be washed and worn round necks, over belts, some made bandanas out of them, we even noticed how John Willie Lees beer-towels were all from East Manc, Wilson's and Watney's from the North side, Boddingtons from Salford and so on. It was a funny sight this lot when coming out all looking like the Ready Brek kids dripping wet.

Nowadays when I think back to that time period when cockneys and tourists from all over the world had started coming to Manchester, it's a crying shame none of them ever got that Scallies-Dome experience, you even had groups who came down to the Dome to just listen to the tunes outside. Only heads from Manchester and Salford used it, no Yonners from the sticks ever ventured in there. A few bad reports went in the newspapers about the doormen coming under attack from shooters and not long after it was shut down. I've been lucky to know three of the DJs, along with Hot Shot, from that time period who knew the dome inside out. Here are their tales.

JAY

From the mid-summer of 1988 to May 1989 there was a social revolution taking place in Manchester and Salford. It marked a change in behaviour for working-class youth in the city, in particular the males. The acid-house craze had broken out, even City's Guvnors and United's ICJ lads put aside their hatreds and travelled together over to Blackburn for the Warehouse raves after the Dome had shut.

People who were a part of this new culture were blown away. There was no going back for them. I never met a single person who said it wasn't for them. I suppose it brought about a sense of pure, carefree enjoyment without the hang-ups that accompanied a night out in the moody old days of clubbing. These included copping off, the constant threat of violence and the pressure to look cool as well as the football rivalries which spilt over at closing time. The Dome was built on word of mouth. There was no media coverage at all, that success totally encapsulated the acid house culture.

We had the likes of the Jam MC's, Steve Williams, Mike Pickering and the Spin masters all playing. For me to play was priceless, a pure pleasure, it was the polar opposite of the Hacienda. It wasn't cool to go to the dome in any way, shape or form. Your whole life revolved around those nights and the kids from the rough neighbourhoods did whatever it took to get the money to fund their nights out there.

DARREN

It had a great sound system and we had access to a wide range of different tunes because we had our own shop, Eastern Bloc, in town. It was a place where kids from council estates could unwind, we played street music to street people. It had a couple of years being right up there at the top of the tree before things went moody. One night a car just turned up and a fella wearing a ballie walked into the entrance where the bouncers were searching punters and blasted away - how the fuck no one died I'll never know, although a doorman did lose a leg.

ANDY BARKER

Although the Dome was a place where a beef was left at the door, you'd always be on your toes. One night we were playing pool waiting to get paid when all of a sudden it sound like a firing range at the fair, everybody was screaming and running about the place. "There's a guy outside with a fucking gat, shooting at the cameras" shouted a terrified passer-by. We couldn't see the point in fucking the game off, surely he didn't have a beef with us DJs, all we did was spin the tunes. So we just carried on for another half hour then nipped over Oldham Road to the estate where we all lived. The next week, just as the club was warming up, a load of coppers swarmed in congregating along the back wall, so we put on a tune with a sample in it that said the word "Babylon" the West Indian slang for dibble. The minute they heard the tune the whole crowd turned around and started kicking off, it was classic brown trouser time for the cops as they all did one via the back exit doors. It was fucking brilliant.

REVIEWING THE SITUATION

By the end of my stint inside, I had lost two good friends; Terry Corrigan and poor old Diller had both passed away. Divy, my best pal, wouldn't be too far behind. Gordon from Wythenshawe had also died plus a few others were soon to follow due to their lifestyles. Life on the grafter's road was taking its toll on a good few of us. Either way I was deported and issued with a lifetime ban from Holland. I remember thinking, "Fucking hell, that's a bit of a radical step, an indefinite ban!"

I quickly returned to Holland as the Dutch girl I had been getting my visits from while I was inside said I could come over and stay with her. She lived on the Liedesplein. Everything was okay for a few days as the lads who now lived there had a whip round so I had Ex's enough for a couple of weeks. Obviously I soon had to start earning again so me and little Brian had sussed a small camera shop and, although it was alarmed, we just went in through the roof – easy peasy, lemon squeezie. We took what we could carry in some silly looking laundry bags, the type you see everywhere now. They were so heavy but we managed to get on a tram, unload what we had and went back for more, then repeated it until we had cleared the shop. Between us we must have looked like right cunts as we could hardly carry the fuckers though luckily the tram and shop were close by. We made 4 trips until we were satisfied we had the best things. It turned out to be a great little earner. It was mid-winter, so after getting a great price from two English guys that flew over to buy them, Brian, me and me Dutch girl fucked off to Tenerife.

The holiday didn't go too well as the Dutch girl was being a pain in the neck all the time and certainly wasn't the happy-go-lucky soul I had been getting visits from. She was constantly nagging about the burglary we had done because I'd said I'd try going straight. What prisoner doesn't say that eh?

On our return to Holland within a short time she told me she was pregnant, this came as a bit of a bombshell. First a relationship, now a father-to-be! This was all new to me. After getting my head into gear and now being 30, I thought "yeah, maybe its time to sort myself out and get off the merry go round". However as any criminal knows, it's just not that easy to go straight after a life time of crime.

> *I'm reviewing the situation:*
> *Can a fellow be a villain all his life?*
> *Better settle down and get myself a wife.*
> *And a wife would cook and sew for me,*
> *And come for me, and go for me,*
> *And go for me and nag at me,*
> *The fingers she will wag at me.*
> *The money she will take from me.*
> *A misery, she'll make from me...*

FATHERHOOD

So now I'm father to a lovely daughter and I'm proudly showing her off around Amsterdam. Having never been part of society, I now had to learn to fit in with normal people, which was a shock to my system after 30 years of living as a thief. But as I was about to discover, being a dad made me re-evaluate my life big time. Watching my daughter being born and the unconditional love I felt for this little human being brought me right down to earth and the realisation set in that it wasn't all about me any more. But old habits die hard...

I soon found myself loading supermarket trolleys to the brim and walking straight through the exit sign past the tills and into the car park. Saturday was an easy shopping day. I'd drive to the supermarkets on the outskirts of the dam where people had pre-ordered groceries waiting to be delivered to them and they would all be lined up ready to be loaded in vans. I would just pick the one I like the look of and put it straight into my boot.

My daughter's maternal grandparents, being Dutch Jewish, had decided that, just in case another Hitler appeared on the scene in the near future, Jasmine was going to be christened a Catholic. So I went straight into what I thought was the biggest church in Amsterdam only to find out that it's a cathedral, the priest telling me that they didn't do baptisms in there, they're done in the local church. Me being me I liked the look of the place, and decided "No, this is where I want my daughter baptised" so spoke to the priest. After quoting the big book to him I told him my name was Mark Peter Paul going on in great length to tell him how much of a devout Catholic my mother was but that she wasn't that well and her last wish was seeing her only granddaughter baptised before she left Holland. "She always comes here to the cathedral to pray whenever she is here," I added.

He still wasn't convinced so as my last card I told him that

Jasmine's mother and maternal grandparents were Jewish – that seemed to get his attention. "Send your mother in tomorrow and we can have a chat" he said straight away. Bingo, we're in, I thought.

So now I have to explain to my mother that the Priest wants to see her and that I'd explained that she was such a devout catholic that the cardinal wants to see her for the Spanish Inquisition. The following day a nervous mother went in to see him and within 20 minutes came out with the biggest grin I'd ever seen. What a result! My Jasmine was getting baptised in a cathedral where they don't even do christenings, that's the Dutch for you.

The night before the big day my mother, DB (Dutch bird) and me were having a nice drink in this famous posh American hotel bar on the Liedesplein when DB decided that she wanted to take my mother to a rave. She would have gone too if I'd not objected. Anyway after what I thought was banter, the missus takes us seriously and starts pointing saying "I wasn't taking your mother to no fucking rave". Things got heated and I'm pointing my finger at the missus and she takes a grip of my finger with her teeth and clamps down hard and wouldn't let go. I wanted to hit her but couldn't. I'm in such pain I thought I was about to faint just as she let go to my relief. After half an hour the tension eased and I asked her for a kiss and let's make up, what else could I do, my poor mother was mortified. As our lips met I couldn't believe it, she actually now clamps her teeth into my lip leaving me looking a right sight at the christening the following day. As you can tell, she wasn't the shy and retiring type!

The next day in the cathedral at 10.30am all was going well although Colin hadn't shown up yet. The entrance was at the side of the building not the front, so who goes "Bang! Bang!" on the front door but our Colin, half way through the christening. It could only be one of two people The Devil or our Colin! Then again when we finally get out after the service, Colin looked like the devil. He'd been out all night and was still pissed. We got ourselves to the nearest pub, the Luxembourg Café, to wet the baby's head, then carried the party on back at home.

We'd only just had our daughter but my relationship with

DB was already tough going. As we all know, there are no hills in Holland but to me it seemed that I had the biggest mountain to climb to try and keep this relationship going for the sake of my daughter. I was 30 now and felt it was the right thing to do, especially knowing what it's like to not have a dad around while you're growing up. I wanted to be a part of my daughter's life. So I was determined to stay around but with the type of guys I hung around with and the things I did for a living, it wasn't going to be easy. Although when the going was good, it was very good. When it was bad it was only just a bit better than being locked up.

Whenever I hit a hard patch and the chips were down the pressure mounted and I started to get stressed feeling trapped and pressured after being free as a bird all my life. I had a big reaction to responsibility and trying to adapt to being a family man.

FAMILY GUY

After such a carefree life it comes as no surprise I found it hard to adjust to family life to say the least. Although I was proud to be a parent I just couldn't fit into a normal life style I felt a bit out of my depth with it all. It didn't help that Colin, who had been locked up since I'd been out, was now getting married to a German girl he had met while inside.

Almost everyone else I knew had moved away from Amsterdam, not because of the police pressure just simply due to the fact that jibbing wasn't worth it anymore, they all mainly got themselves off to Spain as dealing was the in thing now not thieving – thieving had seen better days as now all the tills and safes had daft checks inside with hardly any cash at all, whereas just a few years before it had all been cash. Credit cards and pin code machines had taken over; it just wasn't worth going out jibbing, although I knew nothing else to be honest.

I tried dealing Charlie in the bars in town but that wasn't me, plus with all the time spent out you would spend what you were earning and end up rotten drunk most of the time. I couldn't justify being out 24/7 with the money I was bringing home, so I went out jibbing solo again which never bothered me but it had gone on that long I was bored with it all, I found it all too much and just a year and half after my release I went on what I'd call a self-destruction mission. I hardly bothered coming home, instead I was hitting the town and for the first time ever I started going on major drinking sessions not knowing what day it was or where I'd been at times. Then, following all the drinking, I started fighting people for no reason whatsoever. I can recall that half the fights were over nothing, I'd wake up some mornings not even knowing I'd had a fight till I looked in the mirror and would see myself; eyes all swollen, hands bloodied and sore with bruises all over my body from the scraps.

Family Guy

When the missus asked what I'd been up to, I honestly couldn't tell her, as I genuinely couldn't remember.

Luckily it all come to a head when I got a massive beating one night; I was getting into a taxi, I was with a scouse lad I had recently met called Stigger who needed a taxi too, so I let him go in the first one that turned up at the rank as he was with his missus. I wish I hadn't - the next taxi pulled up and just as I was about to climb in some guy jumped into the front passenger seat, the cheeky cunt I thought.

Before he could close the door I started to punch the fucker repeatedly, again I wish I hadn't, I never saw the other two guys that were getting into the back of the cab! Bish bash bosh crash bang wallop! I got a right old hiding, again being so drunk I just took it all in my stride, you win some you lose some, I don't even recall how I got home that night either.

The next morning I was awoken by my missus with the usual "where you been, who you been with, what time did you get back" questions, Fuck me I put a morning cigarette in my mouth and it felt all weird I couldn't feel anything I had lost the front row of my top teeth - I felt and looked a right mess. I felt even worse when I had to borrow money to get new ones fitted from my new mother in law!

A few weeks passed then one night me and K'ob were in a bar where a mate worked, as we were walking out we passed a typical six foot Dutch guy, then faintly heard our mate from behind the counter "oh fuck not you again". The guy was after money that was owed, the Dutch guy had his back to me so I simply jumped on his back dragging him to the floor - he was a fucking monster and hard work, he fell on top of me and I couldn't move, the best I could think of doing was putting my finger right into the fucker's eyes. This worked a treat and I managed to get out from underneath him. Then, I don't know how but I was stood outside the bar telling K'ob I didn't feel well and I must have hurt my ribs when the guy had landed on my chest, K'ob told me I didn't look well either and was turning blue, I remember saying I'll be ok and that I'd get the tram home, he wasn't having any of it and got us both a taxi telling me something was right. On arrival at the hospital, I told them that my ribs were killing me, the doctor straight away must have known something I didn't, as I'd been stabbed in the back and had a punctured lung!

"Hey, Kev," I joked "I'd have woken up dead if I'd got on that tram before eh!"

We never knew it but while I was fighting the guy, his bird had stabbed me in the back plus what I never saw was Murphy had gripped her hand that was holding the blade and stabbed the Dutch guy using her hand so it transpired he had got stabbed by his own girlfriend! I was put into the waiting ward/room when low and behold whose lay right next to me? Only the fucking guy from the fight, sod's law. We just blanked each other as we both needed medical attention. You couldn't make this shit up. The old bill didn't even turn up as should happen with any stabbing even though they must have known what had happened. This all happened on my 32nd birthday too.

After what seemed like a lifetime I was finally fit again and I gave up on the stupid fights as I had sobered up now and was back on planet earth. This was about the longest time I spent at home with my daughter and missus to be honest.

Colin was locked up at this time but sent word that he was getting married to a social worker he had met while in Oldenburg prison in Germany. I had never even been to any wedding until now and typically it would be in a fuckin jail... Not even a normal wedding for the likes of us lot!

A few months later Colin had been moved and his wife to be had sacked her job so the judges couldn't stop it from going ahead.

When I turned up for this wedding visit, her first request was not to give him any hash and the second was not to ruin her big day... The visit was at a semi-open jail so was lax security wise. I soon gave our kid the first of three chunks of Amsterdam's finest, the prison was allowing us one bottle of alcohol free wine to drink plus a Chinese takeaway, they even let us both go to the toilet where I gave Colin the other two pieces to plug! Hi ho happy days, the new wife never knew so that was my job done, Colin still had half a year to serve yet, so I knew he needed hash to barter with, let alone to smoke. Plus I never knew for certain that I could visit again. Alas it would be to help his mates escape from prison.

LIFE AT HOME

Living with me could never be easy with all the mis-fits I knew coming and going - I would get caught between the two sides of my life; the graft and the family guy. The latter was fine as long as I was earning. When I wasn't earning I'd have to go grafting with whoever was about and there weren't many grafters knocking about anymore; Colin was married and when he got out he had to be at home more and more, problem is money never comes knocking at the door you've got to go and find it.

Another problem was that the Mancs who did come over always wanted to be put up rather than get a hotel/flat of their own. Me being me I always said they could stay, thinking it would be for a few days, it never was though, this used to put a big strain on an already fragile relationship.

"Who's he? Why can't he get a hotel? How long's he staying?" the missus would ask and I could never give an answer to such questions, and the only way to get them to move on was by earning but this was getting harder and harder as time went on.

As an example, once I went across the road from where we lived and saw that a driver had left his car running, I was putting someone up at the time and he'd been at ours about a week, I ran upstairs "quick Tony I've seen a Golf just outside the flat with the engine running. Get off yer backside and go get it, park it round the corner or anywhere... go go go!" He did as asked and was back at mine ten minutes later, "What you doing back here, you got a car now, get out an earn now innit mate yer on yer own pal! I'll meet you tomorrow at Schipol."

"What do you mean I thought we were grafting together."

"Well United are playing tomorrow in the final at Rotterdam, go into town and find someone else mate, I can't you see I'm a family guy here. I'm trying me best to do right with you all week and I can't do no more for you can I?"

Renno came to stay once – he was there for about a week until he came home one night, though not even with me, but before me! The missus wasn't happy when I came home, she wanted him out and woke him up abruptly by half beating him up with his thick leather coat.

The next thing Colin was staying and brought some drunken idiot with him, I never wanted this guy to stay myself but gave in to our kid's request, I was woken up by my DB who was tightly gripping my hand, I knew that obviously something wasn't right, I look over to see this guy having a piss in our bedroom cupboard!

Then when I've jumped up and started yelling at him to get the fuck out the room, he starts mumbling that my bird is fit and he's getting into bed with her! Bang! I twatted him (to wake him up more than anything!)

"Get the fuck out you Yorkshire bastard", the commotion then wakes our Colin up.

"What's going on Marcus?"

"He's outta here Colin, that's what!"

"It's too late in the night, where's he gonna go?"

"Like I give a shit! You go with him for all I care!"

Colin, more in self-interest then callously, slung the guy out without a care in the world.

An Irish guy was staying once. "I'll just go to the car and get my stuff yeah" he says. When he came back he started unpacking his toiletries. There was nothing unusual about that but he only got out a pair of fucking slippers to put on! The missus and me just gave each other that look that says, he's gotta go!

Once the bell rang around midnight, it was K'ob with a scouse lad. They had been pushing a supermarket trolley containing a fucking huge locker/safe they had just robbed from a bar, we got it open after a full night hacking away at the hinges till it was prized open, with the contents liberated we had to get rid of the safe. That was easy enough as there was a canal just over the road; no worries we tipped the fucker from the trolley only to find it didn't sink but it stuck on a mud bank and was still visible for the next few months until it was removed by whoever – looking at it every day did my missus's head in...

The best one of all has to be when I came home one day and my Moroccan neighbour, who usually let on to me and was friendly enough, gave me the biggest 'fuck-off' stare ever, I shrugged it off at first without much thought then went inside. DB told me why he looked so solemn, the guy had opened his front door that morning only to see someone he thinks was me, drunk out of my skull pissing up his fuckin door!

This had to be put right quickly, firstly by finding a photo of myself with our Colin together on it, then having to knock on his door - it wasn't easy but I had to try my best telling him it wasn't me and just hoping he would see it wasn't, plus I got a mop and bucket and cleaned up the mess. He just shrugged his shoulders and gave me his meanest look and disappeared inside. We never ever said hello again after that, fuck knows what he must have thought as I don't think he even knew what I was trying to tell him, as I was half cut too!

The list of 'crimes' was endless. How she ever put up with it all still amazes me to be honest. Though one funny thing was that since I'd been out about three or four years by now, the only cars we had been driving around in were all stolen, she was naively shocked when she found that one out. The only upside for her was when we copped for a good parcel of jewels she always chose something for herself. I've often wondered then and now why women meet guys in prison and are disappointed as to why we ain't like everyday normal folk!

About the only normal thing we had going for us were our holidays at a campsite at Egmond aan Zee, it was only an hour's drive from Amsterdam so the summers were sorted for getting away from it all - much to DB's relief.

Although sometimes I would even ruin the holiday by going out solo. With little cash I couldn't just sit around, I had to go out and at least try to get a bit of money, I never even thought of a real job once. Looking back it was a joke; graft had taken over my life without me knowing it.

I had started to play Sunday football. As I said earlier the Mancs were a dwindling force now and the new kids on the block were all from Liverpool. Stigger, a Scouse lad I knew, had been playing for a team for years, most of the team were pure characters; Paddy owned the Blarneys pub in town, Ricardo was a snooker hall owner and goalkeeper but spent most of the game doing business on his new mobile phone. Our centre forward, Ricardo's partner, sponsored the team; he was shit at football but as he owned it nobody said owt, he only ever scored if the ball hit him and went in rather than him hit the ball! This guy would honestly fly to Holland from fuck knows where just to play every week he was that loaded.

Just before kick off the team talk would usually be what time we all got home and who had got the most sleep the night before, hardly anything about tactics for the game. Either way, not one player held down a real job; I don't think there was a day's work in any of us.

All the other teams we played, especially the Turkish teams, would go all out to prove they were hard, us being English we got stereotyped as Brit hoolies, mind you to look of us all lined up at kick off, they weren't wrong, They wouldn't/didn't know we all looked rough from the night before but we did.

Most games got stopped, as the refs would lose the plot as the games got rougher and rougher. More than one ref ran from the field half crying they got so much stick from the players but the truth was that was usually from the opposition, not us! Either way I loved all the games and DB was getting along fine with Stigger's missus. We also took our daughter as there were always other kids with all the 'Mobwags' that attended. Being more or less a solo grafter now, I went full circle and went back robbing clobber to sell to all the lads in the bar afterwards then on to the goalie's snooker hall to watch whatever games were on Sky Sports. Most of the lads were dealers of some kind but the life I knew dealing wasn't on my list of things to do, so long as I brought food money to the table at home I was happy.

Well for the time being I was...

Family Guy

★

I'd got to know a scouse lad (Joe Pesci) who had only recently just got out of jail in Holland for armed robbery. The failed robbery was televised live on Dutch TV! He knew two lads that wanted ecstasy. Unlike back in the UK these E's still worked as opposed to E's in the UK that were getting cut with god knows what. So people were still coming over to buy parcels. We travelled to Rotterdam and sorted it all with no hassle, on the way back we dropped a tab each, more to see if they worked than anything else. We took the exit off the motorway onto the Halfweg and we were soon hemmed in by three unmarked cop cars. They dragged us out of the car and threw us both to the floor. They were all hyped and armed to the teeth shouting "weapons where are the guns where are they? Where?" all the time pointing guns at us.

I'd been arrested a fair few times before but to say this felt different was an understatement. As we were lay on the floor they seemed to enjoy trampling all over us and giving out a fair few digs just for good measure.

I remember thinking they'd arrested the wrong people here as I'd never even had a gun but then this dreaded thought came over me "what if the Scouser had bought guns on the sly?"

We were loaded into vans and driven to Marnixstraat Police station, still getting roughed up during the journey then dumped into different cells on our arrival. As I sat in mine, I started feeling the effect from the E we'd necked earlier, after a few hours of tripping, I wished I hadn't taken it, even more so as I was brought out for questioning again. The old bill kept going on about fucking guns, it turns out they had followed us to Rotterdam and back thinking we were buying guns not drugs plus the fact there was a G7 political meeting going on in Amsterdam so we had attracted the anti-terrorist squad!

These guys were out of my league and not for the first time on the interview I asked for a cigarette but didn't get one, so I'm saying nothing - they have my passport with my real name on, British visitors passports had just been taken out of circulation, I was then manhandled roughly back to the cell. I was up all night because of the ecstasy and had nothing to do but nurse a massive bump on my napper wondering what the fuck was happening. I'd only given him a lift to get some shitty E's and now we've got the anti-terrorist squad all over us!

Next morning, and much to my relief, the cell door was opened by a normal looking copper wearing a blue uniform – the burly old bill from the night before were nowhere to be seen thank fuck. We were told we were being charged with having five thousand tablets that had been found and as daft as it sounds I was massively relieved, as it meant the Scouser hadn't had guns in the car. There was no more gun talk, thank fuck.

Later that day I was taken up before the Judge in charge of our case and told we were to be charged with the drugs found in the car.

"What drugs?" I answered innocently as always.

"You were driving so the drugs are yours, yes?"

"I know nothing about drugs" I replied clearly.

Either way we were all remanded in Amsterdam's Belmeer jail until they completed their inquiries.

I got word from my scouse mate a few days later that we had been overheard by old bill in a pub just before we left on our little trip to Rotterdam saying the fucking lot should be shot, meaning all the politicians we had seen in some hotel earlier on. The Dutch old bill must have been everywhere that day mingling with the populace and had heard us chatting away! This was why we had been followed. Just bad luck on our part being overheard having a laugh about shooting politicians. Plus Amsterdam's punks had been rioting all that day against the G7 meeting, which didn't help us one bit, as the cops and security service were jittery anyway.

Our case came up three months later and the only defence we had was that the police had made an illegal stop and search but not surprisingly that fell on deaf ears and we were duly sentenced to two years. I wasn't that fussed plus, as every crimmo knows, now and then a break is needed. I was fucking knackered from my lifestyle and needed a lie down plus I've always had the mindset that prison is just a criminal health farm. As long as the sentence ain't too long that is!

I had no problem getting my hash in on visits from DB plus I was lucky and always had canteen money so I just plotted up watching telly content doing nothing. Then one day, around four months into my sentence, my cell door was opened up with a group of prison guards all stood there "we have had a meeting about you Blaney, you must work, you cannot just stay in your cell all the time it isn't healthy for you."

"Wow, hang on a minute. If I could work I wouldn't be in fucking prison in the first place would I?"

They all chuckled and disappeared, two days later they were back, "would you be interested in the cleaner's job on the landing? Just one thing the other prisoners might not be happy, as you haven't worked or been out of your cell in months, so would you work with all the others for a week or two and we'll give you our word you can become the cleaner." True to form they kept their word plus I was lucky as I only did three days work and was switched to cleaner, now I'd gone from pure lock up to being out of my cell all day. A few of the locals were gutted I'd landed the job as I wasn't Dutch but there you go that's Holland for you.

I had got to know a professional hockey player from Canada who had been arrested for smuggling cocaine into Holland hidden inside his hockey sticks, what a character he was! I used to keep lookout while he went into the showers smoking a crack pipe whenever he could!

Between us we had befriended one of the guards who wouldn't have looked out of place as a prisoner himself, I'm still amazed the prison even employed him to be honest. On Christmas Day I'm just relaxing smoking a wee spliff and drinking the alcohol free beer that you could buy at the canteen (the beer not the spliff), when I hear a tap on my cell door and the little hatch opened. All I could see was the friendly screw's big black hands appear holding a chunk of hash and a small bottle of liquid which turned out to be vodka and orange "Blaney Happy Christmas! Enjoy man! This is from Canadian John." This friendly screw made my sentence as easy as it could get, with all the perks I had going on. Looking back it was quite surreal really.

One morning the friendly screw came to my cell asking did I have a razor, as he needed to sort himself out with a shave after being up all night smoking coke with the now recently released Canadian John.

As cleaner I had to be first out to make coffee for everyone, so now I'm a prisoner acting as lookout for a prison guard while he washes up and sorts him himself out in my cell! Talk about double-Dutch! I witnessed the friendly screw slowly developing a coke habit all because of Canadian John who soon had him wrapped round his little finger while supplying most of the prison no doubt. These were yet more surreal moments courtesy of life behind bars in Amsterdam's finest hotel - Belmeer HVB (House of Detention).

During one visit from my DB I had the feeling that things weren't right between us as she looked more than fed up with the weekly visits plus the smuggling in of hash as she had to be searched every time she came in, it was obviously getting too much for her. I went back to my cell to ponder on the visit and decided to call it a day the next time she came to see me. I was thinking I was doing the right thing for both of us and also thought it would be poetic justice for her as we did meet in jail five years earlier and it would give the poor girl her freedom back. So next time I saw her I just blurted out "since we met in jail we may as well part in jail as I haven't even made a go of going straight one little bit since my last release have I?" Much to my astonishment and not to my liking at all, she fucking agreed! She looked made up and relieved! She went from Miss Miserable to Miss World in the blink of a fucking eye. She was so made up she even agreed she would still visit me with my hash and cash every week!

Canadian John came to visit me soon after, "did I know a guy from Manchester called so and so and was he a trusted grafter?" To which I answered in the affirmative to both, he then slipped me a nice chunk of hash, got up and went on his merry way saying if all went well I'd get a drink from it all. I never got time to ask 'all what?'

This just left me pondering on the fastest visit I'd ever had as he was off as quickly as he could, and ghosted out.

True to her word DB kept visiting and we seemed to be getting along better than before, our daughter was six years old now plus DB had been offered a nice house with a garden, anyway we decided to give it another go. I only had a short while to go and for Jasmine's sake it was worth it, I'd been speaking to her on the phone and telling her I was building a fucking motorway from Germany to Holland and the job would take just over a year, being only six she believed me, (what kid wouldn't!) we never considered her visiting me as neither of us wanted that for her.

When arrested I'd been carrying one of them big daft ten year blue passports which was a good ten years out of date as the good old visitors ones had been taken out of circulation in 1995. Having never been arrested with one before, I told myself maybe it was this reason for a gate release that I'd been told about, not deported as usually happened, which made me a bit suspicious. In England that normally meant a gate arrest by the police, although I had nothing to worry about as it was just DB waiting outside wearing her usual characteristic frown, then it was off to town. We went strait to the Star pub just opposite the Flying Dutchman for a tasteful pint of 'ye old Amstel lager' and after staring at each other over a semi silent kinda prison visit, both of us seemed to be thinking 'are we doing the right thing?'

SKIN DEEP

#Many people, tell you that they're your friend#

Not long after getting out I went to see the friendly guard to find out where Canadian John was, as I was looking for the finder's fee that was mentioned at our last meeting back in the jail. Lo and behold they're both smoking from a crack pipe sat in a darkened room. Beside the two of them there were other people in the room, half of whom had been locked up at the same time as me. Everyone was smoking crack, it was just surreal. The last time I'd been amongst these lot they'd all looked healthy. Now they all looked drawn out with grey faces all whispering and searching for lighters that were needed for the pipes. It was evident that my so-called drink from John through meeting and working with the Manc lad had literally gone up in smoke.

★

A lad from Manchester came to Brian's gaff one day and managed to talk his way in to the flat, the cheeky cunt then dragged little Bri around the gaff before tying him up and burning the poor guy with a soldering iron all over his body while demanding money. He didn't stop until he got what he wanted, which was hidden inside Brian's couch.

Brian ended up tied to a chair with severe burns to his arms, legs and feet. The guy disappeared never to be seen again. Luckily some mate had called and found him after two days sat there freezing yet burning from his wounds! Fucking taxers were ever-present, it was just too hard to tell friend from foe.

To make up his losses Brian went to South America to get some cocaine. Having swallowed the pellets he boarded the plane where it refuelled in the USA, only the flight was delayed due to weather, which would mean more time in his stomach/belly. After the plane finally took off and with fours hours to go before it would land in Frankfurt, Brian's belly starts bubbling - he needed a loo pronto!

I swear - just as quick as they came out, he was washing them and sending them back to where they came. He had the cabin staff worried by his regular trips to the toilet, and eventually they got suspicious. The staff's body language told Brian to get back on the toilet ASAP and unload what he could, then on landing he shadowed off to the toilet and did the same again. By the time the old bill took him away he was found to have 200 grams still inside him, he received three and a half years. Even though on this occasion he got nicked, he was one of the bravest smugglers I ever knew and did everything everywhere from A to Z. He even did jail in Pakistan when he was seventeen. He learnt the language and still goes into the lingo whenever he gets the chance. Eventually Brian would move to India permanently - what a rum fucker! He had the nickname 'Dangermouse' as he is only five foot two!

While Brian was doing his sentence, a so-called mate of his came to see me asking if I fancied taking a parcel to some place over a certain border, obviously Brain would get a drink out of it (as it was Brian's contact in the first place). Okay, I chipped in, I knew a border but I needed him on such a bridge at such a day/time. The reason I wanted him there was that I had to walk over customs, so if I was pulled I wanted him to see that I had slung the lot over the bridge into the rapid running river underneath, otherwise if I lost it without a witness I'd be in debt for the shit. He reassured me he would definitely be there, no problem.

A few days later and after a gruelling drive worrying about what I was carrying, as it was normally just weed not powder, I'm sat in the pub overlooking the border and I can't see the fucker anywhere. Local people crossed this border all the time, as it was a little twin village with just the one pub between them. I was just going to walk over mingling with a few people after closing time, simple.

I phoned the guy, "What the fuck, where are you? You said you'd be here?"

"Hey man you're there now, I can't make it. I thought the meet was tomorrow…" which was bullshit, "…can't you just walk through, I'll pay for the taxi?"

"Get to fuck you cheeky Geordie fucking twat! I'm taking the lot back home, you can pick it up when you get to mine, plus I want paying, you fucking cowardly lazy bastard."

So much for people's friends!

I got back in my car and drove another gruelling fucking journey all the way back, although I had to laugh at myself when I crossed the border, I must have been the only smuggler bringing drugs into Holland as opposed to taking them out!

Typical!

★

With the graft now at an end, I started dealing. You would always have to be on your guard when serving up Brits that came over, as you couldn't ever let a buyer meet the dealer or you would be out of the frame as soon as you were out of earshot, they would bypass you altogether and you would be dropped in the blink of an eye.

A few weeks down the line you would see them together, coming out with every excuse they could think of as to why you weren't *in* anymore.

Another downside to it all was the never-ending waiting game, sat at tables looking down at three or four mobile phones waiting for a call. Then, if and when they did ring, it would be "sorry mate tomorrow", "next week", "oh we changed our minds", "we don't want that anymore, we want the other" or "oh it's too expensive".

On many occasions you would find that your profit somehow had been tied up in some fucking dodgy excursion, always the same, "your money will be doubled mate". It was always the same story "oh you'd never guess what happened that deal went sour, everyone was arrested, sorry mate the money's gone". Yeah sure it had you sneaky twats! The drug world wasn't for me, I hated it with every bone in my body and always will. I'd spend days in some shady gaff packing kilo upon kilo of weed or cocaine or speed into vacuumed bags to be transported somewhere and they'd never arrive only to be told the same story, "sorry mate your wages were on the transport that vanished into thin air". Surprise! Surprise! It was always the same story and I was getting really fucked off with this life and being told Walter Mitty stories.

Eventually I got myself involved in smuggling skunk to certain destinations, going over different borders to supply the Brit contractors as there were plenty that loved a smoke.

We all knew the perfect places to cross the Grenz border, plus it was active graft again and not as static as waiting around in Amsterdam. The weed wasn't easy to hide because of its bulk. Usually it was just a case of filling the car boot up and hoping for the best. I would arrive at the destinations with a huge relief, as the car would stink to fuck and just having to unwind your window down would be a giveaway to any old bill if stopped. Luckily we had a scouse lad on hand to offload it all, then I'd have to wait a few days till I got paid, this work was simple and would see me through the next few years with no problems.

All in all it was best for me to just trust myself and stay out of dealing in the Dam, as you couldn't trust a soul. After a while we got lazy and mistakes were made, we started giving credit out and not bothering to go after it all, this led to disaster after disaster with all the excuses coming our way over the phone. On one such occasion I get the usual tale of woe, "You'll never guess what happened to that parcel? Some Russian guy owes us so much cash and ain't paying. Another guy owes us in another town, plus his partner's been nicked…"

Reno was in charge but had lost his focus and we were struggling getting our money back. To us, he was just laying weed out to every Tom, Dick and Harry. In Reno's mind it would all be sorted, it was just a matter of time, they would always pay in the end but we knew it was all going pear-shaped. Reno may have had time but we didn't as it had been credited to us in the first place, so we had to start getting the money back some how.

My scouse mate and me decided to get a guy we knew called Bob. He knew he could sort out the Ruskie for us. This Bob was the hard as nuts stereotype character – an East Ender from London.

He was more than up for it and told us he was made up, as he hated the fucking Russian anyway. Then Reno said he wasn't happy saying he will pay and that there was no need for violence.

Then Bob calls me. "Marco, I've got this facking cant here with me now I'm in a phone box with him," I could hear the kicks and blows going in.

Suddenly there's someone else on the line "Marc, it's Reno. What the fuck man! Bob's lost it."

I wasn't very concerned and could be heard chuckling to myself. I then asked "has the Ruskie twat paid yet?"

"Bob's got the phone cable and he's strangling him with the fuckin' cord now Marc, this is getting a bit heavy man". Two days later Bob got the money owed, Reno wasn't happy and thought it was all a bit over the top and he was convinced the Russians were coming to get us! We never heard a thing though, so with a clean sheet, we started grafting the weed, speed and Charlie again. Happy days!

One guy had my scouse mate and me visit where he was grafting the weed, the three of us had been owed money for too long so we loaded up a boot full of skunk and drove there. We were just driving into the town and the police were just putting down what must have been their last cone on the road (probably for drink drivers as it was late) our hearts went up a fair few notches I can tell you, as it was a right Nazi shit hole. Next thing, we go and see the guy who owes us money thinking it would be nothing more than a simple pick up.

"Oh by the way I've told them you've driven from Amsterdam and you're known to carry guns and gangster stuff," says this other guy.

Gobsmacked I snarled, "You having a fuckin laugh or what?"

I wouldn't mind but the guy telling us this was bigger than me and my scouse mate put together, he was just a gentle giant.

All talk...

I was now in two minds whether we should even enter the pub. Thoughts of getting shot at were going through my mind.

Inside the pub was a bit Nazi looking for my liking; Needless to say it went the opposite way to how we imagined it, the meeting was with some mad looking skinhead, who only ends up being a Brit from Stoke. He just coolly handed us a wad of cash and started pouring out as many schnapps as we could drink, he even took the weed we had arrived with. The shit about guns and stuff was a nasty wind up by the humourless Scouser.

Another time I was sat at a table in Amsterdam with around ten lads and three times that amount of phones on the fuckin table. One lad gets a text "so and so has been nicked, transport's gone". No one mentioned him getting a solicitor or any other help, just nothing, no sympathy at all from us, it was just another day at the office. For those in the top tier, donkeys were ten a penny. Then a dozen mobile phones went into the nearest canal real rapido!

Many so-called dealers would have probably got rich by ripping someone else off, somewhere or other, then bigging it like he was the real deal, while some poor cunt is probably looking all round Europe for their cash back. Some guys would play around with the cash they were supposed to be guarding, doing double deals with other people's money.

One guy I knew needed money getting back to Holland and was asking if any one knew of someone?

"No trouble, I can do that, no worries," some bloke said.

Unbeknown to the guy, the cash would probably go via Turkey, then was put into a shady deal before arriving to Amsterdam, then he had to pay for someone transporting the cash over as a final insult. So long as it wasn't England, I never minded the so-called donkey jobs, so long as I got paid I preferred it solo and it never bothered me driving ten hours to some place on the map.

By now I knew nearly all the best routes to take through Western Europe. I'd had years of practice on the borders, best to trust yourself, innit. Then a car that I foolishly lent out once to a scouse lad I knew, Paul (Bambi), never showed up one night. I thought nowt about it at the time. After three days he came to see me. He had let Donnie drive my car because he didn't know the streets like him, then they both got a pull from the dibble. Donnie was still in the police station, as was my car.

We had by now convinced each other the police didn't deport people anymore because of the Schengen Treaty. Fuck it, I thought, I'd go and get it back. I hadn't been in trouble or anything in ages, so in I walk, half pissed, asking "can I have my car back," even though the motor was on false plates. I was asked for ID, I handed over my passport to the plod at the desk. Tapping away on his computer, I got that stare; the same one I had seen umpteen times before. Then I heard the door just behind me click open, I turned round to see two dibble smiling. "Mr Blaney, this way alstublieft (if you please)" then I was led to a cell, right next to fucking Donnie! After two days Donnie was deported, I was left wondering when I would be interviewed or told why I was being kept in the station. Eventually I was told I would get deported but I had to wait one more day. When I asked what the deportation was about or why they just chuckled "ja daroom manier" meaning simply 'because'.

So much for the so-called Schengen Treaty and the rules adopted under them. In 1999 the Amsterdam Treaty provided opt-outs for only two EU member states: Ireland and the United Kingdom!

The days of being deported by boat had long since ended, as it was planes now. The Dutch old bill love any chance to go fast so no surprise I was driven at full speed (as always) and taken to Schipol Airport. As I was getting put on the plane I saw a copper give one of the stewardesses a big brown envelope; fuck knows what the old bill had said to her. Soon as we landed I decided to approach the same stewardess and smilingly asked for my envelope and without hesitation she handed it over.

I ripped it open going down the stairs and flew into the first toilet I saw. Flushing and tearing all the Dutch papers down the toilet, keeping hold of my passport and what little cash I had and my shoe laces which were in the envelope too, I put them on as quickly as I could, then walked out to join the queue for passport control.

Thinking there would be a copper at the plane by now looking for a deportee. I got through passport control with no problem, but then customs stopped me. Why me? Well I was the only passenger with no fuckin luggage that's why.

I told him I'd just flown in from Amsterdam. "Lost all my things! Stolen! The lot has gone."

I was told to wait while he "went to check things out".

"You lying bastard, you've just been deported," he said when he returned.

"Okay, so it happens, What's next?" I asked.

"Since passport control let you through, you can go."

2OOO AD

With the never-ending cycle of crime going on, it was safe to say I was seldom home, when I was home I'd be shattered from travelling or I'd be cradling a massive hangover due to the fact I'd been out the night before, as you have to be out and about to earn money, it just doesn't knock on your door does it?

Life just wasn't the same, it was all leading downwards, even boring me to be honest and I didn't care for it anymore, it was one hell of a headache to DB I knew that much.

I'd just got back from watching the treble in Barcelona and Jasmine was out playing one day, just me and DB were sat there with not much to say, I blurted out that without Jasmine in the room we never had anything to say anymore, we had never really had a great relationship anyway, So thinking about the way things were heading I decided to jump ship before having to walk the plank as it were. She had that relieved look again from back on our last prison visit four years earlier. I remember two things she said that stay in my mind: that she preferred me in prison, as at least she knew where I was and she didn't have to worry about me in there. Oh and she would gladly send a big bunch of flowers to the next woman who would put up with me in the future!

I decided to end my days in Holland and return to see my daughter as and when I could. Graft as I knew it was over, I couldn't get into the drug dealing world. Dealers and me weren't from the same crime book, it seemed clear to me that I'd actually trust a thief over a dealer any day of the week and that's saying something.

Jibbers, thieves, pickpockets and ticket touts are now seen as old school, they had principles unlike today.

Okay there were some sound guys involved in drugs that I knew but they were few and far between I can tell yer! I was just too trusting with people and easily taken in to be honest.

As regards myself, in my so-called dealing, even DB once said she could do a better job at dealing than me, as I usually always ended up with almost nothing most times. Every now and then I'd end up owing out due to not being paid on time or getting bits of money instead of full whack, so I'd now have to take some money out myself to live on, this all had a knock on effect - debt!

I came from the "honour among thieves" mentality that was now firmly in the past. I'd just had enough of it all, meeting strangers with faceless faces in shady place, at strange times in shady towns. Meeting somebody I never knew but in a way I know type of life; the day of the jibber was gone!

I was still only 40, it was the year 2000, I'd find something else to do but that's another story.

LOOKING BACK

"It was the best of times, it was the worst of times, it was the age of wisdom, it was the age of foolishness, it was the epoch of belief, it was the epoch of incredulity, it was the season of Light, it was the season of Darkness, it was the spring of hope, it was the winter of despair, we had everything before us, we had nothing before us, we were all going direct to Heaven, we were all going direct the other way."

Charles Dickens: A Tale Of Two Cities (1859)

From the mid '70s until the mid '90s Western Europe got well and truly grafted by the travelling Brits, mostly all from the North West!

We had thousands of cities, towns and villages to go at with outlets galore; shops, exhibition centres, fairs, travelling salesmen, sleeping tourists, sleeping truckers. Opportunities on boats, hotels, factories, concert halls and petrol stations, the list was endless.

I can guarantee that almost every one of them would have been visited over the years by some jibber or grafter, without a doubt. I remember years ago when we'd find a place that was 'off the map', and we'd convince ourselves that we were the first grafters to find it and we'd usually be wrong.

Many grafters found their El Dorado and swiftly moved on, investing in swag or drugs. Others didn't but kept on plodding on regardless, after all it was a care-free life; squandering all those ill-gotten gains with an attitude that said "you can't take it with you".

Aside from the all the thieving going on, there was also the good old swag game. In the early days Manchester had its tough firms, run mostly by a family known as the Kavaners, who were the kingpins that grafted concerts all over Europe supplying merchandise for the lads to graft. Most of the Jibbers would attend these concerts/festivals, though more for robbing ticket offices, plus the numerous pubs and bars that were loaded with unattended cash!

The lone grafters that didn't go on the rob as much as us invested in ticket touting. As soon as they were back in Manchester with a nice parcel of drugs or jewellery from abroad it got sold. Then with a few quid in the bank, the rest would be invested in bootleg merchandise.

Everyone kept it tight too, backing up the lads as there tended to be trouble with the security ending up many times with full on mob fights. One firm who hated us with a passion was a German security team who hired biker gangs from all over Europe. It was tit for tat all the way, starting from the punk days right up to the late 90's, for over twenty years it was a roller coaster ride - you had to be on your toes when the fights got heavy, that's for sure.

On one trip to Scandinavia there seemed to be loads of concerts with the prospect of good money to be made but it proved disappointing. The night life was too expensive and from a jibbing point of view the country was far too sparse; it took half a day or more just to get to the next village and even when we did there would be hardly anyone about and we stuck out like sore thumbs. We only ever did well with the petrol stations; they had small safes that we found behind most of the counters but that's all I recall, we only sussed the garages out because we found few towns in the countryside to graft. I just found it took ages to get decent money. Greg and me both sacked going, as one or more times it ended up costing us to be honest.

Amsterdam was our Hotel California ("you can check out anytime you like, but you can't leave") and our favourite HQ in Europe was the Flying Dutchman, finally taken over in the '80s by an old Collyhurst mate called Terry. He even built up a good force of Dutch Reds that still attend Old Trafford through to today, "The Dutch Mancunians" (Jan de Wal MUFC).

Our lot fell in love with the lifestyle there, it was so easy and laid back and the criminal justice system so liberal, it was perfect for us. After a few years we found the Dutch people not only cool but also really down to earth, and after years of robbing them blind I have to admit feeling a tad guilty, as they weren't Nazis either as opposed to the Germans and Swiss.

The truth is they were the biggest hoarders in Europe and should have known better than to not bank their cash. Unfortunately it was liberated from them, making them reconsider their smug and lax attitude.

As for Austria, Germany and Switzerland; we used to joke that if the shopkeepers were old enough then they were definitely Nazis, so it was therefore okay to take their money and jewellery. Switzerland by far deserved that word the most, I even wondered at times if they signed their own Geneva Convention, the smug fuckers!

Spain on the other hand was piss poor but a fantastic place to deal openly and earn a right wad, all the robbed swag we sold went down well; in fact we saw it as doing them a favour as you couldn't get hold of all the latest electronics, especially videos, in the late 70s. Lloret didn't even have one in the whole town! It's nice to know we got accepted and never grassed on; besides we hardly robbed the Spanish, unless it just came our way without trying. Most times that would be lax bar staff or club owners, or on the move at train stations or airports. I know others who made Spain their number one place to graft, and many ended up getting stiff sentences. Their jails can be like dungeons, and you need money to get through it.

★

While writing this book it comes as no surprise that at times I was hardly able to get to sleep after hours digging deep into the memory and getting it all down on paper. There were so many great missions and characters to cover and the overall picture I got every time was us all having not a care in the world. In the early days we had no idea what city or town to aim for and that alone was exciting.

Maggie Thatcher thought it was grim up North and Norman Tebbit told us to get on our bikes and look for work. Well a generation of lads thought "Fuck the bike, we'll get a ferry". We'd jib the rattler or the trams out from the big cities of Europe to the winkle centres and if we had no luck then it was the bus into villages looking for wood and scrap yards, car show rooms and garden centres. After a few years learning our trade it was time to hit the autobahn in our VW vans, Golfs or BMW touring cars. Once safe in Lloret de Mar we'd pull back the sunroof, smell the ganja in the area and blare out some rubber-Dub and UB40. These cars became magnets for the women and opened many doors for us to cop off with the local Spanish darlings.

Saying all that, it's been a task keeping this story upbeat as so many of my friends have ended up in early graves. This was no surprise because of the hedonistic lifestyle, but one thing was for certain; by the year 2000 the jibbing game had run its course, so I finally hoisted up the white flag and called it a day.

My relationship with DB lasted from 1991 to the year 2000. I'd never really settled down to be a family man and have to admit I was hard work. The only reason we stayed together for so long was because of our daughter. I had a good bond with Jasmine, and was a good father but a shit husband. My daughter was the only real thing in my life by this point and it hurt to leave her, although I knew my time was well and truly up. I still deeply regret the fallouts I had with DB in the ten years I was there, and just couldn't settle down to a normal lifestyle. I was hard work and how she put up with me I'll never know.

I'm very lucky to have got through it all, and the most important thing is that I've been able to stay in touch with Jasmine. That truly was worth the effort. After all, it's not all about the money!

STUART

Sadly, just as we were entering the final furlong in publishing this book, we lost one of the authors.

I'd just scanned all the photos and after two years it was finally coming to the stage where Empire were preparing everything to be sent to the printers. So I phoned Stuart with the good news and arranged to meet him in his local boozer. As always when I landed he looked a million dollars and was over the moon to know it would be out soon and he could get back his family pictures. He was going to Stockport to his new girlfriend's, so jumped on the bus into town with me. He couldn't stop saying how much he was buzzing about the book and would have a good session over the weekend. Around 15 minutes later it was my stop, so we had a big, warm hug, bumped fists, and I jumped off.

Sadly, twenty-four hours later, Stuart had died.

Life can be so cruel and yet so rewarding when things are going your way. I just hope his stories remind his family of how loved he was. Having been so close to Stuart I just have to dedicate this book to him.

God Bless Stuart Campbell
RIP

AFTERWORD

Convincing my brother to write a book was always going to be a major task. He must have been thinking doom and gloom trying to follow in the footsteps of my book Grafters, a best seller in 2004. It must be daunting for any first-time writer, thinking they're going to be judged harshly, and the fact is that might happen but he has been up for it, and for that alone you have to give him a squeeze. He had to spend two years getting his stories in order before handing them over to the publisher. It's a tall order what our kid's doing, and I take my hat off to him for sticking with it so long. At times it was hell on earth trying to keep upbeat and focused as Stuart wasn't able to keep up with him due to having a few major health issues mixed in with a crown court case for a fight in the gay village that got ugly. Soon after Marcus said he was thinking of sacking it off, after two years working daily and even taking the day's work to bed with you. But as lady luck would have it Milo publishers asked me if I would ghost-write a project with Hot-Shot, and we began on the story of a little red devil.

What had kept ticking away in the back of my mind over those two long years was the fact that my mother's a really decent writer, having penned pages on local history. We'd both contributed stories about Collyhurst for a book given out to all new pupils at North Manchester schools in 2010, and with that in mind I set about mithering Marcus to write a few pages for Hot-Shot's book. I'm glad to say he soon got the bug and only a few months later he and Stuart both set about writing chapters each for my last book 'The Undesirables'.

I soon realised Marcus didn't need any help with his own writing. The stories are spot on and told from his unique viewpoint. This isn't a rehash of Grafters, Marcus trod his own path around Europe and has his own sense of humour. He had to have being my kid brother…

COCO

There are many special lads mentioned in this book but a quick word about one who was a close friend to me for over 40 years who passed away in 2016. There was no bigger hitter among the grafters than Gary 'Coco' Thompson. He was a true friend, a great guy and it was an honour to have known him so well. Every time I saw him he was dressed to kill, and loved to chat all day long about what street lads love to talk about: football. He said how it's a blag Man City were building more seating areas, as the only time they'd be able to fill them would be on Derby Day, saying "On the other hand, if they sort a deal with McDonald's, the blue noses could buy a burger and get a free ticket for the game". That very same week the latest song sung by United's lads was "If you go down to City's ground, you buy one and get one free" classic Coke.

I first met Coke on the train going to Millwall in 1974. He was sat alone, so I nipped over and got chatting away, and it turned out he'd ran away that very morning from Approved School in Southport to be on this trip. For a young lad determined to get to such an important game he had my respect, plus I loved the fact he was wearing a cherry red Harrington with steel toe cap boots hidden under his brummie pants.

That night game was a fixture the police needed to have control of because of the huge threat of violence. Everyone knew Millwall away could be hairier than a woolly mammoth. After the draw at West Brom on Saturday 14th September it was announced later on radio, then again on the 9 o'clock news, that United's game was to be rearranged and played that coming Monday night. I got the news the next day whilst eating Sunday dinner at my Grandparents', I remember saying to Grandad, "That's taking liberties, such short notice!" Grandad told me some cracking stories about his old man going to one of the most important games in our history, at the end of the 1934 season. Both clubs were at the wrong end of the second division table and the cockneys had the home advantage in a winner takes all game, the loser dropping into the old 3rd Division North or South, a death sentence. Fortunately United won the game 2-0 and rest is history.

Normally after a top Sunday roast I'm ready for the spare room, snoring my bollocks off for a few hours sleeping the booze off. There wasn't a chance that day, I was too worked up, thinking about what lay ahead the next day down in bandit country. I thought I'd best nip to town and see what plans the lads were knocking together. The next day we all met up in the Blackbird café and got bad news; none of the old guard would be able to make it, being much older they held down responsible jobs, and at such short notice there was no chance to jib off work. Not having any top boys was a major blow: no Nutty Norman, Tommy Beard, Crusher, Gaftney, George (Mad Eyes), Big Gibbo or Big Dave from Warrington but it was what it was. It was time to make moves down to the land of jellied eels, light ales and London lunatics by the score.

After five years of hitchhiking up and down dodgy motorways, jibbing coaches and trains, I considered myself a seasoned traveller, proud to be one of the most prolific Red Army youth. On this occasion I totally agreed with the lads, there was no point getting our thumbs out up on that barren Knutsford roundabout. In fact, the only coach going was the team's. Plan B was to hit The Manchester Arms at opening time, neck a few jars of Chester's Mild then soon all the usual banter would be on tap. After an hour we got more bad news; no stolen cars available and not even a hired van to jump in. Plan C was to get the rattler. We were gutted, as Salford Hire Vans were brilliant to get a lift off once they'd parked up on the motorway services. Normally United would have two to four trains booked days before, but that humid night we had just one. As we boarded I remember thinking "Fuck a brick; it's half-empty", with coppers escorting us, no booze and not a chance to jib the train, all having to pay a happy hector. Never mind, on the plus side having so much room meant we could all spread out, soon our carriage was full of snores and farts. We woke up around Rugby with that buzzing feeling inside the stomach, a mix of fear and excitement, the songs started and got louder as we arrived at Euston. It was nice to be greeted by a crew of fellow Reds, and we all bounced round to Euston Square underground. Soon the OB had us all packed onto the tube like sardines, and it became hot as hell taking us a full hour. When we pulled into other stations the police had dogs on big leads swarming all over the platform keeping packs of London's finest thugs offside.

The tube pulled into New Cross and the mob broke into song. We were getting louder all the way up onto the main drag, and the cool night-time air came wafting our way. It was like a shot in the arm, because soon it was time to take in a deep breath, puff out your chest and show them we were here. Fuck the Lambeth Walk, Doc's Barmy Army was akin to a military march, all in tune as one solid pack. We reached Cold Blow Lane, where the name alone could unnerve a person. We were getting plenty of gyp from all the locals outside the pubs, "Fackin' Nawthern Kants!" a few pint pots came sailing over but made no impact on our mob. The area looked so different to the rest of London, proper Jack the Ripper country.

The ground itself should have been called The Dump not The Den. It had one small section of seats, and opposite was what looked like a cow shed with really old dilapidated roofing. Typical of us lot; we came in through the wrong entrance, but luckily once we were in we saw hundreds of lads all packed in behind the goal over to our right, so we made our way over, "safety in numbers" and all that. Talk about speak of the devil, almost as soon as we got to the safety of the mob a war cry went up from scattered units of Treatment thugs as they came charging in from all four sides. The thin blue line of OB managed to split it into smaller groups and diffuse things a bit, so we kept well schtum until half time. I clearly remember being over the moon the score was 0-0. I then walked the plank, jibbing through Millwall thugs to get a much needed pie and drink, it helped me to calm down and get some energy flowing before getting back behind the goal again. The two teams came running out so we sang a song and fellow Reds came back into the fold. We even got a penalty, which Gerry Daley slotted in, yet hardly anyone went berserk like we'd normally do. About ten minutes later a snarling mob converged around us, singing "We're the best behaved supporters in all the land". What a fucking nerve tester that was, catching pure evil looks from old school skinheads and dockers, all making cut-throat gestures, "Fackin' Nawthern bumpkins, we're gonna skin you kants alive!" We gave them V's and managed to stand our ground until the gates opened fifteen minutes before the end. I jibbed off for a slash and noticed every opened exit had small firms hanging about, on the sniff for anyone who looked northern, asking them for the lemon and lime (time). The wrong reply got you dragged offside for a good shoeing, and lots of United fans started to make the classic mistake of trying to jib out early. Even if you jibbed past them it still meant only one thing, "Every man for himself".

Fuck that for a game of soldiers. We linked up with Salford's Little Dessie and co, and a few game Cockney Reds who had stuck with us; Banana Bob, Romford, Sam the Engine and a young Roy Downs, who looked the spit of Michael Jackson. They were saying "Listen lads, plan's simple: just stick together, and whatever happens don't run, if you try to you'll get lost, and their F Troop firm will hunt you down and take liberties. It's best to front them as one unit, and if you go down don't worry as we're willing to all go down together. Easy now lads, don't worry, I'll be sticking to the pack like super-glue". We had a small police escort with a few horses. It had grown dark and you could feel the tension, and no surprise as we came to the very first open corner a Millwall chant went up to charge forward. They even came through the gaps in the horses, landing plenty of punches, and there was no time to think other than return punches and keep moving, staying alert until we were back at the tube station. It felt like a royal result.

Three hundred of us got back into Manchester well after midnight, all agreeing we'd swam the channel getting home in one piece. This was impressive considering me, Dave Willis, and The Ghost were the oldest at 18. Maca McGarry, Rosco, Roy Clarke and the Sunderland Whip were 17. Marshy, Tommy Dunne, Pooley, Boon and B-Burns Syl were all 15. And last but not least there was Coco at a mere 14 years of age. Being known as one of the three hundred over the years got us credit on the terraces, a bit like earning your first stripe in the army. These days it's talked about akin to the three hundred Spartans who took on a full army. I have to laugh, as Coke always said to me "B, if I had a pound for every person who claimed to have been there that night, I'd have a top wedge tucked away."

The next big one in London with Coco was the '77 FA Cup Final against Liverpool, and that win got us back into Europe, somewhere we young ones were itching for. We loved the challenge of jibbing on the continent, and it certainly changed our lives. At the time I had a two bedroomed flat in Hulme with Beverley Ayo; she was a drop dead looker with the same skin tone as Gary, a brilliant dancer who kept the gaff sparkling and always cooked healthy meals, all while working at Castaway Jeans. Coke took the spare bedroom, and I suppose it's fair to say from that point Bev became his surrogate mother. After five cracking years we moved to Rotterdam.

I bumped into Coke at the last Premier league game of the '99 season, a mega important game where we needed to beat Tottenham to get the first trophy in the treble run-in. As always he sorted me out with a cracking seat, and after we won the title he gave me a lift to The Grid's on Barrack Street in Hulme. When we got there, Dicko was saying to John how big the touting game was going to be, and he was spot on. After winning the treble a few months later it was the World Club Cup in Japan. MUFC now ruled the world.

For the next few years touting became on par with working Wimbledon, there was big dosh involved week in week out. Dicko kept getting his fingers burnt on ticket deals, which Coco explained, saying "You'll just get blanked full stop if you're not moving with the right lads and Dicko's City. It's moved up a few gears nowadays, proper dog eat dog." Dicko soon ran the white flag up, moving to Crawley and working with Pim and co in London. "John said his biggest problem were what he called 'S Lads'. These were the inner core of all the firms and each firm had 'S Lads'. They were the backbone of United's firm and loved the thug life, but John was the same stamp as Stuart - he hated bullies and would say, "Why risk going to jail for a punch up with a stranger over football. In his books most inner core lads were too serious and stiff.

The risks are there but you've got to wear the colours at some point. I remember going to a home game against Atletico Madrid in '91. I'd been at my son's passing out in the army the day before and had invited Lee and his army mates to the game. We all met in the Dog and Partridge, and I bumped into Eddie Beef and asked him to keep an eye on the lads while I went touting for five seats in K stand. Beef soon had the lads in stitches telling them about a Cat House in Madrid, where after the game the lads paid top brass a fortune with bent visa cards, even getting them to cook steak and chips, typical Eddie.

Once I'd got the tickets sorted I bumped into The Grid working on Malc's stall outside Lou Macari's chippy. I'd not seen John for a year, so we nipped back into the pub. While we were at the bar ordering a pint someone blurted out "Spread the word lads, we don't wear colours". John put me in the picture, saying that that snide quote was meant for us. It seemed like one of the lads had seen The Grid giving the United swag to my son and his mates, and whoever it was had them down as some kind of weak link within the group. Remember these were the pre-Premiership days, when no foreign firms dared to bring a mob; even the Russians and Eastern Bloc countries would've got a good hiding back in the day, so silly statements like that one just went over my head. I'd heard the same bullshit quotes at the football for over 20 years. "We Don't Run Lads" is a classic; I've seen top lads from all football firms saying it as they're giving it legs themselves!

The next day John said "B, don't you think it's time you stop running with the pack and grow up, Bro". It was a pivotal point in my life as I took on board The Grid's advice. John only ever worked with his Uncle Malcolm on a stall outside the United chippy, and I thought it was a good move keeping it in the family, so today I only ever graft with our kid from a stall we have inside United's fanzone at Red Square. I still see some lads at OT but there's no fist-bumping and chatting about the 70's and 80's, about how exciting it all was. With us all being senior citizens now it makes sense to stay civil, so we just nod or say hello as most times we're out doing our own things graft-wise and need to move on.

John and I agreed touting with heads like that, who can't drop the thug life, was too much like hard work, yet Coco loved the challenge and over the next decade blew them all out of the water. What made him so different was being liked inside the club itself, from the top brass and players down to the car park attendants and the tea ladies. He had all the right connections, never needing to open an office, create a website or hire out rooms in the nearby hotels to sell tickets. Coke did all his business on trust alone. He retired in 2012 having regular holidays in the Caribbean, skiing in the Swiss Alps, lots of shopping trips to Milan and a new Range Rover as soon as the football season ended. Not bad on trust alone.

What really made him stick out from everyone else was his dress sense; even when on the jib up in the alps in the late 70's, where the people were as white as the snow, that was never a problem for him, he had the knack to look a million dollars no matter what. I remember the first time we landed in St Moritz after a few days jibbing around Hamburg in January '78. We stepped down from the rattler onto the platform into crisp snow that covered our desert boots, I swear it came up to ours knees. First thing next day we all paid about 300 Swiss Francs each (which worked out at about £100) for the only sensible footwear you can really wear in those top jolly ski-resorts; those huge, white, furry boots that come up to your knees. As soon as we got home and showed the boots to all the gay hairdressers in Spring Gardens, all of us bar Coco doubled our money, having kept them in mint condition over those hectic five days in the Alps. Come that Saturday, United had an away game in London. We all met early in Virgin Records off Piccadilly and there was Coco: all pent up, sporting a snow white Swiss Ski hat, red ski-gloves, a red Lacoste sleeveless puffa jacket, a white cashmere polo-neck with a thick gold chain on show, jet black original Lois jeans with creases stitched perfectly down the middle, with, you guessed it, those fuck-off snow-white ski boots! Classic Coco! Now he was ready to rumble.

He was lethal when it came to combat on the terraces, feared and respected as a true gentleman, an ICJ legend and the king of cool, who always kept his cool. He loved shopping in the January sales in Milan, and his famous 'Cast Off Sales' were a must: every other month certain items he got sick of after a night's wear he sold on at amazingly cheap prices.

Coke loved to know people's thoughts on things, and never stopped asking questions to the lads as we sat in The Nag's Head after games. "What's your favourite buildings in Manchester and why?" "What's your top gigs in Manchester and why?" I remember Wimbledon's manager saying "If I was in the trenches going into battle, I'd want Fash the Bash and Vinnie Jones by my side". Soon Coco's asking who mine would be, "Nobby Stiles and Micky Farrell," I said and it took him a few weeks before blurting out "Got it lads, Fireman Sam and Harry the Dog." Next he'd be asking who the Top Ten Jibbers of all time are. I'd say so and so then a week later change my mind, as did Coke, so we never did get around to finishing that list...

One fact about 2016 was the number of celebrity deaths, experts say there were more in six months than you'd normally get in six years. In my case it started when Coco called round on Christmas Eve 2015. Over the years he would give me a parcel of clothes, a monkey or a bag of sand and a box of chocolates for my mother. This year he was stressed out, telling me Ronnie Ross had passed away, before stunning me again by saying "I've no use for this anymore" and handing me his pride and joy; a perfectly scaled replica of the European Cup that took him years, and a few bob, to get made up. Old Trafford even used it for photos with tourists, so you know it's a good copy.

A few days later I went to see Renno, who loves a drink yet in forty years I'd never seen him be sick. When I got there he was bent over the balcony spewing his ring up, as he'd just got tragic news about his brother's death. The very next day Long Legs phoned me; Coco was dead. Bev drove up from London, and I'd not seen her since '88 when we split, so I was pleased to see her. We called over to Anne Marie's to find out the facts, and after Bev dropped me off a few hours later I had a serious heart attack! How's that for brotherly love, coming out in sympathy with a near-miss of my own. At my age it's a toss of the coin; you're either off to the bone yard or off to the hospital. I was lucky and after surgery and two weeks' rest I was back. It was the day before Coco's send off, and the Dean asked me to say a few words, but it was too much to attempt off the cuff, so Joe Brown did a speech that had everyone chuckling about Gary's antics. It was more like a state funeral; the last time I'd seen a turnout like that at Manchester Cathedral was George Best's service. Pete Chap had made up a wreath and placed it on the coffin, it read "Farewell Coco, Inter-City Jibber Legend" with the British Rail logo in red roses. His wake has held in the Sir Alex Ferguson lounge, how about that for respect. Three months later at the Stretford Enders yearly reunion in the Nag's Head, we all drank to Coco. While at the bar I had the '68 goalkeeper Alex Stepney on one side and Paraffin Pete, United's most prolific supporter, on the other as we watched the red devils beat Everton to take us back to Wembley. So I decided against my doctor's advice to make this my last ever Cup Final. I'd had a fantastic run seeing so many games, but health-wise you have to sack it off and keep healthy. Even if I cut myself shaving it bleeds for hours, I have shitloads of tablets to take daily and other stuff in case stress or excitement gets too much.

Luckily for my heart, there was not much in the way of excitement at Old Trafford under Van Gaal; with us playing crab football where virtually every game is 0-0 at half time. Soon it was time for his last meal at Mr Wings and retirement to the sun, while Giggsy went back to grassroots with Salford City FC. My doctor's orders were that I'm not allowed to fly or use the gym for a year, can't get in a crowded lift and should never run for a bus. I was happy to avoid the gym for a year but still took Coco's cup to the FA Cup Final for good luck and as a farewell to him. I can't help thinking what a shame it is that he never got to see Marcus Rashford in action, because at 18 Coco was the spit of him; same skin tone, size, haircut, and both having that ultra-coolness about them.

Now under Jose Mourinho we've bagged a cup double and we're back in the Champions League so things are definitely on the up and up.

My motto for over thirty years was "Get it spent and be content". Now it's "Health is Wealth". These days the icing on the cake for me is rising early, opening the balcony's winter windows and breathing in the fresh air, surrounded by greenery. It's hard to believe that it's pretty much the same view as when I was a kid in the 60's. Well, the same place, not the same view. Back then it was a damp, ugly, black and white world; the railway viaduct on Collyhurst Street had satanic-looking steam trains rolling over them 24/7, and now it's got colourful smooth metros gliding by with lots of smiling faces. There's also a new logo that's been sprayed brightly on the old black bricks; a cherry red smiley face with a joint dangling out the side of its crooked mouth, and underneath it reads "United's lads are off to Stockholm, while City's are off to Rusholme". The more things change, the more they stay the same.

That's it from me. I'm off to get the Manchester Worker Bee tattooed on my chest and put some money in the pot for the victims of the Manchester attack. Us Mancs pull together when the chips are down. Always have, always will.

Colin Blaney

JIBS, JACKS AND RATTLERS:
A GLOSSARY OF JIBBERS' SLANG

Arnie: Women's purse
Approvey: Approved school for young offenders
Apple Crumble: Rumble

Banging Jacks: Stealing cash from tills
Bandit: Criminal
Bareback Rider: Cider
Bacon Sandwich: Language
Bees and Honey or Bugs Bunny: Money
Battle Cruiser/Watering hole: Pub
Bubble: Grass fellow thief to the police
Blocking/Chalking: Distracting the target whilst somebody else can pick the pocket
Brief: Solicitor or ticket

Cucumbers: Numbers
Currant: Sun newspaper and Son
Cloggy: Dutchman

Dan Dares: Flares
Dibble: Policeman (Officer Dibble being the name of the copper in Top Cat)
Dipping/zapping: Picking pockets

Face: Well known Jibber or a tough cookie in the jail
Farmer Giles: Piles
Frank Nitti: Pity (Nitti was a top henchman for Al Capone)

Gat: Gun
Gerannie: Purse
Gear: Heroin
Goon: Idiot

Grafter: Professional criminal

Hit and Miss: On the piss
Hammers: Your fighting fists
Hector: Ticket inspector

IPP: Imprisonment for Public Protection

Jam Jar: Car
Jack: Till (Jack and Jill)
Jekyll: Fake (Jekyll and Hyde – snide)
Jib: Avoid paying at all cost
Jimmy Boyle or Joe Royle: Tin Foil
Jib off: Leave
Jolly: Someone posh and stuck up

Kettle: Watch (kettle and hob = cob, as in cob watch)
Kipper: Face (Kipper and Plaice)

Lad: Thug on the streets and also at the football
L-Plates: Life sentence
Little Fellas: Ecstasy pills
Lemon and Lime: Time
Long 'Un: 100 pounds

Mars Bar: Scar
Micky: Scouser (Micky Mouse = Scouse)
Midnight Mass: Grass
Millwall Brick: Makeshift weapon made from tightly wound up newspaper

Nasty: Smack
Nifty: 50 pound note
Nitto: Stop whatever you doing at once
Newton Heath: Teeth
Night Boat from Cairo: Giro

Old Queen: Mother

Pen and Ink: Stink
Persian Rugs: Drugs
Peter: Safe or a prison cell

A Glossary of Jibbers' Slang

Poke: Money, from the Irish phrase "Phoca" meaning "in your pocket"
Puff and Blow: Slow

Rattler: Train
Read and Write: Fight
Rice and Barley: Charlie (Coke)
Rogan Josh: Nosh (Blowjob)
Russell Harty: Party

Salford Docks: Socks
Sausage Time: Sexual Activity
Stretford-Enders: Suspender Belt with the silks
Snide: A Fake person or money
Straight-Goer: Law–Abiding Citizen
Stripe: Slash mark on a person's kipper
Swag: Merchandise sold outside Stadiums, also means a parcel of stolen goodies
Sweaty Sock: Scotsman (Sweaty Sock =Jock)
Suwannee River: Liver (a river that runs through Florida and Georgia in the USA)
Spare Rib: Jib
Skin and Blister: Sister

Twine: Trick a shopkeeper into giving you too much change
Tool Merchant: Dangerous Lad overly reliant on weapons
Trips/Window-panes: LSD
Twirlers: Keys

Uri Gellar: Stella Artois
Wrong un: Sex offender

THE JIBBERS SONG

Jibbers song, sung to the tune of David Bowie's "The Laughing Gnome"

HA-HA-HA, HE-HE-HE,
I'm the laughing gnome and you can't catch me

Just in case you don't know who we are, we're the famous ICJ
and we Jibbed it all the way to Brussels and back, and that is a fact.
And the last time I was captured was in my early days before the ICJ
for our own reasons we don't like to pay Especially in the day,
Oh you cannot fail jibbing on the Great British Rail.
Hector, Hector - coming down the train, bit of pain,
good news lads, he ain't got a brain.

CHORUS

HA-HA-HA, HE-HE-HE I'm an ICJ and you can't catch me
HA-HA-HA, HE-HE-HE Just made bail - got my Inter-Rail - so I'm
Laughing now!

VERSE TWO

Happy as Larry, all drinking in Harry's.
Get through the door, sticky feet on the floor.
Time to hit the Dam, first stop Birmingham,
We banged a till, it was a top thrill,
The damage was done, we'd copped for a ton,
So we jibbed a trian, taxi and a tram, that was the plan,
So after the game, in which we did win,
Next stop was Berlin.
No bee's in our bin, never give in its a mortal sin.
Ha ha ha he he he I'm a ICJ, and you can't catch me.
Ha ha ha he he he, just made bail and my inter ail,
I'm laughing now!